China Diary

The Life of Mary Austin Endicott

Life Writing Series

In the **Life Writing Series**, Wilfrid Laurier University Press publishes life writing and new life-writing criticism in order to promote autobiographical accounts, diaries, letters, and testimonials written and/or told by women and men whose political, literary, or philosophical purposes are central to their lives. **Life Writing** features the accounts of ordinary people, written in English, or translated into English from French or the languages of the First Nations or from any of the languages of immigration to Canada. **Life Writing** will also publish original theoretical investigations about life writing, as long as they are not limited to one author or text.

Priority is given to manuscripts that provide access to those voices that have not traditionally had access to the publication process.

Manuscripts of social, cultural, and historical interest that are considered for the series, but are not published, are maintained in the **Life Writing Archive** of Wilfrid Laurier University Library.

Series Editor
Marlene Kadar
Humanities Division, York University

Manuscripts to be sent to
Brian Henderson, Director
Wilfrid Laurier University Press
75 University Avenue West
Waterloo, Ontario, Canada N2L 3C5

China Diary

The Life of Mary Austin Endicott

Shirley Jane Endicott

Wilfrid Laurier University Press
WLU

We acknowledge the support of the Canada Council for the Arts for our publishing program. We acknowledge the financial support of the Government of Canada through the Book Publishing Industry Development Program for our publishing activities.

National Library of Canada Cataloguing in Publication Data

Endicott, Shirley Jane, 1930-
   China diary : the life of Mary Austin Endicott

(Life writing series)
Includes bibliographical references.
ISBN 0-88920-412-8

   1. Endicott, Mary Austin.   2. Endicott, Mary Austin—Diaries.
3. Missionaries' spouses—China—Biography.   4. Missionaries' spouses—
China—Diaries.   5. United Church of Canada—Missions—China.
I. Title.   II. Series.

BV3427.E51E54 2003   266'.792'092   C2002-903297-0

Cover design by Leslie Macredie. Front cover photograph
of Mary Austin Endicott taken by Vida Peene.
Calligraphy by Xianjing Chao. Back cover photograph
of Shirley Jane Endicott taken by Doug Garland.

Permission to quote from Anna Wickham's poem "The Tired Man" (p. 52)
courtesy of Margaret Hepburn and George Hepburn.

Printed in Canada

Dedicated to

Suzanne Michelle
first of thirteen grandchildren
asked by my mother to call her
Grandmary

and to

the spirit of Green Jade
everywhere

What I would like to do is a personal account, much as I wrote it in those long letters from China when I was so lonely, and the letters, giving the details of our life, were my chief outlet.

— Mary Austin Endicott, 1963

Contents

List of Illustrations

Acknowledgements

I am indebted to the National Archives of Canada for access to my mother's letters. A special thanks to Wilma MacDonald who personally retrieved letters on several occasions, saving me an extra trip to Ottawa.

When I felt I was truly "drowning in letters," Mary Bird offered support. She became my midwife, and without her I would never have survived the struggle to pull together a manuscript. She never lost faith even when I had. Donald Willmott and Jim Taylor read early drafts; their comments helped me decide on the parts of my mother's life that were central to her extraordinary journey.

My three brothers often contributed their memories and their perspectives. In addition, Mike helped in the research by going to the Toronto Reference Library and the York Township Board of Education archives. He also provided invaluable assistance with the proofreading. Stephen graciously gave me permission to cite a letter he wrote and provided photographs from his store of precious family albums. As well, he drew my attention to the Chinese name Dad gave Mother—Yuehua, or Moonflower—which combined poetically with Wen, his Chinese surname. (The three Chinese characters are used as a break symbol in the text throughout this book.) Norman, my mother's firstborn, is struggling with Parkinson's disease. For over a year I made weekly visits to Sunnybrook Hospital's L Wing, clutching a draft chapter or a letter in my hand to read to him. His comments often gave me new insights and his ongoing interest in my project was important to me. Illuminating anecdotes came from my sisters-in-law, Kathleen Fouracre, Lena Wilson and Isabel MacIntyre. The next generation gave me moral support. My niece Valerie Endicott, in particular, listened as I struggled with my own feelings about what I was learning. My children, Sylvia and Brian Cook, played similar roles, as did a number of close friends. I am grateful to all of them.

My partner, William Small, not only became house husband but was a living encyclopedia about the China my mother experienced. Bill grew up

文月華的中國日記

in Szechwan, returned there to work as an adult and knows the complex history of twentieth-century China. To him, especially, I say "fei shin" for your help, your "extended heart" on behalf of my project.

Many thanks to Leslie Macredie and Carroll Klein of Wilfrid Laurier University Press for their combination of personal warmth and professional insights.

Finally, I wish to thank Mina Wong for finding Xianjing Chao, the calligrapher who added so much by his talented touch.

文月華

Xianjing Chao, a retired chief architect from China, now lives in Toronto. Trained in childhood to write with Chinese brush and ink, calligraphy has been his lifetime hobby. He has been asked to write for different events and occasions. His calligraphy was published in the first issue of *Canadian Martial Arts Magazine* when the magazine was launched in 1996.

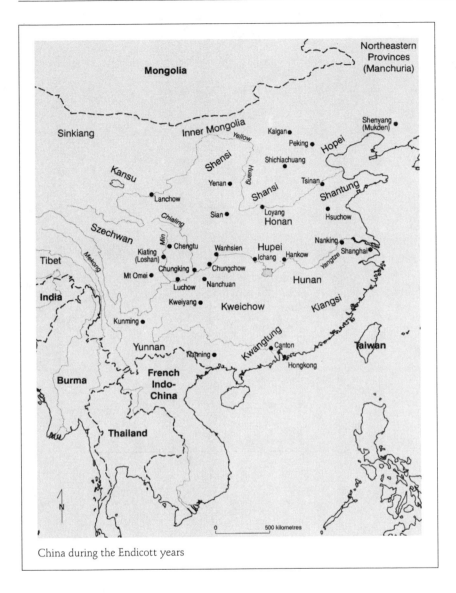

China during the Endicott years

文月華的中國日記

Introduction
Who Was My Mother?

In the early 1950s my father's name was a household word in Canada. Jim Endicott was either revered as a peace champion or pilloried as a "Communist stooge." The Endicott Uproar, as I call it, began in the United Church of Canada when he resigned as a missionary to China and returned home. He plunged into a one-man crusade urging Christians to stop military aid to the corrupt Nationalist government in China. The Chinese Communists were becoming victorious, he said, because they gave land to peasants; the revolution was not being instigated by Moscow.

Soon he became the leader of the Canadian Peace Congress and spearheaded the first "Ban the Bomb" campaign. In the spring of 1952 the media dubbed him "Public Enemy Number One" when he accused the United States of using germ warfare in the Korean War. To this day his family members, including grandchildren, are asked: "Are you one of The Endicotts?" Hardly anyone asks about my mother.

Within the family, stories about my father ("Popeye") abound, while the life of my mother ("Grandmary") has faded like an old photograph.

文月華

One such family legend—The Turtle Soup Incident—began on a summer day in the early 1940s, at a wooded site on the shores of Lake Muskoka. My Uncle Norman and his wife Betty left their three children, ages six to ten, in the care of my parents for several days.

The afternoon of the first day my cousins were horrified when my father, their beloved Uncle Jim, caught a huge snapping turtle—and gleefully announced it would make a "wondrous" soup. In spite of their protests he went ahead with this plan. Outraged, they declared they were leaving until their parents returned. Gathering up their sleeping bags, they traipsed off indignantly into the woods. This act of civil disobedience was the heart of the legend.

文
月
華
的
中
國
日
記

Over thirty years later, I paid my cousins a surprise visit at that same Lake Muskoka property. The Turtle Soup Incident was in my mind. I was hardly out of the boat before cousin Clare was relating my mother's role in the affair. Her face was animated and she spoke with great gusto and delight. I had never heard this part of the story before:

Aunt Mary came through the woods like a gentle storybook Pied Piper and sat down by our sleeping bags as if what we had done was perfectly natural. She spoke softly and wove a magic spell over us. I'll never forget it. In the most matter-of-fact manner, she informed us that supper would be ready in half an hour. The menu was described—no mention of turtle soup. Then she gracefully stood up and disappeared into the woods. We picked up our sleeping bags and followed her back to camp.

How typical, I reflected, that I knew my father's actions but not those of my mother. Why was her role not part of the family legend? Was this an inevitable fate for the wife of a famous man?

I knew that my mother's life with my father had not obliterated her as a person. There must be many such stories, I thought.

My mother was an inveterate letter writer. She considered the ones written to family and friends during her sixteen years as a missionary to be her "China Diary"; they were preserved by her family and a close friend, Freda Waldon. My mother's filing cabinets bulged with carbon copies of her correspondence, now mostly stored in the National Archives of Canada in Ottawa.

At first my intention was simply to select some of the most interesting letters and let them tell the story. But letters are written to a specific audience and for a particular purpose; they do not always speak for themselves. An anecdote from my sister-in-law, Isabel MacIntyre, illuminates this truth:

In the early 1960s I helped my mother-in-law, "Grandmary," review her life in China, based on her letters, which had been stored in a trunk by her mother and sister.

I commented once on what a wonder it was that she was able to cope with the difficulties of a strange country after having led such a sheltered life as the mayor's daughter in Chatham. She replied, "I didn't always cope so well."

"But," I said, "you'd never know it from your letters."

She was quiet for a minute, and as she spoke, tears came to her eyes. "You've no idea how many pages I had to tear up because they were stained with tears. I couldn't let my mother see them; she would have worried and there was nothing she could to do help."

I came to understand that my mother used her pen (and typewriter) to find a way through various crises and important events in her life. What emerges is an intimate record of her rocky personal odyssey. She had "married China" (my phrase) without an iota of knowledge of the hardships that would entail. These letters contain her fears and triumphs—surviving perilous trips through the Yangtze Gorges, overcoming her terror of speaking in public, glimpses of a marriage between two forceful personalities and the importance of spirituality in her life.

文月華

The title chosen for this book—*China Diary*—expands my mother's definition of that term. Reading through her correspondence, I became convinced that the years my mother lived in China laid the foundation for everything that happened after she returned to Canada. In addition, her sense of mission about China—interpreting developments—continued on. In a sense, she never stopped being "married" to China.

文月華

Towards the end of her life my mother became discouraged by many health problems. To provide a meaningful distraction from her infirmity, Stephen suggested she review the letters she had sent from China and make an account of her years abroad for her grandchildren. She called the unfinished memoirs "Life with Jim." It proved to be invaluable in my research of her first few years in China. However, as her energy flagged, her ability to process memories of her own life declined and she simply asked her assistant to type letters describing my father's life, which is why excerpts from the memoirs appear only twice after chapter 9.

Solving Editorial Dilemmas

The circumstances under which my mother began her memoirs explain why they omit her first twenty-eight years. Writing about that part of her life in chapter 1 became a major challenge. This chapter is a piecing

文
月
華
的
中
國
日
記

together of fragments from many sources—"The Gates of Eden" in *Rebel Out of China*; a lengthy 1927 letter to her friend Freda Waldon; a 1929 report to the Department of Child Study at the University of Toronto; a 1942 account of her religious quest written for her children; and fragments from letters written as late as 1947. I have imposed the framework of interpretation here: the fragments are hers, the piecing together is mine.

Although my mother's correspondence has been cited extensively, this is not a collection of letters. For one thing, the sheer volume of material ruled this out. I estimate I read perhaps 5,000 pages of single-spaced typing. The letters I have chosen to cite are those that highlight the way she responded to the unusual circumstances of her life. Thus, many interesting exchanges or narratives have been omitted because they do not speak to this theme. The emphasis is on what is unique. The treasure trove of "kid stuff"—our cute sayings—has been omitted. Likewise, the extensive correspondence prompted by my Grandfather Austin's decision to remarry only six months after his wife's death is not cited. These letters document the opposing reactions of my mother and her sister Jane to this development but family reverberations are common at the time of a parent's remarriage. The facts of the case are given briefly in the narrative, but the letters are not quoted.

When an anecdote appears in both the original China letters and in the "Life with Jim" account, I have chosen the source that reveals more of my mother's feelings. An example is her reaction to living for four months in the city of Chungking upon her return in November 1929. The memoirs, in this case, are more forthcoming. On the other hand, the memoirs sometimes gloss over or omit events that had deep meaning for my mother at the time—her long quest to find a cure for her stammering, for example.

In selecting the material to be included I have assumed that the letters written nearer in time to the events are more factual and less likely to be shaped by wishful thinking or other changes in perspective, which often occur in later years. The most illuminating example of this is found in the two accounts of going to a conference of the Oxford Group in Quebec City in 1933. As I compared what she confided in a private document written just after the conference with what she said in her memoirs, it was hard to believe it was the same event. Looking back thirty years my mother asserted that the evening she spent walking the ramparts of Quebec City with an old friend, grieving the death of his wife, "remains now as the one 'real' bit about the whole week-end." She included a poem she

文
月
華
的
中
國
日
記

had written during the conference and explained it was her reaction to the conference. After considerable thought I omitted the memoirs' account because I found her explanation of the theology contained in the poem difficult to follow and assumed my readers would share my problem.

Because the earlier description of the Quebec City conference comes from a personal "stream-of consciousness" account, not intended for an audience, it has some puzzling aspects for which I have attempted to provide some interpretation. What follows my question "What are we to make of this...account?" are my speculations, backed up by evidence I found in other letters. In this case it is impossible to be certain what was truly my mother's voice.

In addition, reading the memoirs one would think she had virtually no use for the Oxford Group after her return to China in 1934. Her letters at the time, however, paint a different reality, and again I have assumed what was written at the time was more accurate.

An important issue for me was deciding how much of my parents' private life to reveal. For example, the 1928 correspondence (during an involuntary separation) contains a conversation on their sex life. I decided to include parts of this because, according to one historian, during the 1920s "sexuality and sexual attraction began to occupy a more central place in modern ideas of personalty and identity, and sexual happiness came to the fore as a primary purpose of marriage."[1] My parents were part of that social development and deserve credit for being willing to talk about the intimate side of their marriage. Also, this issue turned out to be relevant to a major marital crisis years later. The problem here was that most of my father's more explicit letters about sexual matters were missing from the National Archives files. However, the highlights remain because my mother refers to his remarks in her replies. I have selected those excerpts which not only illustrate the general tone of frankness but are also germane to the overall story of their marriage.

Another informative exchange took place in the course of their two-and-a-half year separation during World War II. One problem with the letters was sheer volume, particularly on the part of my mother. Because of wartime conditions, often she would receive multiple letters within two or three days—after weeks of silence—and reply to all of them at once. Many of these letters are particularly long-winded and rambling, which

1 Karen Dubinsky, "There's Something About Niagara Falls," *The Beaver* 81, 1 (February/March 2001)

文
月
華
的
中
國
日
記

was my mother's style when in a state of emotional upheaval. My strategy was to delete the daily life and family news sections and pick up those threads which I believed both shed light on my mother's character and were most pertinent to the ebb and flow of the relationship.

In the interests of clarity I changed terminology in chapter 15. In the excerpt from her paper "On Finding Life," she describes the ideas of Fritz Künkel on overcoming "egocentricity" and becoming genuinely altruistic. This ideal state was translated as one of "objectivity," which could be confused with its use in academia as meaning an unbiased stance. I replaced "objectivity" with "concern for others."

There are two places where I have constructed stories which my mother originally told in letters written over many months. The foster mother experiences (chapter 14) came from many letters to family and a 1938 report to Dr. W.E. Blatz. Likewise, her time as school trustee (chapter 20) was pieced together from snippets to family and friends. I felt justified in doing this because, in these cases, she was not trying to protect her mother or influence a family member—she was reporting on her interesting work.

Deciding to leave out topics was also an important part of the editorial process. In chapter 20, for example, some Board of Education issues were omitted because they did not significantly add to the portrayal of my mother's character and value position. Chapter 22 describes her drastic shift in political loyalties without giving myriad details of the differences between the social democrats (Co-operative Commonwealth Federation, or CCF) and the communists (Labour Progressive Party, or LPP) with which my mother wrestled for over a year. One evening, for example, she invited an LPP functionary to her house to explain these differences to her. They were joined by some friends, including Avis and Jarvis McCurdy, both staunch CCF supporters. Avis wrote a two-page letter advising my mother, "For God's sake, stay away from [the LPP] with a ten thousand foot pole." My mother had taken detailed notes about the evening and was puzzled "that two people could get such different things" out of the same event. I hoped there might be an accessible story in this interchange. However, both letters concentrated on itemizing the convoluted CCF/LPP conflict of the time, which, after several readings, I decided would not be of interest to today's general audience (and can be accessed elsewhere).

Chapter 25, "Life—in the Cold War—with Jim," remains a personal account, even though much of it is taken from items she wrote for publication. The excerpts chosen have the flavour of the circular letters she wrote to friends from China. They illustrate her unique contribution to the peace movement and to explaining the Chinese Revolution.

In chapter 26 I was again faced with choosing from the "banker's box" of letters she wrote to a prisoner in Kingston Penitentiary. I chose ones that highlighted the intensity of her involvement in this project. To protect the man's identity I have omitted the context in which they met, changed his name and left out most specific dates.

I have kept the Wade-Giles style of spelling Chinese names that was in use at the time rather than Pinguin, the current method.

Finally, where it seemed helpful, I have, from time to time, inserted personal comments based on my own memories.

How Writing My Mother's Life Influenced Mine

When my granddaughter turned five she said "Grandma, tell me about when you were a little girl." She wanted stories—but all I had were fleeting recollections, too fragmented to weave into a narrative. Furthermore, my most accessible memories were painful—no other little girls to play with, the hostility of Chinese crowds when we went out of our compound ("running dogs of imperialism")—and did not seem suitable for one so young. I felt sure my mother had faithfully recorded her children's birthday celebrations, travel adventures and cute sayings—all the sorts of things a five year old would find enchanting. Finding them was my original motivation for exploring the hundreds of China letters. Pushed by the bond with my small granddaughter, early in June 1995 I began the onerous task of picking out letters to be photocopied in the National Archives. I was looking for "kid stuff," which I found in abundance, but a quick glance at each letter told me they recorded many facets of my mother's life about which I was hungry to know. I spent the whole of my first pension cheque paying for photocopies of that initial batch of China Diary letters.

The strength of that hunger was my first surprise.

When the large box of letters arrived from the National Archives six weeks later, my husband urged me not to read them until I had put them in properly labelled chronological files. I ignored this wise advice and

文
月
華
的
中
國
日
記

grabbed a letter from the middle of the box. It described why my mother chose me to go with her on the "Mad Truck Ride" to Chengtu—she felt that I was the one most deprived of playmates. Unaccountable waves of gratitude swept over me. Not long after, I read about the time and energy she took to copy down the words she heard me chanting and call them "poems." I felt like a child opening a magic Christmas present.

The outcome of this first level of retrieval was a satisfying sense of how important I was in my mother's universe as well as a stock of material for "grandma stories." I made a scrapbook of anecdotes about my China childhood and that of my three brothers, giving copies to the extended Endicott tribe that Christmas.

It seemed to satisfy the original hunger to become better informed. I didn't think writing my mother's life would be a significant personal learning experience and besides, I had already written an account of my own life story. The jacket cover of *Facing the Tiger* (1987) described it as "Confronting and conquering one's hidden fears..." Each chapter had a "tiger"—and the one entitled "Almost Strangers" was about the ambivalence I felt towards my mother when I was seventeen. "If I had kept a journal throughout these periods," I wrote, "this is how it might have chronicled my relationship with her."

1947

What has happened? I'm still the same Shirley but Mother is so different. Why isn't it like it was before she went to join Dad in China? I miss the good times we had together then. What has happened?[2]

In *Facing the Tiger* I went on to describe how I finally reached out to my mother in the early 1960s and initiated a close woman-to-woman relationship. I had made my peace. By 1995 then, I felt no urge to write my mother's life to satisfy my own emotional needs.

A feminist call to retrieve a case history of "herstory" whispered in my ear, but I brushed it aside. Facing a hip replacement, I felt I lacked the stamina to do the complicated story justice. The surgery, however, left me plagued with problems; after a year I decided I needed a project to take my mind off my troubles. My husband agreed to take over the kitchen and I groped my way into this project.

---

2 In *Facing the Tiger* I erroneously dated this "journal entry" 1948.

Almost immediately I began to feel a kinship with my mother that I had not experienced during her lifetime. In 1973 I had taken a six-week tour of China, just after my marriage to my second husband, William Small who, like my father, spoke Chinese like a native. I barely remembered a few phrases from childhood and, if I did say something, found it impossible to understand the response. At the time I had been a competent university teacher for almost a decade, but in China I found myself reduced to the status of a kindergarten child, dependent upon my husband for everything, even telling the waitress what I wanted for breakfast. Unable to make small talk when the curious crowds pressed in around us, my anxiety rose and my self-esteem plunged. Reading the voluminous letters my mother wrote when she first arrived in China, I relived my 1973 experience—when I was a guest of the Chinese government—and felt an overwhelming empathy for her during her "ghastly first year," an empathy that replaced my childhood embarrassment upon hearing her dissolve into tears as she struggled to do the weekly accounting with her Chinese cook.

Now that I have read my mother's letters, reread, laughed, wept and wept some more, the anguish of my teenage cris de coeur—"What... happened?"—has evaporated. As I have learned of so many of the "tigers" my mother faced and conquered, my admiration for her has risen dramatically. When I ploughed through the World War II correspondence between my parents and the six-month drama in 1947 Shanghai, I understood why I had not been given the emotional attention I craved when she returned to Canada. There remain questions I would like to have asked, but that wound has healed.

An unexpected gift of writing my mother's life was gaining a vicarious emotional connection with both my grandmothers. Sarah Endicott died before I was born and her importance to my mother was unknown to me. I found myself strangely moved by the 1926 account of how meaningful my mother found a photograph of her mother-in-law.

I met Minnie Austin when we returned to Canada on furlough in 1933. I was only three at the time. Well into this project, I found a letter to her recalling the time of my birth—how lovely that she had been present at this happy time and how helpful she had been. The date told me it was probably the last letter from my mother that Grandmother Austin received before her death. I shivered to think that reliving my birth must have been one of her final pleasurable moments.

文
月
華
的
中
國
日
記

I wept when I read the excerpt from *Five Stars over China* that is reproduced in chapter 25. The Chinese woman described there is almost biblical in stature, a grassroots Miriam leading her people across the Red Sea to liberation. My mother clearly hoped the experiment she had witnessed in 1952 would lead to a contemporary Promised Land.

But now, at the beginning of the twenty-first century, the ideals of the Chinese Revolution have long been betrayed. I struggle to believe Green Jade's sacrifices were not made in vain. I struggle to understand the Promised Land as a metaphor for hope, not an actual place.

Finally, several times during this project I have had vivid dreams of my mother—vibrant and vitally interested in me. I have come to miss her more than ever, but we are no longer "Almost Strangers."

Part 1

文月華的中國日記

1

From a Background of Privilege

> Although we were only a few yards from shore the yellow waters swirled by
> ominously. I looked at the gap between the ship and the nearest sampan that
> had hooked on to the side of the steamer and I wondered if I would make it
> with my precious bundle in my arms. A fellow missionary went first and
> stood in the sampan with a reassuring smile, while Jim went to the baggage
> hold to supervise the unloading of our trunks and bags. I looked at the rush-
> ing waters, then at the two British officers whose coolness and confidence
> inspired me to go ahead. The captain held the baby while the chief officer
> handed me down to our colleague in the sampan and then gave me the baby
> without dropping him in that gap of terrifying river. ("Life with Jim")

Nothing in her twenty-nine years had prepared Mary Elsie Austin for
those fearsome moments on the Yangtze River. For the chaotic reality that
was warlord China in 1926.

Born April 13, 1897, she grew up surrounded by silver candlesticks and
white linen tablecloths. Her home was a large custom-built turreted mansion on the banks of the placid Thames River that ran through Chatham,
Ontario. Her father, Charles Austin, owned the largest department store
in Kent County. When Mary was thirteen, he was elected mayor. The
Austins were the first family in town to own an automobile. At age fifteen, taking a year off from school, Mary accompanied her family on a
three-month trip to Europe, visiting museums and art galleries and staying in fine hotels.

Mary was intensely close to her mother, Mary Elizabeth (Minnie)
Chapman, the daughter of a Methodist preacher.

> As long as I could remember [Mother] had been keenly interested in public
> affairs and for several years was the president of the Women's Canadian
> Club as well as the Women's Missionary Society Auxiliary in our church.
> Although her education was somewhat limited she kept herself informed

文
月
華
的
中
國
日
記

and was able to chair public meetings as well as to be hostess to distinguished guests who were the speakers and usually stayed in our home. The guest she enjoyed most was Mrs. Pankhurst, the leader of the suffragettes in England, whose views Mother heartily shared. ("Life with Jim")

Minnie Chapman Austin. Charles Austin. Photos: Margaret Edmunds, Chatham.

Mary's relationship with her older sister Jane was intense and turbulent. Candid in their criticisms of each other, both remained fiercely loyal. Jane was scathing in her criticism of the psychoanalytic insights that were to become so dear to Mary's heart, but never missed sending parcels for Christmas and birthdays. For her part, Mary thought Jane was over-preoccupied with keeping up appearances, foolishly sentimental and domineering, but often wrote to her personally about family and other matters. In spite of mixed feelings, the connection remained important to both of them.

As a young child, Mary was seriously ill three times—diphtheria at age six, scarlet fever a year later and typhoid on another occasion. Her stamina was permanently undermined, which she experienced as a humiliation. In addition, soon after she started school she began to stutter. Over time, she grew to believe that her stuttering was her "chief personality disturbance."

After turning thirty she wrote more about this part of her life than any other which suggests how deeply she experienced stammering as a major physical and psychological handicap, one that even influenced her choice of university courses. In 1927 Mary revealed details of the struggle to overcome her disability in a long letter to her chief confidante, Freda Waldon, a librarian in Hamilton and godmother to her first child:

> I remember my mother telling me to go slowly or say it over again. She said she had also stammered when a little girl and Grandfather cured her by stopping her and saying, "Take your time, my little dear." She used to tell me this, and tried the same dodge on me but it only made me very angry and hot inside, although I wanted very much to do it....
>
> When I was fourteen I spent six weeks in the home of a minister who cures stammering. His methods were solely mechanical, breathing exercises, practice in reading slowly and so on. [Although I was repelled by his personality] I improved for a while but a few weeks...back at school and I had slid back, and by this time I was most sensitive about it. The fact that I dreaded reading essays and so on aloud kept me from going into an English and History course at college, which was my natural bent, and turned me to the labs of Household Science, which is probably partly the reason why I reacted to it so strongly. (to Freda Waldon, 28 June 1927)

Mary turned to the new discipline of Freudian psychoanalysis in hopes of finding a cure for her stammering. She became convinced it was a new and important science—"the handmaid of truth." At age twenty-four, doing graduate work in New York, her hopes soared when she heard that Dr. E.A. Bott, the head of the Psychology Department at the University of Toronto, knew a Mrs. Scripture who did "splendid work in curing speech defects." With great enthusiasm Mary relayed the details of the first interview to her parents:

> She attacked the subject from the psychological and neurological standpoint. This interested me at once, as I believe it to be the most vital, at least in such cases as mine....
>
> Almost from the first instant, I felt she had just the [right] type of personality...keen insight, confidence and cordial sympathy, with a background of unmistakable sincerity and refinement....She asked me about previous treatment, and I told her briefly. She said I did not need drill...but [rather] personal contact, intimate help to form new habits. And, of course, that is what I have known for a long time was the only thing that could really help me. And I don't believe I will ever do it by myself, for I can never try harder than I have done....

15

文
月
華
的
中
國
日
記

I [am to] spend December and January under her supervision, with perhaps only one or two interviews a week, but living according to her program of rest, relaxation, study of the underlying psychological principles, practicing the new habits until I am at the stage to do some public speaking and gain absolute confidence in myself. (to parents, 30 September 1921)

This program also failed because, Mary told Freda, it turned out that Mrs. Scripture's "methods were mostly mechanical" and "she was not analytical at all, though she assured me that my trouble was largely psychological...."

Later Mary secretly took a correspondence course from which the only valuable suggestion was "autosuggestion": "I had already discovered this for myself and it often helped me over definite situations but left me tense and exhausted. By this time I was quite discouraged but I felt sure this weakness must be overcome by scientific methods sometime and I kept on the alert by reading and enquiring whenever I could as to what was being done on the subject" (Report to St. George's School for Child Study, 1929).

In the spring of 1925, not long before going to China, she made one more attempt to solve the riddle of her stammering. She consulted a psychoanalyst, Dr. Margaret Strong, who gave her "a sympathetic though, of necessity, hasty analysis." Mary was asked to give her earliest memory:

On the last day of the Fair it rained and my father carried me on his shoulder: "Little Mary has been such a good girl." The phrase sticks in my memory.

A midway show, DARKNESS AND DAWN, was filled with horrible dead men, sitting beside the fires of hell. Skeletons flitted among the crowd with icy fingers; one of them stole the purse of a woman.

I was between three and four and I remember all this most vividly. Dr. Strong suggested that whether it happened or not, the fact that I remember it among so few details at such an early age, signified it probably had symbolic significance for me. It is a general symbol to indicate loss of virtue....

She thought some incident of a sexual nature occurred very early which made me feel I had been wicked and, in order to balance this, I became good and pious and always strove to have my parents and others think well of me, so that I might think well of myself.

She concluded that, instead of the inferiority complex I imagined I had, I really had a superiority complex, probably resulting from the use of a defence mechanism in childhood to hide a sense of guilt. In her opinion this guilt arose from sexual sources. (to Freda Waldon, 28 June 1927)

文
月
華
的
中
國
日
記

It was also Dr. Strong's opinion that due to the repressive type of childhood training there was also "an elimination complex and probably a food complex." All these, she thought, accounted for Mary's "lack of robustness and for the emotional disturbance, of which the stammering was a symptom." Mother Austin believed her daughter's low energy began after a debilitating attack of scarlet fever, but before leaving for China Mary passed a thorough medical examination. This result led her to believe there was no constitutional cause for her lack of stamina and reaffirmed her acceptance of Dr. Strong's explanation for the stammering.

The problem remained, however, and so did her frustration. She confessed to Freda that if "my stammering…is a symptom of disharmony that affects me in other ways, such as my health and vigour, then that is a defeat not to be tolerated while there is opening to seek for a way out."

The quest for a perfect solution continued for many years until the ideas of a non-Freudian psychologist entered Mary's life and she tried an entirely new strategy.

文月華

A preoccupation to find an absolute cure for her stammering was, of course, only part of her growing-up experiences. While still in her teens Mary challenged some of the Austins' cherished religious beliefs:

> I had a battle royal with my parents over the principle of dancing and card playing in our home. It had been contrary to the rules of the Methodist Church but times were changing and when I finally convinced them that I could not entertain my friends without these amusements, they gave in, and then said, "If bridge is going to be played in this house, we may as well learn it." ("Life with Jim")

She also began to have great arguments about evolution, much to the alarm of her parents, especially her mother. And how could anyone take some of the Bible stories literally? The story of Jonah, for example. Furthermore, she was not comfortable with the prayers and rituals in the Sunday morning worship service. By the age of seventeen, when she went to Victoria College at the University of Toronto, she was about ready "to throw religion in the dust-heap."

Nevertheless, "just for a lark," after her second year at Victoria College, she went to a student conference at the elegant Muskoka resort, Elgin

文
月
華
的
中
國
日
記

House. Here she was deeply moved by a challenge "to give up all that was unworthy and follow the supreme example of Jesus who gave himself to a cause." The speaker was Samuel Hooke, a controversial non-conformist Old Testament scholar at Victoria, later driven out because of his unconventional views. Mary left Elgin House determined to search for a satisfying religion—to follow Professor Hooke's admonition and leave herself open to Truth.

Mary, about age fifteen, perhaps before leaving on a three-month family trip to Europe. Photo: Margaret Edmunds, Chatham.

Her quest, however, was interrupted by the disastrous outcome of a secret affair of the heart. Since the age of sixteen she had been in love with her cousin, Allen Austin. When Mary was seventeen she and Allen went to college together for a year and a half: "The first shy kisses became much more ardent embraces....There was a very strong bond between us, and had we not been related, we would almost surely have married. Sometimes we thought we would anyway" (to Freda Waldon, 28 June 1927). All this

文
月
華
的
中
國
日
記

was kept a secret for fear of parental disapproval. Then, early in 1916, Allen left to go overseas to serve in World War I. Three years later he informed his cousin that he was going to marry an Englishwoman. Mary, now twenty-one, was devastated, and she plunged into a debilitating depression.

Mary with her sister Jane, brother-in-law Charles, and nephew Austin Wright, circa 1919. Family friend Lester B. Pearson is on the right.

After a few months, however, she had rallied sufficiently to begin an internship as a dietitian in a hospital in New York. A year later, encouraged by Miss Margaret Addison, a professor at the University of Toronto, Mary returned to New York to take a five-month graduate course in household science. The 1921 letters home bubble with enthusiasm about her extra-curricular activities—going with fellow dietitians to the theatre and to lectures on art and sculpture at the Metropolitan Museum of Art, taking a course on modern drama and—best of all—a short story course in the Journalism Department at Columbia University.

She had a rare capacity for friendship and made friends easily. For example, she wrote at some length to her mother about the pleasure of meeting a Mrs. Neuser, a Jewish woman who sat next to her in her first art class:

Last Saturday her husband was in New Jersey for the week-end, so I went with her to do some shopping (They call it the ghetto because it is all Jewish.)...We got some fresh vegetables on the street market & went home to the apartment to get our dinner....We had lots of fun cooking in the tiny kitchen & I enjoyed the meal immensely....

文
月
華
的
中
國
日
記

I have often wanted to know people like that who are so different from those I have known—and I am glad to have this opportunity. They have been married a little over a year, but they are not like most couples. She goes to night school five nights a week learning Latin & chemistry. She is going to go through for medicine or dentistry. She says she never expects to practice unless something happens to her husband, but she will use it for charitable work in the slums. They are Socialists, but not of the extreme type, and her great idea is to help humanity—to give everybody a chance. (to Minnie Austin, from New York, 23 October 1921)

Although she was grateful for Miss Addison's interest in her, it seems clear that Mary's heart was never really in her household science course. In fact, she cut the last two months of the practical work in order to take the ill-fated intensive program with Mrs. Scripture to cure her stammering.

In any case, returning to Canada in 1922, Mary made no effort to pursue a career as a dietitian. Almost twenty-five years old by now, her parents still insisted that she live at home rather than find her "own way in the world." Although resenting this, she made no strong objection. The chief reason she did not break away completely was because her "speech difficulties would have made earning a livelihood a matter of considerable strain."

For two years after New York she wrote "spasmodically" for publication. She was paid between $6.00 and $11.00 for each item, which was a reasonable fee when a book might cost as little as $1.60. However, as she confided to Freda, she found she was not suited for a life where one had to find a topic to write about just for the sake of writing.

Living off her father's money she was free to do volunteer work. She formed a girl's group at her local congregation and served on committees—the executive of the Chatham Literary Guild, the Girls Work Board at the Methodist Church headquarters. She was also able to attend student conferences and resume her quest for a satisfying religion. The first breakthrough came with the founding of the left-wing Student Christian Movement (SCM) in the spring of 1922, not long after Mary came back from New York. She joined the editorial board of *The Canadian Student*, the SCM's magazine, along with her "beloved" Professor S.H. Hooke and Helen Bott (wife of the psychologist who had recommended Mrs. Scripture).

She had walked through the valley of despair, reached new ground and was ready for a new challenge.

Mary's religious search, begun at age nineteen, climaxed seven years later in a deeply felt spiritual awakening during the summer of 1923. She found what she was seeking when she went to Bon Echo Park for a five-week seminar led by a University of Toronto chemistry professor, H.B. Sharman. She felt his two books, *Jesus in the Records* and *Jesus As Teacher,* provided "a scientific method of study" and gave an understanding of Christ she found both "reasonable and real." In a Student Christian Movement publication, she told how she came away with a concept of God as "a Power waiting to be used" and a belief that Jesus had discovered the means of "drawing upon that Life-giving Power."

Finding this theology was not as easy as her public statements implied. One evening—perhaps after climbing the Great Rock to see the setting sun—Mary retired to her tent and began to "talk with God" using pen and paper.

Be with me, O God, this night.
  I am with you, now and always.
Guide my feet in the right path.
  Put your hand in mine, child of my love.
Give me strength not to stumble or turn away
  Would you feel my strength, the strength that guides the universe through time and eternity?
Oh, that is too mighty for me. I am only a girl living for a generation, a citizen of one country.
  True. But you are part of me who hath been since Time begun and shall be when your mortal frame is dust blown about the earth.
The thought of death frightens me. The thought of living frightens me too, sometimes, when I look about and see how difficult and terrifying it can be — But I know that if I lean on Thee, I'll get through the hard places without breaking down.
  Better still would be to realize that I am in you and you in me even as life makes the tree green, beautiful and strong. Make my will your will and you will walk with unwavering step.
My will be lost in yours? But then I couldn't do what I like. I am young and don't want to be always thinking about what I ought to do. I want to be happy and free. Maybe, when I am old — Maybe then —
  Why not explore the way now? My will is never imposed on man. You are free to accept it or reject it whenever this choice becomes clear to you.

文
月
華
的
中
國
日
記

It is an opportunity life holds for you and upon your choice depends the direction of your whole life. My son Jesus, long ago in Nazareth discovered the secret of the way. You, too, can discover it from 3 short books about his life — But you are tired now. Lay chattering aside and go to sleep. I am always here. We can talk again.

Good-night, Father. I am sleepy now, but I want to know more about all this. It sounds like something I've been looking for without knowing I was. We will talk again. Good-night.

She kept this handwritten "Dialogue with God" in her red tooled-leather writing case for the rest of her life.

At Sharman seminars, discussions were conducted in small study groups, allowing each participant to relate the material to their own lives and come to their own conclusions. Mary emerged believing that the self must be changed so that a new creature would come forth dedicated to one great purpose—to do that which is right and that only, which is the will of God. This was a central issue in her "Dialogue with God" and remained the core of her faith.

While at Bon Echo Mary also found an approach to the miracle stories in the Gospels that did not violate the findings of modern science: "The story of the disciples appealing to Jesus on the stormy sea is so much richer in meaning if we interpret it that Jesus stilled the fears of the disciples rather than the waves of the sea. They would have to be in storms again many times but they could always remember his calmness and even his acceptance of what the forces of nature might do to them. It would help to steady them and make them better able to meet another emergency" (to family, 28 March 1938).

Mary's friendship with Miss Effie Lafferty, a Chatham woman doomed to live her life in a wheelchair after a railway accident, confirmed the social importance of her new-found theology:

A famous singer, who was on the same train as she was, came to the hospital to sing for her and the patients. He did it with a kind heart, but to her it was ironical he thanked God that he had escaped being hurt on that tragic occasion....She looked a bit bitter, and I know she was asking: "Did God save Harold and let me be crushed?"

I do not believe God "gives" good fortune to some, and sends pain to others....What happens to any individual is dependent upon the circumstances

文
月
華
的
中
國
日
記

in which he finds himself, circumstances both natural and man-made. God is Goodness, which implies truth and love....It is left to man to express that Goodness in his actions. (to Jane, 21 June 1947)

Thus, by her mid-twenties Mary's ideas about God were a far cry from those of her parents. But what was she to do about the church? "When I found a personal religion which was satisfying to me, it was so different from that found in the church that it was difficult for me to feel at home there at all." On the other hand, it was only within the church that she could pass on what had become real to her. She decided to get along as best as she could about "church observances" and threw her energies into leading the Canadian Girls In Training (CGIT) group she had founded.

She also wrote a course of study for a 1924 CGIT summer camp based on the records of the life of Jesus—using the methodology of small-group discussions that had been so powerful at Bon Echo: "It is hoped that leaders will relate the discussions as intimately as possible to the conditions among girls today....Start the girls thinking and questioning in their minds. Do not settle things permanently....Truth discovered for oneself is doubly precious and vivid."

文月華

The Bon Echo experience gave Mary a sense of mission and "in spite of the tension and strain involved at times in speaking up in committees or teaching groups," she managed "to be reasonably content." Presumably her heartbreak over Allen was now mended, but none of her subsequent friendships with men blossomed into anything more than fleeting romantic involvements.

As 1924 drew to a close, true love seemed out of her grasp. She would have to make a life for herself—alone. But how? The church seemed to provide a solution. The Austins had always supported foreign missions, which offered one of the few respectable career opportunities for middle-class unmarried women. For some years she had hoped that some day she might go abroad and spend a year each in China, Japan and India as a visitor and write "human-interest stories for church publications." While there perhaps it would be possible to do work among older girls or lead Bible study groups. This dream of widening her horizons led her to register for a missionary conference in Washington, DC, in late January 1925, a decision that would change her life forever.

2

Prelude to Adventure

The weekend of January 10, 1925 was proceeding like any other—two university friends for dinner and prospects of Mother's superb Saturday night stewed chicken. On the agenda for me: a new dress to try on at Father's store and then bang head-on into a new life! A revolution could hardly have been more drastic.

The unconscious herald of this new era was a tall youth with light brown hair and eyes that matched his broad smile as he and my father stood together on a tour of the store. Father was obviously relieved to see the three girls come along. "Take this chap off my hands," he said. "He has several hours to put in between trains." We were not averse.

Where had I seen that confident, buoyant face? [When Father introduced him as] the son of his old friend, Dr. James Endicott, for many years Foreign Missions Secretary of the Methodist Church of Canada, [I remembered]. Back in 1922 at the founding national conference of the Student Christian Movement (SCM) held in Convocation Hall at the University of Toronto, young Jim Endicott had led the Toronto delegation, rising so often "on a point of order" that he automatically caused a ripple of amusement....When a revolt broke out on the need for more time to discuss the causes of war, Jim [was chosen] as the *pro tem* chairman. He was one of many veterans present who had vowed in the trenches of France to dedicate their lives to peace.

Mary's memories of how her "Life with Jim" began. She cherished the belief that the marriage was one of those in which "heaven had a hand," and took pleasure recalling details which supported that hypothesis:

That chance meeting between trains in Chatham on that fateful weekend was not, as it seemed, a matter of blind fate which brought our lives together. Several years earlier Jim's father, after being our house-guest over a Sunday's preaching for missions, had said to him, "I met just the right girl for you on this trip!" Jim [a divinity student] was so astonished at this remark that it occurred to him when he was invited to preach in Dresden in January 1925. His father, discussing time-tables said, "You'll have several hours' wait between trains in Chatham. You might drop in to see my old friend, Charles Austin, in his store." The name rang a bell with SCM associations and with that earlier remark of his father. Jim wondered if he would meet the Austin daughter! He did.

Moreover, after Jim's brief visit in the Austin home between trains my mother said to me…"Now that's the kind of young man I'd like to see you marry!" I laughed and said, "Well, this one's booked!" and thought no more of it.

Two weeks later, however, Jim, too, would attend the Washington International Missionary Conference because since the age of thirteen he had wanted to become a missionary like his father and go to China, the land of his birth and childhood. Although meeting Mary Austin at the conference set in motion a whirlwind romance, his first priority remained the childhood dream of following in his father's footsteps. Nevertheless, to cite *Rebel Out of China*, her effect on him was "overpowering." In her memoirs Mary validates that claim:

> Unknown to either of us a miracle was taking place in our hearts and minds that weekend as we met at meal-times and walked the beautiful avenue between the Capitol and the Lincoln Memorial, exploring each other's ideas and experience as only newly-found friends can do. We each felt the inner excitement of the discovery of mutual interests but were unaware that our faces shone and that one old friend among the delegates was so struck by this radiance that she went home and reported to relatives of mine that we were engaged!
>
> There was no basis in fact for this report but within a matter of weeks it was true. Jim and I had discussed my idea of going overseas as a visitor and journalist and he had promised to find out what travel arrangements could be made when the next batch of missionaries would be sent out. This formed a basis for meeting again when I went to Toronto a fortnight after the Washington conference to attend the National Girls Work Board.

February 19, 1925, was the crucial day. Jim met Mary in the morning in the Victoria College residence where she was staying. Here he said: "I've come to ask you to go to China with me." She quickly agreed, even though she knew he had not yet broken off his engagement to another

文
月
華
的
中
國
日
記

woman—Nina Yeomans, whom he had met while still an undergraduate at Victoria College.

In great anguish, Jim went to Belleville the next day and asked Nina to be released from his promise. A major scandal broke out among his circle of friends. His father, too, was highly displeased at his impetuous action, much as he admired Charles Austin's daughter. The storm blew over, especially when Nina moved to quell the criticism. She came to Toronto to make public her personal good wishes for Jim, and sent Mary a strong letter of assurance. Nevertheless, the latter retained some residual uneasiness. "I cannot be sure we did the right thing in rushing things so," Mary confided to Freda, after two happy years of marriage.

As time goes by people often come to believe that what they wished had happened was indeed the way things were. In Mary's case, towards the end of her life, as she dictated the story of her fairy-tale romance, she reversed the chronology of events: Jim knew something new and overwhelming had occurred, but he "talked over the matter with his parents and one or two older church friends" who gave him conflicting advice. After these quiet consultations he asked Nina to release him from the engagement and only when they had agreed to "remain as friends and go their separate ways" did he ask if Mary would come to China with him. In this revised version, then, Jim did not propose to Mary until early March—in a car beside the railway tracks in Chatham.

"How characteristic it was for him to have come to the point at once, without any build-up or waiting for a romantic setting!" Mary enthused in her memoirs. "As for me, my whole being leapt to accept. I knew something unique and full of wonder had happened to me."

The reality of what happened was described in a letter Mary wrote her father one year after "Jim spoke the magic words":

This is the anniversary of the week of revolution.…When I think of poor Jim's haggard, distracted face when he came to Annesley that morning to have a talk with me, of our walk down the muddy sidewalks of University Avenue and over to the King Edward Hotel, hoping to find you still there that we might talk over with you our bewildered discovery of mingled joy and pain.

I know Miss Addison's words are true and that our happiness was born of great sorrow. So far I think it has risen to the heights [our critics] would desire, but I have to laugh when I think of the two of us that morning sitting in the mezzanine of the King Edward because we had nowhere to go and we were too exhausted by the shock to walk further.

I must have given Jim some inkling of how I felt but I remember when he asked me if I loved him, I said, "You don't want me to tell you here, do you?" and we had to be content with holding hands under his hat and not caring how foolish we looked to the occasional chamber-maid who flitted by.

I remember he said we'd have to buy a stove in Canada to use in China, but that was as far as he had gone in calculations of loot and he rather terrified me by saying that I would have to bake the bread. I think I inwardly resolved we would live on love and imported soda biscuits but outwardly I felt sure that all things were possible. Then we went for lunch at the Mission Tea Room but all we could gulp down was some thin soup and a glass of milk. (to Charles Austin, 19 February 1926)

From a much later letter Mary wrote to her father, we know the next drama in the fairy-tale romance recorded in her memoirs is faithful to the actual historical events:

Early in March Jim asked to come to Chatham. I met him with the car and we waited at the Canadian National Railway crossing for the long train to pull out. Ten minutes later we suddenly realized the train was gone and the traffic had moved on around us, probably thinking we were stalled. Far from it; we were rushing through space to the stars!...

He'd brought a gold ring with a blue lapis lazuli into which the outline of the Capitol dome had been carved. It was his interpretation of my preference for a ring, which had personal significance for both of us. Blue and gold were the colours I wore that weekend in Washington and the stone itself came from China.

I remember how we sat in church and looked at it—with all the choir staring at us—and how it matched my blue-and-gold hat and scarf. (to Charles Austin, 8 March 1936)

For ten weeks they wrote each other almost daily. Mary summed up her feelings for Jim in these words: "You are strong enough and experienced enough to go with me through any garden of pain...together we shall not be crushed...somehow in a way I cannot know, now, through you I shall find the Loving Purpose behind and in all life." They would be a "mutual improvement society," she said, talking freely to one another, from time to time, about personal problems. She had already inaugurated

文
月
華
的
中
國
日
記

it in her letters, asking Jim to be more sensitive to other people's feelings, paying more attention to conventional etiquette, for example.

Jim was dubious about the notion of a "mutual improvement society," but said he would try to be more thoughtful.

At this time Mary had her consultation with Dr. Margaret Strong, the psychoanalyst. She also asked Jim to visit Dr. Strong so that he might understand her psychological difficulties. He went for one visit—all there was time for as they were booked to leave for China early that summer. He found Freudian analysis confusing, but his willingness to go gave Mary the courage to discuss sexual matters freely with him. Jim responded in kind. A remarkable achievement for two people trained to believe "sex is sin."

Jim had not had a deeply felt spiritual awakening equivalent to Mary's 1923 experience at the Sharman seminar at Bon Echo park. He had attended a Sharman study group at Victoria College but, unlike Mary, was not convinced by the importance attached to the small group methodology in which individuals found their own truth. He had however, a great respect and deep affection for the ideas of Professor H.B. Hooke, whose eloquent plea for students to "work for a cause" had so impressed Mary. Of course, they had both participated in the founding conference of the Student Christian Movement and were committed to its ideals of peace and justice. Thus, even though Jim was committed to become an ordained minister and Mary had discarded most of traditional theology, they felt their agreement in values and general purposes outweighed any conflicting ideas.

In that fateful spring of 1925 their theological differences faded into insignificance: the potent promise of sexual pleasure was uppermost in both minds. Just before their June nineteenth wedding Jim penned an impassioned love letter:

> You are more than a symbol of life, you are a challenging spirit—God's way of stabbing my spirit broad awake—and my life rises to meet that challenge and the joy of battle is in my eye. So while you may have lost faith in my maturity and judgement—and my manners—I care not just so long as you do not lose faith in what is now a reality, that my love for you and the meaning of yours to me is a real challenge to growth.
>
> I wish you were here in my arms at this moment. The overwhelming thought has just struck me that this is the last letter I shall write you before

we are given the freedom of love and the social cherubim lift the flaming swords that guard the gates of Eden.

Mary cherished that last phrase; "Eden" became her code word for the heart of their marriage.

文
月
華
的
中
國
日
記

Mary Austin and Jim Endicott on their wedding day, 19 June 1925. The flower girl is Mary's niece, Joyce Wright.

On June 19, 1925, she floated down the long lawn outside the Austins' mansion, on the arm of her father, "precisely as the sun sank below the horizon leaving rosy clouds in its train." The honeymoon was at the Endicotts' summer cottage in Muskoka:

We tried to read aloud from a book on Cobden and Bright and one on Garibaldi, which had especially impressed Jim in his history course. We made little progress in these books but had better luck exchanging poems as we drifted lazily in the canoe or watched the wind lash the rain in fury. We took pictures of each other by the rocks and in the daisy-fields and in a tiny cove on a protected side of the island, which served as a Garden of

文
月
華
的
中
國
日
記

Eden setting—with Adam wearing a wristwatch, and Eve a floating white veil. ("Life with Jim")

Amidst the bliss of Eden-in-Muskoka, and in spite of reading Marie Stopes's *Married Love*, Mary unexpectedly became pregnant—contrary to the advice given by the Mission Board to all young missionaries. They urged a delay of two years in founding a family to allow time for language study and to get used to a new country.

Because of a great wave of anti-foreign feeling in China (See "Warlord China," Appendix B) their sailing date kept being postponed. In the interim they often visited Jim's mother, Sarah Diamond Endicott, who was mortally ill with cancer.

Finally, in early October, the call came. Now there were farewell parties and church services. Most of the time it was Jim who spoke, but at her home church, in spite of her stammering, she did too:

As I stepped into the old pulpit at Park Street Church in Chatham, my parents were especially astonished and delighted. It seemed like an unexpected parting gift I left with them....My mother seemed frail and I felt I might never see her again.

Hardest of all was our last visit to Jim's mother in hospital shortly before our train left. As we wept together in the narrow berth of the transcontinental train that night, Jim's mind kept recurring to trivial things—times when he had forgotten to empty the ashes or the garbage. They were like daggers in his heart now. He remembered, too, the advice his mother had given him with her marriage blessing: "Don't scold her, whatever she does."

At last we were on board the beautiful Empress of Asia, on which we had first-class cabins (this was the custom until the Depression). As we stood by the rail watching Vancouver recede into the distance, I looked up at Jim. For him the weighing of the anchors was the opening chord in the symphony of his life's work. He was returning to his first motherland, his first language and the familiar sights and sounds of childhood.

Suddenly, as the ship swung out to sea I felt alone, with a stranger whose ways had not been mine. Then unexpectedly the first flutter of new life stirred within me....I pinched Jim's arm as the shoreline became faint and told him about the flutter kick. He was properly thrilled too, and sensing my feelings, he told me how his parents, in pioneer missionary days, had stood by the rail in Yokohama on their way to China. As they gazed at the snowy crown of Mount Fuji floating above the mist, his father's face was radiant with anticipation of their new life; his mother was winking back the tears in apprehension for the future. ("Life with Jim")

文月華

As Mary sailed into a new life she thought a lot about what her mother-in-law must have experienced and recorded in her memoirs the very different circumstances of Sarah Endicott's life as a missionary's wife.

There were about 8,000 missionaries in China when Jim was a child, most of them bringing a narrow, rigid gospel calculated to save the heathen from hellfire. Our Mission, of the Methodist (and later The United) Church of Canada, was of the Protestant Liberal minority, with a strong accent on humanitarian activities—hospitals, schools and a university, nursery and literacy classes as well as preaching the Gospel of Love and Redemption.

In Mother Endicott's time there were few such facilities; only Mission schools admitted girls for many years after education began to spread. The abolition of foot binding for girls began with missionary concern and became law when the old empire gave way to a republic in 1911 under Sun Yat Sen.

A woman showing her bound feet. Although foot-binding had been made illegal in 1911, the practice continued for several decades, especially in the countryside.

文月華的中國日記

文
月
華
的
中
國
日
記

Jim's mother had been especially concerned about these two reforms in the status of women, which became our Mission policy during her time in China. She was completely absorbed in the care of her five children and never acquired fluency in Chinese but she watched each step in the emancipation of women with keen interest and was deeply moved that one of her sons dedicated his life to carry on the missionary work his father and other pioneers had begun.

She had hoped to hear news that we were settled in language study in Chengtu [before she died], but the end of her long suffering came the day after we arrived in China. We felt very lonely and far away, although we were thankful for her release from pain. ("Life with Jim")

文月華

Before meeting Jim, Mary had wanted to come to China and write human interest stories for her church publication. Upon her arrival in Shanghai, she began to take notes that would eventually end up in the first of many circular letters to family and friends:

Shanghai's streets are crowded and chaotic, in spite of the beautiful and imposing foreign buildings in the financial centre on the Bund. Such endless mobs of unkempt, bare-footed rickshaw coolies in ragged, faded blue tunics....Oh, the dirt and the struggle for a livelihood; the competition for every little way of earning a bit!

An unbiased observer could not help but feel the Chinese have some justification for their anti-foreign feeling. Many of the foreigners act like conquerors. The kicking of rickshaw coolies by half-baked youths from abroad, the parks that are closed to the Chinese (the French allow them in on permits, the Brits not at all)—these create an impression with which it is difficult to cope....

We stayed at the Missionary Home, which exists for the benefit of transients of every faith and creed....All the guests were expected to assemble morning and evening for prayers, which included a 20–minute homily from one of the elder defenders of the faith. The one morning we went we got...the hottest warning about hell fire that I have ever heard. Apparently, hell is the backbone of religion and the chief reason for the life of Jesus and for all missionary effort.

We learned that this traditional-fundamentalist introduction to China is a standing joke among most of the missionaries, and that the back stairway leading from the dining rooms is known as "the prayer escape." As if by a special intervention of providence, our room was at the head of these stairs. (circular letter, 9 December 1925)

文月華

On November 23, 1925, the Endicotts began their 1200-mile trip up the Yangtze River from Shanghai to Chungking. There were three stages to this voyage, each one in a slightly smaller steamer. A large well-appointed British ship took them as far as Hankow. This was a treaty port with a foreign concession where, a year later, anti-foreign feelings would explode, an event that would dramatically disrupt the Endicotts' life. At Hankow the travellers disembarked and went for five days in another vessel to the city of Ichang, gateway to the treacherous rapids of the Yangtze Gorges. Here they transferred to yet a smaller but more powerful ship, the only type that could navigate the perilous waters ahead:

The trip from Ichang to Chungking is one of the most exciting stretches of river in the world. Jim remembered the power of the rapids and the majesty of the gorges from his boyhood, and, for once, it was impossible for him to exaggerate. Our expectations were over fulfilled.

The river is so narrow in spots that the cliffs come very close together until, from the side of the deck, they seem to fill the sky. The formation of the rocks and caves therein, with tier upon tier of mountain peaks fading into a ghostly distance, were sources of never-ending delight to us....

The thatched shacks "stuck like the horns of a bull" on the steep sides, while tiny patches of cultivated land around them spoke of life reduced to its simplest state. No wonder ancient Chinese poets used to come here to meditate.

When we rounded the curve into the Wind-Box Gorge, the siren gave a long blast of warning of which you could count six distinct waves of echo. That shrill whistle of the siren is one of the weirdest sounds I have ever heard—like the shriek of a lost soul, with the volume of a dragon's roar....

The channels of the mighty torrent are always changing and the water levels vary considerably from day to day. We saw two steamers perched high and dry on the rocky banks and heard from the captain of two ships that have gone to the bottom within the last two years. (circular letter, 9 December 1925)

As they approached the notorious Yeh Tan or Wild Rapids, Sarah Endicott's experience on her first trip up the river by Chinese houseboat in 1892 came to Mary's mind. In her memoirs she recollected how "the passengers

文
月
華
的
中
國
日
記

had been walking along the towpath while the trackers tugged at the bamboo ropes. The roar of the rapids almost drowned the trackers' rhythmic calls as they heaved on the sturdy boat when lo! one of the ropes snapped, the boat was knocked hither and yon on the rocks before they could pull it in. A piece off the bottom had been smashed and Sarah Endicott's precious portable organ had gone to the bottom. Her pregnancy nausea during the six weeks by steamer and houseboat must have become acute" ("Life with Jim").

Mary's private thoughts about her mother-in-law were not recorded in the circular letter the Endicotts sent to Canada after arriving in Chungking. It told a different story about this part of Mary's first trip through the Yangtze River Gorges:

The Yeh Tan rapids, situated below the 25-mile stretch of the Witches' Mountain Gorge, were in an angry mood; the large whirlpool near the left bank looked very fierce with the centre about four feet lower than the edges. The spray from the force of the current hitting our boat, as it entered the rapid near the right bank at full speed, blew up over the bows.

In spite of all the power we could muster, the effect of our full speed against the current was to ferry the ship straight across the river onto the edge of the whirlpool where it seemed as if we would surely be thrown up on the bank. We hung on the edge of the whirlpool for some minutes and then tried to cross the rapid at an angle, only to land back where we started on the right bank.

Once more we butted up into the current only to be driven toward the whirlpool again. By this time the funnel was getting very hot. While the ship hung on the edge of the whirlpool once more, the crew threw a steel cable to trackers on the shore. As two hundred men pulled it up and fastened it to a high pile of rock, the ship stood still on all the power it could summon, with two fire hoses playing on the smoke stack. The water ran down in boiling streams.

The vessel swayed back and forth on the edge of the raging, swirling water until the cable was fastened and the anchor engine heaved on it and pulled the boat through. The captain said we used three or four tons of coal in that half hour. (circular letter, 9 December 1925)

3

Struggling with Culture Shock

Before she actually arrived in the country, Mary's knowledge of China came mainly from a short course she took in Chinese Art at the Metropolitan Museum of Art in New York while doing graduate work at Columbia University.

> I marveled at the delicacy of the paintings...felt the excitement of movement in the swirl of draperies, drawn, carved or embroidered. The same aliveness was conveyed by the white-capped waves, the dragon's graceful scaly body and swishing tail, the lone bird swooping over a valley. The beauty of these objects of bygone centuries made China an enchanted name.
>
> The real China [was] vastly different from romantic, ancient China, whose treasures I had studied. I was overwhelmed, in our early years in Chungking, by the sight of ragged, underfed, blue-clad millions, crowded into tiny mud farm huts or dingy, jerry-built, open-front shops. (*Five Stars over China*)

The real China in 1925 was also a war zone. Stories abounded of shootings along the Yangtze River which Mary passed on in her first of many circular letters to family and friends:

> We...had no trouble up the river...from civil commotions or soldiers firing. The latter fire on steamers, sometimes apparently for a little sport, at other times to attempt to collect illegal taxes. Two months ago some soldiers in junks fired on an American steamer, presumably because they were annoyed at the wash from the steamer [threatening to engulf] them. After they had fired nine shots, the Mei Ren opened with a machine gun and killed one and wounded eight. There was a great commotion here in Chungking and the bodies of the victims were deposited on the desks of the office of the steamer company until they could get satisfaction. This is a favourite, and one must admit a rather dramatic method used by the Chinese to keep a grievance from being overlooked. (circular letter, 9 December 1925)

文
月
華
的
中
國
日
記

That same letter explained that the danger of a new outbreak of hostilities toward foreigners lurked just below the surface. During their first week in Chungking, Mary and Jim were invited to the homes of missionaries and foreign businessmen where they heard graphic details of what had been going on the previous summer:

> To be slapped or stoned in the streets, as well as reviled, to have their servants terrorised into leaving them so that supplies were cut off, to have to leave their homes with a few minutes notice and crowd on to the gunboat to go down river, sleeping on decks, to hear their summer houses had been looted half an hour of their leaving is an ordeal to shake the stoutest....However, things are quiet now and most of the servants were waiting to receive them when they returned in October, glad to get work again.

A few weeks later, Jim had two personal experiences with overt anti-foreign hostility. In one case students were holding a street corner meeting. They shouted anti-foreign epithets and threw some overripe oranges at him. Later the same day he came across another group distributing pamphlets urging students not to attend Christian schools. "These dog-teachers teach history only to the Ming Dynasty because they are afraid to teach recent history....They turn you into a foreign dog and you must dance to their tune." The mothers of "foreign dogs" were also singled out for criticism in extremely unflattering terms.

Jim recognized these actions simply as signs of a growing Chinese nationalism; still he urged Mary not to take any unnecessary trips into the city that winter. She had begun attending the provincial Mission Council, enjoying the contact with other missionaries but now that came to an end.

文月華

Chungking was as far as the steamers went. Foreign passengers on their way to other destinations stayed at the Mission Business Agency, run by Gordon and Clara Jones as a small hotel. The Endicotts, waiting to go on to Chengtu for language study, stayed at the Agency until arrangements could be made for this last stage of their journey. While they waited, Mary recorded her first stark impressions of Chungking, for her friends:

> If any of you lack the inspiration for a creepy nightmare, I wish you could go through the streets of Chungking at night, carried in a chair, to and from a dinner or meeting. It is like going through a labyrinth of winding tunnels

lined with caves on either side, weirdly lighted with torch lights or oil lamps except in a few sections where there are electric lights. Until about ten o'clock the labyrinth is crowded with unfamiliar forms and faces jostling each other and all talking at once. The caves are the little shops and eating-places with food of all sorts exposed. Later, boards are put up for the night and one catches glimpses of piles of bedding being made up for the night.

文月華的中國日記

The type of sedan chair Mary would have ridden through the streets of Chungking when she first arrived (and later, in 1929, with two small children, chap. 9). Chair carriers wore straw sandals to protect the soles of their feet.

Chungking is built on hills and one has to go up long flights of stone steps to go almost anywhere. I don't know which is worse for a newcomer, being carried in a sedan chair up the steps or down. Every few minutes the chairmen stop and change shoulders, often abruptly. The streets and steps are so narrow that two chairs can barely pass, and even one chair in a crowded street creates a disturbance; people get poked with the poles in spite of the shouting of the carriers.

I can't get over grabbing the arms of the chair tensely when I see their poor thin shoulders getting a gibe, especially the women, and once a woman nurs-

文
月
華
的
中
國
日
記

ing a baby as she went along. I keep wondering if they are feeling resentment for their discomfort, how much of it is directed towards the person riding in state, and how much towards the carriers who stop for nobody except a group of soldiers drawn up before a shop to arrest someone.

I gave up chair riding and insisted on walking everywhere, clinging to Jim's arm on one side and to any other strong male on the other. The streets are slippery from the water slopped over the pails being carried up from the river and the rats dart across from one side to the other just before you step on them. All this in the eerie light of a coal-oil lantern carried by one of the male escorts.

Whether I ride, high above the uneven, slippery steps and the rats, or whether I walk, tense with apprehension, it is like going from purgatory into heaven to pass through gates opened at our call by a friendly gateman into the quiet cleanliness and comparative spaciousness of a foreign compound where the dinner or the meeting brings cheer and renews confidence that it is possible to become accustomed to much that startles the nerves and rends the heart. (circular letter, 9 December 1925)

文月華

Canadian missionaries sent to West China were expected to devote their first two years in the country to language study. Usually year one was in Chengtu, where there was a thriving foreign community because of a mission-supported university and hospitals. The second year would be spent in a more isolated station.

While she waited in Chungking before continuing on to Chengtu, Mary grew anxious about the advanced state of her pregnancy:

I had been quietly worrying about this last phase of our extensive journey ever since our long delay in sailing had taken me further and further along in my great adventure. I had been in excellent health but there was always medical help within call.

On the last lap, from Chungking to Chengtu, we had the choice of ten days overland, sleeping in Chinese inns where sanitary conditions were primitive and no medical help available, or going up by junk for three or four weeks, under cleaner conditions but still entirely alone except for three single returning missionaries who were to go along with us. They would interpret for us but be as ignorant and helpless as ourselves should an emergency occur or even be threatened.

I knew that Jim's mother had made a much harder journey—in the same condition—from Shanghai and mostly by Chinese houseboat, but at least there was a young missionary doctor in their party if things went wrong. I am inclined to think now that Jim thought we should count on my good health and good luck to see us through and proceed normally, but he did not make it difficult to accept the advice of older missionaries to remain in Chungking....

When Harold Swann, a college friend of Jim's and his wife Donalda pressed us to make our home with them for the time of language study in Chungking, the die was cast. We stayed.

Barely had we got settled in the Swann's Nest when a senior missionary's wife, returning from furlough, insisted on medical escort on the overland trip because of a bad heart condition. It was arranged that a doctor would go with them five days up the road till they were met by a Chengtu missionary doctor who would be with them the rest of the way.

Executive urged that Jim and I join this party. There was great discussion but I was well into the seventh month by then and showing signs of fatigue induced by the long journey. I was much relieved when it was decided to leave things as they were.

I didn't want to make a fuss; indeed I was determined not to let Jim down as one incapable of a harder life than I had been used to. Perhaps that very effort to hide my feelings was part of the strain of the journey now beginning to show when I could relax. ("Life with Jim")

"Leaving things as they were" saved the cost and difficulty of transporting the enormous cargo of wedding gifts, which Mary's father had insisted on providing. Charles Austin had crated up a houseful of elegant furnishings—linens, dishes, appliances and furniture, including a piano—and sent them across the ocean. Bringing the many large crates up the Yangtze had been laborious, frustrating and expensive. The missionary who led the party and oversaw this endeavour became exasperated and declared that Chungking was quite far enough.

So it was that Mary's first winter in China was spent sharing a house with Harold and Donalda Swann—across the river from the teeming crowds of Chungking—in a compound at Duckling Pond, a peaceful hamlet nestled in fertile valleys of rice paddies.

Jim settled in quickly, setting his sights on becoming a language specialist, a goal made easier by his having been born and brought up in

文
月
華
的
中
國
日
記

Szechwan. In addition, he seemed to have a natural linguistic gift. He would become one of the few foreigners who spoke Chinese like a native. In her memoirs, Mary describes her own very different experience with learning the language:

Jim soon began to sound like the native to the country, which he was. Alas, for the contrast to me....I had a teacher for a short time twice a day—which was about all I could take that winter with spring and the child not far behind. Try as hard as I could—and perhaps that was part of the jinx—I could not reproduce the sounds I heard; they just came out all wrong....

Quite a few new missionaries struggled in vain to become fluent and natural but the result always sounded like a distorted version of the English translation. Sometimes the husband would be at ease with this accursed language but the wife would not; sometimes it was the other way around; for some the discouragement was too great and led to the termination of their work at the first furlough....

It may have been disappointment with life in China; it may have been an unconscious desire to protect me from having to converse or speak in

Peasants ploughing rice fields with water buffalo, outside the Duckling Pond compound where Mary was to spend her first winter in China. In background is the Gin I Middle School, where Jim taught in later years (chap. 13).

public under strain, which increases my natural difficulty. I just know that I could see a look of disgust on the faces of the various Chinese teachers who throughout our years of study turned from Jim's perfect reproduction of the Chinese idiom and sounds to his dumbbell wife.

At one time our teacher was an old-fashioned scholar with the long fingernails and wispy beard. He noticed me typing and asked Jim how it was that I could use this complicated machine. When Jim told him I was a university graduate, his wonder knew no bounds and he began to treat my faltering response to his teaching with more respect.

Before a month had passed Jim was able to define a new idea in simple words he had already learned and so to acquire, through free conversation with the teacher, a new vocabulary of his own.

I was not so fortunate. Once at dinner, soon after we began housekeeping I rang the bell and asked the Table Boy with perfect confidence, to bring in the tea strainer. He looked deeply puzzled and turned for interpretation to Jim who could not restrain a twinkle in his eye as he gave the correct version. As the Boy discreetly vanished Jim answered the question in my face by saying, "My dear, you asked him to bring in the kitchen stove!" My sense of humour upheld me but I could have cheerfully thrown both stove and strainer at their two heads. The sounds are law and lu with different accents—a double trap for me!

Jim comforted me by reminding me of our friend Marguerite Brown who was trying to train her Table Boy to wear the new white serving gowns she had supplied. When he appeared again without it, she asked sternly, "Where is your apron?" He looked startled then quickly retired. Her husband was in a gale of laughter and her red hair was rising until he managed to tell her she had actually asked: "Where is your tail?" The words are "wei-yao" and "wei-ba." The accents or tones used to say "wei" differ. Some sounds had four or five meanings, depending on the accent. For instance the word "ma" means mother, horse, curse, or wipe depending on accents only. ("Life with Jim")

Surrounded by unimaginable poverty and hostility towards foreigners, pregnant and lacking the language, she was stranded in a country that was pulling her down like the Yangtze Gorges whirlpool. Like the steel cables thrown to trackers from the steamer on the edge of the whirlpool, Mary used her typewriter to avoid being sucked into the whirling maelstrom of despair. She wrote many long letters to family and friends during the first few months, unfurling one lifeline after another:

41

文
月
華
的
中
國
日
記

Dear Family and Friends,

At Chinese New Year's the beggars flock into the city, and you can walk only a few feet on the busy streets without having to step close to one, if not over one. I suppose [people] get used to beggars after [they] have been in the east for a while, but certainly no westerner has any idea what the term really means until he comes here. Picture the most degraded-looking creature your imagination can conjure up, less than half-clothed, dirty, deformed in some way perhaps, with horrible sores...on almost any part of the body exposed prominently to arouse the pity of the passer-by. Then, imagine this poor wretch wailing and moaning and holding out his or her skinny hand, perhaps clutching at your coat or arm....The [deaf and] dumb beggars run their hands down your back to attract your attention, making queer sounds. (from Chungking, 22 February 1926)

Dear Freda,

The doctor is betting on a boy from the number of heartbeats, so we have been trying to take boys' names seriously. David seems to have waned in our affections and we feel James would be sure to be Jim some day and Jim would become Daddy and so we are trying out Mark. It sounds a bit harsh for a wee baby but would be nice later on....Anyway, I hope he <u>will</u> be the first of four "gospels" of Endicott, some of them "gospelles"....

I think the Jim of a year ago would have been rather astonished, could he have pictured the Mary of now. His first impressions of me were of my independence of thought and spirit, which were symbolized in my walk, the way I liked to swing along.

I think it has rather amazed him, since our marriage, how much I have counted on being with him and doing things with him. I know it has amazed me whenever I realize that it is almost as if I count all time lost that is not spent with him. It has been unusually so in our case, because of our nomadic life in contrast to the business-and-bungalow style of most newly-weds, and particularly since we have been surrounded by so much that is strange if not repellent.

I have remarked after an ordeal of going through the Chungking streets that the day of the chaperon or the escort for the feminine is revived in Chungking. Even Lal Swann says she wouldn't go about the city without her husband and certainly I would not. All of which amuses me when I remember what store I used to set by feminine independence. Jim and I still have good arguments and we don't claim to see eye to eye on many things, but to

a far greater extent than I ever imagined possible, I have taken on the attrib-
utes of "the clinging vine." Hardy's picture of "The Ivy-Wife" was a most
interesting discovery, with its dreadful warning at the close. (from Chungking, 11 February 1926)

"The Ivy-Wife" describes a woman with a "soft green claw," cramping
and binding her husband until he became "bark-bound," then flagged,
snapped and fell on his wife, destroying them both. Mary, who had con-
fidently driven a car in Chatham for ten years, was now trapped in a place
where foreign women like herself, who had previously felt safe to go out
alone, no longer did, even those who spoke Chinese.

Her colleagues perceived her strengths and talents, even if she had lost
sight of them. Early in 1926 the annual Provincial Mission Council met in
Chungking. The agenda included unequal treaties, extraterritoriality and
gunboat diplomacy:

> In the heat of the discussion on the floor of Council in Chungking Jim
> crossed swords sharply with some of the older and conservative members
> who believed things should stay as they were. When it came to gunboat pro-
> tection Jim got carried away and said, "The missionary movement was not
> based on a commission to 'go ye' into all the world and shoot the gospel into
> every creature!"...
>
> When I heard about it, I realized for the first time that I had married a
> firebrand....I still remember Harold Swann's brotherly advice to me: "Jim
> will get along fine with the Chinese; you will have to smooth the way with
> his missionary colleagues sometimes." ("Life with Jim")

文
月
華
的
中
國
日
記

4

Spring in the Golden Valley

The Small Dictator who altered all our plans is holding us to a strict schedule of walking from one to two hours a day. For a good brisk walk we prefer to promenade on the verandah each day but on sunny days promptly at four o'clock when the language teacher departs, we set out for a hike in the hills, which look so beautiful on our horizon.

Spring is already in bloom in the valleys where the crescent-shaped rice-fields, still standing in water, alternate with fields of rape-oil plants, which have the brilliance of mustard and all the fields are bordered with the purple flowering bean. When we raise our eyes from this Golden Valley we see the odd plum tree in blossom and the new green is beginning to show on the bamboo clumps. Sometimes the peasants in the little mud huts, aroused by their fiercely barking dog, come out to reassure me, smile and wish me joy for the birth of a son.

The "Golden Valley," where Mary and Jim walked while awaiting the birth of their first child.

These walks through the Golden Valley as we call it, have become a symbol of our happiness in the second spring of great events in the building of our life together and the founding of our family. We have decided to come back on a sentimental pilgrimage whenever we can as we recall some lines Jim sent me a year ago:

Know this: That every year you live I swear

I will make Spring come everywhere. (circular letter, 1 March 1926)

文月華

Anticipating the birth of her first child not only sustained Mary through those first harsh three months in China, it became part of her personal cosmology. Early in March she confided to Freda "it must be the most thrilling anticipation there is in life, the mystery of travail and then the wonder of having a baby." Joyous and poignant.

Well, Mother darling,

Here I am on the tenth day,[1] sitting up in bed for the first time and seizing the opportunity to write my first letter.

I am propped up by the backrest, which we had made, painted white, & Jim covered with canvas....I am writing this on the little bedside table, which the Hospital lent me....It's convenient for meals, even when I have been lying down, leaning on my elbow for them....

I am just longing for the time when I can bathe and dress him myself—or even when I can hold him in my arms and get a good look at him.

When the doctor told me I could work if I wanted to, I went to it as if it was a rowing race. My arms ached for days from pulling on the bed-head and Jim's hand, and my middle muscles were quite paralysed for about three days afterwards....

Jim stayed right by me[2] and next day one knee was all black and blue where he had pressed it against the iron side of the bed every time I was pushing. He said it was not as bad as he expected and he was most interested in watching the actual birth of the baby. He said when the head appeared his face was like a masque, no expression on it at all.

Immediately the baby began to breathe and gave that dear little cry, which is like no other for sweetness, his face began to have the expression of a living being. It makes me think of Genesis—"And God breathed into his

1 Western medical expertise at the time advised complete bed rest for two weeks after a birth.
2 The active support of her husband may seem commonplace now, but it was unusual at that time.

45

文
月
華
的
中
國
日
記

nostrils the breath of life and man became a living soul." I think the writer must have got his inspiration from watching the birth of a child. (to Minnie Austin, 3 April 1926)

Norman Austin Endicott was only five weeks old when Mary had to face the full reality of missionary life in warlord China. For five months she had lived peacefully behind compound walls at Duckling Pond. Now, like The Lord forcing Adam and Eve to leave Eden, the Szechwan Mission Council decreed that Jim and Mary move to the small town of Chungchow, 125 miles down the Yangtze River from Chungking, and continue their language studies there.

The move was made in two instalments. First, Jim took their thirty-nine crates of furniture by junk to Chungchow because it was not a treaty port and steamers were not allowed to dock there. "The thought of him being away for a whole week is appalling," Mary told her sister Jane.

Travelling by *huaga'r*, a kind of deck chair slung between poles, outside Duckling Pond compound.

In her memoirs Mary recalls with transparent honesty her feelings of panic and terror during that "appalling week." It should be remembered she'd only been out of bed for three weeks and new mothers often experience similar exaggerated feelings.

On May 4th Jim left home at 6:30 A.M., took the junk across the river to the city fore-shore below the mission business agency to load the furniture we had brought from Canada (except the piano) as well as various staples and canned goods not available in Chungchow. Then the junk came back to the south side to get the things we had been using all winter.

I was to go down to see them off and was looking forward to the sight of our first junk load and the romantic idea of my husband sailing in one. Unfortunately, by the time I was warned they were almost ready and had got half way down the bank to the river, I met carriers coming back: the boat had already sailed. The boatmen were grouching lest they might not reach a town ten miles downstream before dark. They wanted an early start from that place before the customs men arrived on duty.

I could have wept with disappointment for I had been ready for two hours. This was the opening of a new era in our life together, a step forward towards our own home, where I expected to put down my roots into life in China....

It was a perfect May evening with the scent of blossoming trees drifting from the little farmhouses as I climbed the long hill with patient gateman just behind. The rice fields were bright green and the excitement of new life bursting out filled the spring air. It fitted in with the thrill of being on our own, but still, all was fraught with uncertainty and apprehension.

Inevitably there came into my mind stories I had heard of junks over turned by the swift current or bandits who had fired at random and in one case had killed a child sleeping in its mother's arms. These blood-curdling perils had actually happened to members of our mission....

I was determined to be cheerful before the Swanns but I was painfully aware that robbers broke into houses. In fact, the very room where I was sleeping was the one that had been entered the year before. The compound wall—topped by pieces of broken glass in the cement—no longer seemed a strong bulwark.

Moreover, I had not lost the feeling that oriental servants had been known to murder their employers in their beds so I welcomed the sugges-tion that Hal should lock the door of my bedroom leaving open the window which opened on to their sleeping porch. He and Lal must have chuckled together over my exaggerated anxiety.

5

Chungchow Diary: Living with Uncertainty

Mary's letters during what she later called "that first ghastly year" were valiant efforts at sounding upbeat. When terrifying or painful experiences were over, she called them "adventures." The move to Chungchow, for example, was announced to family and friends as "the beginning of our real adventures as missionaries." After the passage of years, however, there is a greater ring of honesty. In this "looking back" account of that same move, based closely on the original letter, Mary inserted the phrases "that terrifying gap of river" and "my first adventure in dangerous living."

Travelling in China is of all things the most haphazard. You never can tell when a steamer is to leave or when it is likely to arrive. The uncertainty of the height of the water made it doubly uncertain at this time of year. We had four hours notice to leave Chungking, the said notice arriving while we were still in bed one morning.

Fortunately, our trunks were packed, in the main, and what was in use or left out could be thrown into suitcases or the korrie, a huge basket suitcase which is a standing joke in most families out here as the place where one looks first for lost articles. The neighbours came in to help, and in two hours time we were sitting all ready and the carriers had returned for the second instalment of luggage. They just got back in time to carry my chair and the leftovers to the steamer to get us there a few minutes before she was due to sail.

In the general confusion Jim packed all my dresses but a gay flowered chiffon so that I set off in state in the drizzling rain.

The Swanns loaned us their *bay joudze* for the baby, a sort of covered bamboo box in which he can lie down and which is carried on a coolie's back. It was the first time we had taken him out and Jim kept close behind him to keep the people in the village from peeking in at him or to rescue him from a rice field if the coolie should slip on the muddy path. He looked very proud striding along behind his son, both of us trying to picture his father doing the same years ago....

文
月
華
的
中
國
日
記

Landing at Chungchow early next morning in the drizzle (me still in my party dress) was unforgettable. The steamer was turned to face upstream but the anchor was not lowered. As we came in sight of the town, the captain had blown four whistles to alert our friends but the engines idled only while we got our luggage and ourselves off.

In the meantime, all the little sampans moored along the shore rushed out to get our goods and us. Some of them carried Chinese passengers who had been waiting for a lucky break, and scrambled as best they could aboard the drifting ship. All this with much shouting and shoving.

Although we were only a few yards from shore the yellow waters of the Yangtze were swirling by ominously. I looked at the gap between the ship and the nearest sampan that had hooked onto the side of the ship and I wondered if I would make it with my precious bundle in my arms. Dr. Anderson, who is making his annual dental itinerary, went first and stood in the sampan with a reassuring smile, while Jim went to the baggage hold to supervise the unloading of our trunks and bags.

I looked at the rushing waters, then at the two British officers whose coolness and confidence inspired me to go ahead. The captain held the baby while the chief officer handed me down to Dr. Anderson in the sampan and then gave me the baby without dropping him in that gap of terrifying river.

My first adventure in dangerous living, I thought, as I smiled with relief and waved my thanks. Next came Evelyn Morgan, aged nine, who had been in school in Chungking and took this rare chance of escort home for the summer holidays. She was beaming with a child's love of adventure....

Before the sampan had reached the shore, the big white ship had moved off, turned downstream and was on her course again. I had a sinking feeling for a moment that this was our last link with the civilized world, as I knew it.

Dr. Alex Pincock had heard the four whistles and came down the city wall to meet us, followed by his sedan chair for me. As we had no way of warning him that we were arriving a few days before schedule, we had to sit in the little sampan at the shore to wait. The shouts from the boatmen had spread the news that some High Noses were arriving. In a moment we were surrounded by a crowd of curious people, mostly ragged children with running noses and scabby heads who had scrambled down the bank with incredible speed.

I felt unable to cope with them if they should push their way onto our end of the little boat. But Dr. Anderson was there to reassure me and the

文
月
華
的
中
國
日
記

boatmen spoke roughly to anyone whose natural curiosity seemed about to get the better of him.

Jim and Mary, happy in Chungchow, 1926, even though life is uncertain.

At last the chair and three carriers arrived and soon we were climbing the steep hillside on which the city is built. I was relieved to be more or less separated from the crowd who followed with delighted shrieks of laughter and no doubt rude remarks about the foreigner. Before we had made our slow laboured way up the 1000 steps of the incline along the city wall, the crowd lost interest, even in the tiny foreign baby cuddled in my arms who had been, of course, the main point of their curiosity. ("Life with Jim," based on circular letter, 29 May 1926)

文月華

The Endicotts stayed in the Pincock's compound while renovations were made to the house they were to stay in:

The chief point of interest in Chungchow for us is, of course, the little house, which is to be our first real home together. It is quite different from the other foreign houses, being a Chinese made-over house, now sadly in need of repair....My heart sank the first day or two when I went down from the Pincock's compound to see our house, but the more often I went the more possibilities I saw in it. Now I am impatient for the fall to be here and we can get settled in it.

文
月
華
的
中
國
日
記

They are making some alterations which will overcome the defects of darkness and dampness, adding a fireplace in the living-room and one in the bedroom for cheer and then it will be not only liveable but possessing a charm of its own in its squat, rambling lines....

The really old Chinese houses do not have windows and I imagine this one did not have any, originally, for they all look as if they had been hacked out and were hanging on by the eyelashes, so to speak.

Jim has spent a good deal of time unpacking the furniture and now everything but the stove has seen the light. I try to go down every morning to be in at the post mortem, as a good deal of the furniture has been damaged in one way or another, a leg off here, a back off there, and so on. There are no total casualties and almost all the damage is done in such a way that it can be mended. Our lovely walnut dining table is intact, not even a scratch on the surface and the surface of the buffet is untouched. As they were our most handsome pieces, we are fortunate....

I'm ever so glad we could bring some furniture because it is quite different from that which is made out here and it has really come through the wars very well. (circular letter, 29 May 1926)

Jim christened their dream-home-to-be with Chinese characters, which meant "Luxuriant-Growth-Of-Happiness House." They were to take possession in September after returning from "The Hills," where the missionaries went to escape the stifling heat.

Soon after the Endicotts arrived in Chungchow a letter came from their friends the Swanns, describing the fighting that broke out in Chungking just two days after Mary and Jim left: "Everything has been tied up...no word from the city, no connections with the medical property, and the people of the countryside hiding lest the retreating army should press them into service. For three days a picket of soldiers watched everything we did from the top of that big grave near our compound wall."

In Chungchow itself the presence of soldiers of a warlord on the run meant it was dangerous for any Chinese servant to be out on the street alone less they get pressed into service. The workmen repairing the Endicott's Luxuriant-Growth-of-Happiness house ate at the Pincocks' compound and had to be escorted back and forth between the compounds every day.

文月華

文
月
華
的
中
國
日
記

Soon after arriving in Chungchow Mary found a way to disguise her fears by using props and dramatizing her "adventures."

> I have had two new thrills since coming here. The first time I went from the Pincock's down to our compound alone I felt like little Red Riding Hood making her maiden trip to Grandmother. With the memory of Chungking beggars in mind I felt sure that someone would be sure to touch me with their dirty or diseased hands if not actually carry me off for ransom, but nobody did. I took the coolie with me several times at first but then I was able to go alone and ceased to feel panicky.
>
> Wearing the pith hat we bought in Shanghai (the second thrill), I saw myself as a northerner living under semi-tropical skies in a picture in the National Geographic Magazine. "I must be a formidable figure," I said to myself, "with my sun helmet, dark glasses and cane to ward off the dogs that guard every Chinese farm-house, and nobody would guess that I have become a veritable clinging vine."
>
> I smiled to remember a poem I had once quoted to Jim in our courting days:
>
>> I am a quiet gentleman
>> And I would sit and think
>> But my wife is walking the whirlwind
>> Through night as black as ink.
>
> That was the kind of person I wanted to be but coming to China had set me back a few notches. ("Life with Jim")

文月華

The month of June brought intense heat. Killing the two or three mosquitoes inside the netting over their bed became a nightly routine. Dr. Pincock believed in prevention, and everyone took quinine two consecutive nights a week to avoid malaria.

Dysentery was also common in the summer season, brought by flies from the open cesspools, which stored the nitrate-rich human waste or "night soil" used for fertilizing crops.

> A newcomer, walking warily on the narrow stone paths between rice fields had to learn the technique of manoeuvring his way past a peasant carrying two huge buckets of this essential commodity at the ends of a shoulder pole. It was difficult to convince an illiterate house-coolie that flies could carry debilitating, and sometimes fatal diseases, from this source.

文
月
華
的
中
國
日
記

This was one of the basic points of public health education. Big posters in the clinic showed a hand swatting the fly to save the baby nearby. I learned that dysentery had been the cause of most of the deaths of foreign children over the years and my anxiety to protect our chubby little son became acute.

The fear of illness paled in significance, however, when truly unexpected risks occurred:

Then the terrible news came that Mrs. Sibley of our mission had been decapitated while walking along the street at noon. This news was so horrible that it seemed hardly credible but there were the stark details: She and her husband lived in a small out-station off the beaten track like our own Chungchow. She had gone up to Chengtu for dental work and had gone out on the street to do a bit of shopping when an unknown assassin who attacked her from behind, cut off her head with a sword, put it into a bag and threw it into a public toilet. (circular letter, 29 May 1926)

Mary went on to assure her family and friends that the authorities had things well in hand. She subsequently confided to her sister, however, that the news had upset her milk supply and that Jim was "almost laid out, ill, off and on for several days."

文月華

By July it was time to move up to "The Hills," a widespread practice in all mission fields of escaping the summer heat. Szechwan summers were extremely hot and humid. The Endicotts rented a bungalow of their own. It was a special time for the young couple but not without its problems:

The country people around here are friendly but very, very curious. I suppose it is like a visit to a museum or a zoo to come and stare at the foreigners and their things. At this moment there are about ten boys and men squeezing themselves in the open doorway of the study, craning their necks and watching this marvellous machine and the two monkeys writing.

We try to keep them out of the house, but yesterday we came home from our walk and found them in the back *hong dze* looking at the food in the windcupboard and one lout drinking out of the dipper in the big water jar. Jim tried to remonstrate with him politely, and he asked why he shouldn't drink it, wasn't the water good? That is one true answer, but Jim explained to the

文
月
華
的
中
國
日
記

cook that we did not want to offend our neighbours but it was not the foreign custom to have strangers inside the house.

Every morning when I am studying outside with my teacher, I am sure to have one or two audiences of a half dozen or so—women grass-cutters, students and little children who watch the water buffaloes at pasture. I suppose it is a good initiation to speaking in public, but rather embarrassing when one is going over a new lesson. (to family, 10 July 1926)

That summer at "The Hills," the Endicotts spent a lot of time together. Several "fault lines" in their relationship surfaced, one of which is candidly revealed in her memoirs:

I had been brought up on a flat Ontario plain and never tired of the panorama of the distant mountains and the valley of the Yangtze River thousands of feet below us, curving in and out for fifty miles....

Sometimes the moon would rise from behind the hills and flood the valley with its weird beauty, making the river a serpent of silver, a fantastic giant dragon of Chinese lore.

Jim spent his leisure time collecting butterflies and moths. I often went with him in my golf knickers, scrambling down a steep gully and up over a wooded hilltop. But sometimes the gullies were too steep for me and I would wait at the top while Jim dashed nimbly around. Once I called to him in an agitated manner. He came up promptly and was dumbfounded when I told him that I was in terror of some water buffaloes grazing nearby....They seemed to be coming towards me and I could not see how to escape without scrambling down the steep sides of the gully or exciting them by running away.

Jim spoke firmly to the little buffalo boys and they turned their beasts in the other direction. When he turned to me I saw that he was exasperated by my timidity. The look in his eyes seemed to say, "I may have to send you home to your father."

I turned and walked quickly away feeling like a parcel marked "Return To Sender." Jim went back down the gully for the moth he had missed. I found myself heading for my favourite lookout on the cliff. As always, the beauty of the river and the hills beyond acted as magic to my spirits. For a moment I felt perilously close to the edge then quickly realized this was a morbid fascination.

I hastened back to the bungalow to my laughing baby and an anxious, remorseful, young husband who held me close in his arms without even looking to see if the servants were around.

A few days afterwards a small buffalo boy was gored in the abdomen by his ugly charge. His mother carried him to Dr. Pincock's bungalow. Jim helped Alex in his attempt to help save the child with the primitive means of surgery available but the patient did not survive.

We worked out a new plan for our recreation time. Every sunny day Jim went off for a short period of bug hunting by himself then joined me in a hike or on the tennis court. Jim had been a tennis champion at university and I was an untrained, bumbling novice. Seeing that it was a nervous strain for me when we played doubles with the Pincocks, Jim proposed that we plan to have short periods of singles in which he taught me the proper strokes.

In spite of the number of adjustments I had to make during this period I look back on that summer as one having a special aura of happiness because we spent so much of our leisure time together. Best of all were the hikes, where I was not inhibited by inadequacies or fears. And there was a unique pleasure on stormy days when we put on our rubberised gear, breasted the stinging rain and wind and listened to its moaning through the pines.

Always there was the baby to come back to—the baby whose development was a series of discoveries for us....In our healthy, happy offspring, I found a satisfaction denied me in other roles.

When dinner was over and the baby tucked into bed we usually went for a stroll on the levelled terrace in front of the bungalows. In the starlight or guided only by the dim lamp light from the bungalow, we walked up and down discussing our views on life....Inevitably our talk turned to our ideas on religion and our philosophy....For some years I had been using George Bernard Shaw's terms "Life Force" and "Creative Evolution," when the traditional ideas of God as giving physical protection to the good had faded out.

Jim agreed with me that the comforting assurances in the 91st psalm, a great favourite with my parents and most church people, could not be applied to preservation in danger, a concept very much in our minds since the murder of Mrs. Sibley. We discussed the meaning of one phrase in that psalm: "His truth shall be thy shield and buckler." That was the important part, to be willing to discover new meaning of life as we went along and not to lean upon what had seemed valid for others. ("Life with Jim")

During this time Mary often thought of what her mother-in-law, Sarah Endicott had endured: "Every time I look at [her] photograph she seems to be smiling at me encouragingly as if to say, "I know, my dear, I've been

文
月
華
的
中
國
日
記

through it all, and I know just where it is hard. Then I think of her pride in Father and Jim and all of [her children] and I know she thought it was worth it. I shall never be worth her salt but she is an inspiration to me" (to Jim's sister Enid, 7 September 1926).

文月華

As the summer of 1926 drew to a close, the political situation in China worsened. British gunboats had opened fire at Wanshien, a mere sixty miles away, and killed about three thousand Chinese civilians and troops (see Appendix B, The Wanshien Incident). The British consul in Chungking advised all British nationals, which at that time included Canadians, to be prepared to evacuate.

The Endicotts returned to Chungchow from "The Hills" and finally moved into their own home, which now might well have been renamed "Living-With-Uncertainty House":

> We feel distracted these days. There are so many conflicting things to do and the general air of suspense makes one feel like doing nothing at all....Looking after Sparkplug is our chief relief from unpleasant thoughts....
>
> It is a combination of the ridiculous and the pathetic, the way we have been packing and unpacking, settling and tearing-up at the same time. We are torn between two feelings, to use all the nice things we can—lest we have to leave them behind and never use them at all—and the desire to save our canned goods for a possible boycott and pack our valuables away in case we can take some trunks. We have the big korrie packed with the necessities for a change in clothing, the baby's junk and a couple of lightweight blankets for use as deck passengers if we get on a crowded steamer....
>
> We are at a loss to know what we think about it all. We are so happy here, in settling our little home, and this place is so lacking in demonstrations or disturbances, it is often hard for us to realize that anything drastic *could* happen....
>
> I agree with Jim's desire to stick it out if that would help our purpose in coming here. We hate to be identified with the business and military interests of our own country, when there is so much to be said against them. We also hate to suffer too much on account of being identified with them in the minds of many of the Chinese, whether we wish it or not.
>
> I feel I would like to stay with Jim under any circumstances, but Norman is absolutely dependent on us and could stand less stress, and I can

see where single-handed men could look after themselves better in a pinch than with women and children along, and perhaps make a temporary escape into the country....

We have finally decided to use our nice things while we can....Last Tuesday we had the other two mission families in for an evening meal. We got out the sterling silver, used candles in both dining and living room, coffee in the living room with our darling coffee cups, big silver tray, silver coffee pot and so on. The menu was mostly canned goods, with olives and Mother's cranberries as a special treat. It was cool enough for a dinner jacket for Jim so we were quite festive....

We hear that a family in Foochow have asked for immediate furlough, two years and a half ahead on account of her health. It is the result of mental worry and strain, sleeplessness and so forth, which is quite serious in this country where people go over the border of mental balance more easily....Makes me hope very hard that I am the wiry though thin kind that can stand more than you'd think. I'd awfully hate to ever have to leave Jim out here or take him away on my account. (circular letter, 26 September 1926)

Safely through another week—and we are even dropping that poised-for-flight feeling. It is too soon to unpack the trunks, much less the korrie, but nothing has happened to make us feel the clouds are gathering except the Chungking report of a wireless that the British are sending eight more units to China, besides the three that are on their way. (to family, 2 October 1926)

Part 2

文月華的中國日記

6

Hijacked on the Yangtze

Christmas Day, 1926

The Endicotts received a telegram from Chungking saying that at last their piano would be coming on a steamer set to sail the next morning. Jim went down to the shore to wait for the steamer. It turned out to be a fruitless week-long vigil, but not without incident. The first morning he learned that the night before, some soldiers had fired on a small boat which had refused to carry any more people because of the approaching dark. They killed the boatman's wife and the little baby she was carrying on her back. The boatman laid the two dead bodies on the shore for exhibition, sat there and howled for justice.

New Year's Day, 1927

The Pincocks and the Endicotts wondered how the men would get to the annual mission council given the lack of steamers. Someone got the bright idea of going to Chungking by junk, leaving the women and babies there—where a doctor was nearby—while Alex and Jim would go on to Chengtu, see the great sights, then proceed on to Kaiting (Lesan) to council. Mary was tickled pink to have the chance to go by small boat on what was reputedly one of the nicest experiences one can have in China.

Her intended destination was Duckling Pond, where Norman had been born. She ended up at the Foreign Settlement in the port of Shanghai. There she wrote an account of their adventures for family and friends:

> By ten on the morning of January 3rd, we were down on the little junk and away by noon. I wondered where on earth two families were going to stow even their necessities. We had Evelyn Morgan with us, too, on her way to the Canadian School at Chungking, so there had to be room for five cots and Jamie Pincock's kiddie-coop. Norman slept in a big flat basket, the top of the

文
月
華
的
中
國
日
記

famous korrie. The space where the cots were was curtained off; there was just room to walk outside of it, as the boat would be about ten feet wide.

A complication set in when we discovered the boatmen had to keep taking up some planks in the floor and going down into the hold to bale out water every little while. It was decided to leave the planks up and everybody watch their step across the gap. No accident occurred until a few hours before we left the boat when Evelyn, who is rather a dreamy child anyway, stepped into it and disappeared from sight without a sound. I had visions of her flopping around in the water as there was considerable there, but Jim hauled her out before she had time to be much more than astonished and she was only wet to the waist.

I enjoyed watching the boatmen, twelve men counting the captain, the cook and the two pilots. The other eight rowed or tracked. I loved to watch them row, standing on the prow with their huge oars, swaying so rhythmically as they pulled, usually singing in time like the Volga boat-song. When there was wind, they unfurled the big brown sail and they sang for wind, a queer wild-sounding call and grinned all over when the sail filled out and we flew along.

View of a junk on the Yangtze River, taken from another junk, the kind Mary describes here.

Most of the time they walked on shore each in his own place on the rope, which was attached to the mast and slung around each man's shoulder in turn, bandoleer fashion. A certain man was the leader and another

文
月
華
的
中
國
日
記

ran behind when they were climbing over rocks to keep the rope from being caught on a rock. When they would be pulling us up a rapid, they would bend over 'til they were on their hands and knees just crawling along and usually both the captain and the front pilot would be poling for all they were worth.

We often struck a rock and had some quite exciting times getting off, with the water swirling all about us. We used to run up to the front to watch at such times and I felt great respect for the skill of the boatmen and very little fear. Personally, it did not bother me as much as when we were coming up in the steamer last year and would run aground. A little boat seems so much nearer to jumping off....

One day some soldiers commandeered our boat. They were wild-looking troops on the run because the local warlord, Yang Sen, had disarmed their general as untrustworthy. They said they had to have our boat to take their men across to the other side of the river. In fact they paid the captain ten dollars for the use of his boat. By the time we had taken the first lot across, the bank we had just left was alive with soldiers and they began to fire at boats on the river to call them over for passage.

As ours was a large junk, it had to go up stream a few hundred yards or so and then cross so as not to be carried down too far by the current. About ten men rowed the boat across. When the soldiers saw us heading up stream, they began to fire over our heads.

It was my first experience of being under fire and I wish you could have seen me sitting flat on the bottom of the boat with the baby on my lap wondering how much more scared I was going to get. Soon it was decided to get off the boat and find a place on shore safe from the bullets if possible. I suddenly realized I didn't have the baby's Klim prepared for the ten o'clock feeding and the poor little chap didn't get it until nearly twelve, but there was never a whimper out of him.

I have to laugh now when I think of myself getting off that boat. The gangplank was a narrow board, rather shakily arranged and considerable water between the boat and the shore. I stood on the boat with my granite pot of bottles in one hand and a small bag of baby necessities in the other, my big coat weighing me down, and looked at that plank. Jim was already on shore, the baby on his back in the little chair and the shots whizzing through the air, from both directions.

"Come on," he shouted, "You've got to come. Your life's in danger." I took a deep breath and went, almost as I would leap over a precipice in a

文
月
華
的
中
國
日
記

sane moment, but the stars were with me and I didn't get a ducking. We scrambled behind the big boulders to wait till all the party were together before proceeding to more permanent quarters. Evelyn was ahead with Jim carrying the lanterns and everybody had some weird-looking bundle. Two of the boatmen carried some food and bedding which we had hurriedly picked out. It came on rain, the road was slippery, and we had quite a climb up the hillside to an old temple outside of the town of Fungdu.

By four o'clock all the soldiers were across. Jim and Alex went down to the shore to see if the boatmen were still there. The junk was, but all the boatmen but three had been impressed to carry loads for the soldiers. Jim and Alex ran around town and found two or three of the most important and by presenting their cards, managed to get them released. It was decided that Alex should stay on the boat that night but that the women and children should stay up in the temple until the morning should "see what it should see." Norman was laid in a wicker basket and Jim and I spread our two blankets on a heap of dried leaves on an upstairs verandah of the temple.

The next day the local military assured us that the situation was all clear and that we could go on. We were anxious to make all speed to get to Chungking in time for the men to go to Chengtu before council. We had just started off down the hill when bang went a rifle and we turned back. Jim and Alex went down to see why the shooting and found it was the local police calling in a boat to be examined. It had a lot of ammunition, which had been stolen during the previous day's excitement. Since it did not concern us, Jim came back and got the rest of us; we started off once more and anchored at Fungdu.

The general there had turned "red" and his troops were all wearing the southern badge. Turning "red" seemed to have improved them, as they were quite polite. A boatload of captured ammunition came in and instead of impressing the boatmen for service, they came to us and requested us to ask the boatmen to help unload and paid the men for their work. That night a little "red" officer came to search our junk and he, too, was very polite.

...At Foochow a telegram from the British consul urged all British to leave because of the seizure of the British concession at Hankow. The next day we were rejoicing at our reunion with the Swanns and the others at Duckling Pond, when at nine o'clock in the evening, a message came from the British consul that he was walking over to the hospital property and would all the men please go there to meet him. The women stayed together until the men came back from the interview in the other compound. I shall long remember

文
月
華
的
中
國
日
記

the moment when the door opened and Alex and Jim burst in to say that this time we had to go. The consul had reported that the consulate at Chengtu was being closed, and that all British in the nine consular districts west of Nanking were being evacuated. He pleaded with the men to take the next boat, which was to leave the next day at noon (see Appendix B, The Hankow Incident).

It was nearly midnight when we scuttled back to the Swanns and helped them pack for a couple of hours before we retired. In the morning we repacked our baskets and boxes to have them as compact and convenient as possible as we expected to be crowded on the steamer, and by two o'clock we were off.

We went to Ichang on a very small steamer. Seventy-six of our people came down on it this fall from up Chengtu way but where they put themselves I can't see. Our party of nine adults and eleven children seemed to overflow into every corner. There were only three first-class cabins so we were two families to a cabin with the men sleeping on cots on the decks. Lal Swann and I had our three 'enfants' in one small cabin and it was quite a squirm getting about. The saloon was just big enough to get us around the table, children first and then adults but the captain was a good sort and let the children play in his cabin.

The real thing in thrills was when the word got around that the captain wanted us to go on the bridge because there was likely to be firing. Such a counting of noses to be sure nobody was asleep in a cabin or no child playing in some corner. Once I had a chilly feeling when the firing started most unexpectedly and Jim started out to find some of the people after he had thrust the baby and me in on the floor behind the plates. The bullets were cracking through the air very close and, as we expected, when he had made the rounds of the cabins, he came back to find they had come in on the other side of the bridge just after he left.

The steering apparatus was in the middle; we couldn't see over and we could not make much noise lest it rattle the pilot or the steersman. I don't know what those 76 people did when or if they were fired on, for we covered the floor. I suppose in such a time one could be two or three layers deep. The children were wonderful and nobody showed any signs of being afraid but we all laughed as we ducked as low as we could. We were inspired by the Chinese pilot who was more concerned with rocks than with bandits, and had to put his head out beyond the armoured plate to watch the channel.

This only lasted for two or three days and there was much of that time when we moved about quite freely and enjoyed the scenery so it was not so

文
月
華
的
中
國
日
記

bad as it may sound to you. In fact, since nothing more serious occurred than the riddling of Norman's panty-pail and some of his clothes, I can look back on it as rather a lark, the chief regret being it kept us from seeing the prettiest part of the gorges.

This kind of casual firing has been going on for years on the upper river by bandits and by military who wish to stop boats for passage or taxes, and most people have had at least one experience, so I am glad we had. It is comforting to know that one doesn't faint or go into a fit or run mad like Jane Austen's romantic heroine when there are bullets whizzing around.

It gave us a queer feeling to go sailing past Chungchow. We could glimpse our property away up the hill and wondered if the Morgans were watching out the attic window or on the wall. The captain would not slow down at all for fear of being boarded but we anchored a few hours' walk below and the women servants got off at dawn and took letters back to the Morgans. I did hate to see our amah Dzang Da Sao go and she was quite broken up—a combination of leaving the baby and losing a job, I suppose....

We had always planned to be the last ones to leave so the laugh is on us that we should be in the vanguard of the run, but one never knows how circumstances will find one, and certainly we were caught out this time—almost like being kidnapped on a stroll. (circular letter, 5 February 1927)

7

Shanghai Exile

China's revolutionary history reached a watershed in 1927. The Nationalist Party led by Chiang Kai-shek had recently formed a coalition with the Communist Party. During the year the Endicotts spent in Shanghai, this coalition was secretly (and brutally) sabotaged by Chiang. There was much tension in the air, but most non-Chinese, living in the seclusion of the foreign concessions, had little understanding of the significance of the political developments going on around them. The Endicotts were no exception.

In spite of the uncertainties during this evacuation, Mary's morale improved because of living in a thriving exile community. It became a time of making subtle but important changes in some of her views. Until then she had taken her affluent background for granted. Within a short time of arriving, she was forced to re-examine this attitude. Later her views on China turned around.

The first item on her Shanghai agenda, however, was a concern about her parents' plan to come to visit her in China:

Dear Family,

The more we think of it the more we feel it might be unwise for Mother to attempt to come out here now....We are concerned lest the strain of the past months has undermined her health....Then, of course, there may be a crisis here which would be unpleasant for a few days, though it is difficult to think that it could be seriously dangerous to the lives of foreigners here. (to family, 4 February 1927)

Perhaps, thought Mary, it would be better for her to return to Canada right away, risking a few months of separation from Jim in order to lessen her mother's anxieties. To go or not to go? The question—made possible by her affluence—preoccupied her for weeks, even as the Chinese Revolution swirled around her. After several cables and numerous letters, the Austins agreed to visit their daughter at a pleasant summer resort in Japan.

文
月
華
的
中
國
日
記

While Mary was negotiating the Austins' visit, atrocities were occurring outside the Foreign Settlement. The Shanghai Trade Union Federation called a general strike on February 19 to celebrate the coming of the Kuomingtang Northern Expeditionary Army. However, Chiang Kai-shek halted the advance of the KMT army, allowing Shanghai warlord police to kill labour leaders, beheading many in the streets. Jim was shocked when his language teacher took him to see the heads displayed on lamp posts; Mary took care not to reveal these and later brutalities to her mother.

文月華

The "Mayor's Daughter's" private income from dividends was a mixed blessing; she and Jim used it to pay for some of their exile expenses (thus saving the mission money), but this extra financial freedom led to an unanticipated blunder: shortly after arriving in Shanghai they moved into a comfortable flat in the French Concession, vacated by a couple going on furlough. Then, to their dismay, foreign refugees poured into Shanghai from all over China and were forced to live in cramped quarters.

Mary explained to her mother that they would move to a smaller place as soon as possible because it was not seemly to be the only family really comfortably situated. Jim's father, now the Moderator of the United Church, would soon be coming on an official visit, making it particularly important to avoid engendering negative feelings from other missionaries.

文月華

On March 20, as the Kuomintang Army again approached Shanghai, the city was taken over, in advance, by radical trade unionists, becoming the "greatest mass insurrection in history," according to the 1998 TVO documentary *Soong Sisters: Destiny's Children*. The next day, March 21, workers seized control of the police stations and raised the new Nationalist flag on all government buildings outside the foreign concession.

Seeing the new flags, the Endicotts assumed (mistakenly) the Kuomintang Army, coming from Canton, to the south, had captured Shanghai:

> Dear Mother,
>
> The fall of Shanghai to the south has not upset us, so far. The fighting has been in the Chinese territory adjacent to the Foreign Settlement...and we are trying to carry on activities as usual. It is thrilling to see the southern [Nationalist] flag flying all over the place—a white sun on a blue square

in the upper left-hand corner of a red rectangle....One hopes that it is the symbol of better days for China. (to Minnie Austin, 22 March 1927)

Several days later on March 24, the city of Nanking was taken by units of the Northern Expeditionary Army. Several foreigners lost their lives, which led to the shelling of the city by British and American warships, killing and wounding about 2,000 soldiers and civilians. Chiang Kai-shek blamed this "Incident" on Communists and used it to encourage anti-Communist opinion. Mary realized news of this would appear in Canadian papers and wrote to assure her family:

Dear Mother,

I expect that the Nanking tragedy heightened your feeling that I should go home. I don't think you need to worry. If anything, the Nanking affair has increased our safety for it has put everybody more than ever on guard & the defences here are on an entirely different scale. Then, this city has definitely changed hands now. The only fuss will be if they try to secure the return of the concessions by force. In that case, the British & other foreign authorities will know fairly well how things are going & will guard the safety of their nationals in accordance. You can be sure the press will exaggerate the worst.

We considered leaving for Japan at once instead of renting this house for three months. However, if we leave here now it would imply that we believe Shanghai is not safe. We do not feel that way & so think it would be bad for the morale of others to create that impression.

A later trip to Japan would be considered as a summer vacation and so quite in line. (to Minnie Austin, 2 April 1927)

Jim was also writing to Mary's mother. For him, "One of the good results of the Nanking tragedy is the upsetting of the Red applecart and letting the more moderate elements of the Kuomintang have control." Years later, when the Endicotts understood these events very differently, Jim would find it hard to forgive himself for his 1927 analysis. In her memoirs, Mary simply acknowledged, "We held all the conventional wisdom of the day."

The brutal suppression of workers and leftists escalated. On April 12 Chiang Kai-shek turned on the left in his party, launching a pre-planned reign of terror. The sign for public execution was a telltale scarlet stain on the neck. Thousands were beheaded in Shanghai and other centres. Sun

文
月
華
的
中
國
日
記

Yat-sen's widow, Soong Ching Ling, was devastated at the shattering of her husband's dream.

Paradoxically, in the midst of this upheaval and tension, the Endicotts experienced a strong sense of community, which Mary described in her letters home:

- A "Sharman group" sprang up among "the younger set" in the Endicotts' neighbourhood, using *Jesus in the Records*.
- As the city curfew eased in mid-May, that same younger set began a literary group. Mary and Jim joined the poetry section and led the first night.
- Weekly Wednesday teas provided a chance to discuss news from the mission station in Szechwan and other topics of concern to all.
- There were opportunities to attend lectures on Chinese history and to meet a wide circle of Chinese Christians who spoke English.

Taking part in these community activities led Mary to change her feelings about China. Later that year, when a letter from her father included a sweeping negative evaluation of the Chinese people, she wrote a spirited rebuttal:

Dear Dad,

I have become convinced that most people are unfair to China. It is an accumulation of things I have heard and read, an accumulation made gradually, because I did not feel that way when I came out here....

Can you imagine Jesus despising, practically condemning, a whole nation of people because of the vices that are glaring in certain groups?...I *have* faith in the inherent value of the Chinese people, and also in the ultimate outcome of their present struggle to make their nation into a modern democracy....

I have two comments regarding the report of your shipboard friends: "Every Chinese who has been educated abroad soon returns true to type when he comes back to China—self-aggrandisement, squeeze of all public funds etc. is the natural and proper order of procedure." Firstly, the speaker obviously was not acquainted with the majority of Christian leaders who have studied abroad. Secondly, many of the Chinese who have such low ideals of social relationships find so much of the same thing abroad that they are encouraged to believe it *is* "the natural and proper order of procedure" for the human race. (to Charles Austin, 18 October 1927)

In early April, at the height of the political chaos—a ten o'clock curfew was still in place—Mary became pregnant, by choice. At that time it seemed likely that Jim would not be sent back to Szechwan until early 1928, which meant he could be at the birth and help her during the baby's first six weeks or so. By summer, however, there loomed the possibility of Jim being sent back in the fall. She confided to Jane that if he stayed until February or March it "might mean spoiling his work this year."

> I insisted on having the baby now and I won't let it interfere with [Jim's] work if I can help it, though it would be a great disappointment not to have him see it for so long. Jim's father [as United Church Moderator here for a conference] thought we were crazy to have another now and I won't have him blaming it for holding Jim up. I must do some more thinking. I must find out who will be staying in Shanghai and who might be going home in March. (to Jane Wright, 7 July 1927)

She wanted four children and no amount of political turmoil was going to stop her.

文月華

Changes in Mary's interior life occurred, facilitated by a spontaneous life review in a lengthy letter to Freda Waldon. It began by responding to Freda's suggestion that her friend might benefit from some independent creativity activity—beyond her role as wife and mother, Mary disagreed:

> I do not react positively to your suggestion that I should have some outlet apart from Jim, such as writing. I feel no urge for it at all, and when I recall how I used to struggle to find something to write about for the market, I recoil. Just writing for itself appeals to me but I have plenty of outlet for that in letters....Then, I do feel I ought to devote whatever mental energy I have to studying the language....Also, this is the childbearing and rearing time of my life and I regard that as a vocation in itself and my first consideration.
>   By the way, I think Jim and I have progressed quite a bit since the time I wrote you that outpouring. I don't know just what the difference is but I sense a growth, a firmer basis for relationship, a greater inner conviction that all is well with us. (to Freda Waldon, 28 June 1927)

This was followed by pages and pages of unburdening. Detailed confessions of the four times she had violated her strict sexual code: "a nice

71

文
月
華
的
中
國
日
記

girl saved her kisses till she got engaged." Next, a list of the childhood memories that Dr. Strong, the psychoanalyst, believed were connected to her stammering and her lack of robustness. Finally: "I think even writing this long confession to you has done me good; I feel an added sense of peace and relaxation."

文月華

After the summer visit from the Austins at a Japanese summer resort, the Endicotts returned to Shanghai and Mary's letters home bubbled with enthusiasm. The picture conveyed is a "Chatham-in-China":

- "We have rented a piano: It is lovely to have a piano again—it is almost three years since I used one much. I bought a book of Chopin's nocturnes, a book of Schumann and one of old British songs."
- "We've bought a new gramophone—a Viva-tonal Columbia, which only plays records made in the new orthophonic style! When you are in the next room, and cannot see the machine, you would swear it is the real thing….Jim has christened our house 'Endicottage' and types up programmes for community Saturday night concerts."
- A close community surrounded Jim and Mary: Earl and Katherine Willmott, fellow "Sharmanites" and members of the literary group, were neighbours, with no phone, so there was "frequent running back and forth." Nell Rackham, whose husband George had returned to Szechwan, was also living close by, and the three families were "together or in pairs almost every day. For once, things are what one hoped they would be." (autumn 1927 letters)

Well, almost. There was "one small fly in the ointment": a number of missionaries had begun to explore the value of extramarital "intimate friendships." This term did not mean "free love" or sexual promiscuity. It was about having an emotional attachment to a member of the opposite sex with whom you shared a common interest. According to the theory, the marriage would be enriched because of the variety and contrast such intimate friendships entailed. If sexual feelings arose, no one should feel guilty, but what we would call sex today was not necessarily part of the equation.

Lively discussions ensued. Then, sometime in the autumn of 1927, Jim—briefly—put the theory into practice. We hear about this in their 1928 correspondence, after Mary has returned to Canada.

文月華

By the end of November 1927, it was known that the happy life at "Endi-cottage," in the French Concession, was not going to last much longer. Women with families could definitely not get up river before the following fall. The plan was for Mary to go home with two-year-old Norman and a very young baby on February 19, 1928, accompanied by Marguerite Brown and her two children. Jim would then go up river with Marguerite's husband, Hal.

Shanghai childbirths took place in hospitals and husbands were only admitted if the doctor consented. Undaunted, Mary overcame this obstacle by telling the doctor how helpful Jim had been at the first birth. The universe was unfolding as best as it could, under the circumstances, and she began to line a bassinette with blue satin.

Barely a month before her baby was due, Mary was diagnosed as having trachoma, a much-dreaded and highly contagious eye disease that can lead to blindness. Over 30 percent of China's population was afflicted by it. Hard pustules form on the inner eyelids. The treatment was lengthy and painful. Furthermore, Norman's amah had a mild borderline case. Both she and Mary wore dark glasses when attending Norman to lessen the risk of infection.

Then, just two weeks before Mary's due date, Jim came down with chicken pox: "Jim was really very miserable for about a week and I felt quite desolate till I got used to the situation. The Willmotts, Rackhams and everybody were ready and anxious to do anything they could....The worst thought from the start has been that Jim will not be able to go to the hospital with me as we planned" (to family, c. 15 December 1927).

文月華

In late December, expecting the baby any moment, Mary received word from Jane, of a "disaster in family fortunes": her father had had a severe financial setback. The "Mayor's Daughter," overcome with remorse at her many extravagances, felt compelled (against Jim's wishes) to confess all to her family:

> We have not been accustomed to even living on our salary. It will not hurt us, of course, and may be good for our souls to have to watch the dollars closely and be happy on necessities. Our present regret is that we can't recall

文
月
華
的
中
國
日
記

some of the luxuries of the past. We have taxied where we might have ridden on the dirty slow cars with endless waitings on corners, we have bought a bed and a wardrobe which we might have done without, we have had cream and bacon and other things which we can't get to eat in Szechwan but which we can do without nicely—and will from now on.

The gramophone is the most obvious recklessness, also the one which has meant the most to us, so it is the hardest to regret.

I have bought very nice things for Norman and the baby which need not have been so nice, also a few Chinese things for ourselves and for gifts, all of which mounts up the list in an astonishing way. We have also indulged in two servants instead of the one most people have, in order to leave me free to study and to rest and walk a great deal.

Jim thinks it would be better if I did not go into detail about it but merely told you how dreadfully sorry we both are that we did not heed father's warning and put aside from the 1927 dividends enough to have taken me home....However I thought you would be interested to know the details.

I have not been economical about housekeeping. Our grocery bills are higher than other people's and I just let it slide because I didn't realize how much it was getting out of hand, nor, of course, that I was likely to regret it keenly. I feel better to confess this frankly to you and then you will know I mean it when I say that, aside from this trip home, I really don't mind if we do have to be really economical for some years. It will probably be good for us, and we can have a lot of fun out of it, and, as we are living among others who are doing it, it will be nothing unusual. (to family, 29 December 1927)

Mary assured her father that if he were unable to find the $500 needed to pay for her trip home, she would be willing to cancel her trip. In spite of the alarmist tone of Jane's letter, Charles Austin was still a wealthy man and immediately cabled the needed money. (The company he had expected to sell his business to had gone bankrupt; the "great disaster" was losing the expected profit.)

文月華

When the much anticipated birth finally occurred, it joined the story of "The Ring" and the Yangtze hijacking in Endicott oral history. Mary recorded this legendary event in her memoirs:

On January 5 we made a mad dash to the Country Hospital in the car that we shared with another missionary family....Elaborate plans had been made in contrast to the home delivery of the first baby. I was to have two of our evacuation group, Dr. Retta Kilborn and her daughter Cora for anaesthetist and Special Nurse. Fortunately Cora came to our house for dinner that night and was with me when the first demand "knock, knock, let me out" was followed by three others in close succession. She called to Jim that we must go at once, waiting only to call the doctor but with no time to call the hospital.

The route seemed endless and Cora kept saying, "Hurry, Jim, hurry," whereupon he almost ran into a blank wall thinking it was the street ahead. The night supervisor was flustered at our arrival without warning and said to Jim rather haughtily, "Is this your first baby?" to which he replied, "No, I've had dozens but none like this." The doctor arrived and barely had time to scrub up in time to deliver the baby, twenty minutes after our arrival at the hospital. Cora was on the telephone calling her mother to make haste so the anaesthetic bottle was given to Jim to administer under the guidance of the doctor as he had done at Norman's birth. ("Life with Jim")

The birth of Stephen Lyon was the climax of Mary's Shanghai exile. The anticlimax came ten days later when she was allowed to go home because of the quiet conditions:

The next morning our cook, anxious to do his part to celebrate this momentous occasion, built an extra heavy fire in the dining room grate and set the house on fire. Jim and Cora were having breakfast when I called down that I could hear something crackling in the chimney. Jim thought it was just a case of over-anxiety but Cora said he'd better look. He ran outside and saw flames shooting out through the chimney. He called the Fire department, then bundled me up in blankets and carried me to the neighbours. Cora had the baby and the amah carried Norman....

Fortunately we were able to get a one-room apartment nearby where we could have meals with several of our missionary families in the same compound. We lived in this rather confusing atmosphere for the four weeks that were left to us in Shanghai. ("Life with Jim")

On February 18, 1928, Mary boarded the *Empress of Canada* with two-year-old Norman Austin and six-week-old Stephen Lyon.

8

Eight Months of Separation

Once again, Mary was travelling with a young baby, vulnerable to anxiety about real and imagined dangers:

> The uncertainty of when Jim and I would be reunited and all that might happen before that time took the edge off the joy of my first return home. In the previous year, at the time of evacuation, Nan Dickenson, whose husband had stayed with the skeleton staff in Chengtu, had started for Canada with five children. Her three-year-old was stricken with diphtheria in Japan and died soon after the doctor arrived. Nan continued her journey but on board ship her eldest boy came down with scarlet fever. In Vancouver, friends put the other three children on a train for their grandmothers while Nan stayed in the isolation hospital until her son died. Her experience put terror into the hearts of the mothers travelling with children.
>
> On the third day out to sea, Norman came down with tonsillitis. The ship's doctor assured me it was not serious and that I need not get off in Japan but my anxiety [was high] and its effect on the child I was nursing changed him from a strong healthy infant to a whining baby, losing weight in those crucial first weeks of his life. ("Life with Jim")

Because her travelling companion, Marguerite Brown, was so incapacitated by seasickness and unable to look after her two young children, Mary took them under her wing. Understandably she arrived home in a state of exhaustion. Her early letters to Jim were consequently unfocussed and rambling in contrast to the account in her memoirs:

> It was good to be home again with my family but after a few weeks when the excitement had worn off and the baby had been rescued by Doctor Allen Brown of Toronto, one of the pioneer paediatricians, I was ready to return....The trials and tribulations, even the necessity to cope with the

Chinese language, all seemed less important than being with Jim again and getting on with the founding of a home.

Out of the blue came a cable from Chungking, saying that Jim had come down with typhus fever three weeks earlier. Our friend Gordon Jones at the Mission Agency had delayed sending the cable until it was certain that Jim would recover. He guessed I would know that the disease was usually fatal and of the other three in our mission who had been stricken by typhus, two were in the little foreign cemetery above Chungking and the third completely lost his memory....Jim had been out in the country on his first itinerary to the small stations and no doubt had picked up some lice in a Chinese inn while travelling. ("Life with Jim")

"It seemed so near to my worst fears," she wrote Jim's father. "I felt as if I had been leaning over a precipice and almost fallen."

文月華

Mary left China carrying a number of inner burdens, which in the excitement of giving birth and the subsequent house fire she had not been able to work though with Jim. One of the benefits of the eight months of enforced separation was that a number of these were brought to the surface and discussed through the letters they wrote to each other.

Before he succumbed to typhus, Jim wrote various detailed confidences to Mary, all of which served to lighten her mood. The first was about his inner struggle to justify his chosen vocation:

Dear Mary,

Why am I...going on my lonely way up the Yangtze? With a "Gnat" that has a very nasty sting in her tail escorting me? Will future historical research show that this was a futile effervescence of surplus altruism?...Or will we show up as badly as the Crusaders, the egoists of the white race seeking to conform all people to our ways of thinking, as a sort of insurance that our ways will survive?...

One thing I do feel is that since I have met you and joined my life to yours, I haven't been as successful in [bringing together] thoughts and philosophies as I had hoped to be....[Also] I feel that our next achievement is going to be the sense that we are on a great stream of common philosophy, and attitude, going forward and exploring all love's married possibilities. Probably I will get that sense of freedom when I am not defending any belief, but experimenting with all beliefs; I will then be more successful in attaining real oneness with you....

文
月
華
的
中
國
日
記

I used to feel that in order to meet [my religious] ideals I would need elaborate creeds to back me up, oratorical purple patches and eloquences.... [But now that has changed]....I am happy and lonely and believe in what I am doing—so far. (from a steamer on the Yangtze, en route to Chungking, February 1928)

He had spoken to one of Mary's inner burdens:

Dear Jim,

I can remember a time, at the Chungchow hills when I began to feel that we would have to be content to see life from different angles....I was disappointed, and felt an emptiness, which I realize more now than I allowed myself to then, and maybe it had something to do with those periods of depression when I felt myself so inadequate to share the life you wished to live....

However, I feel now that we have gone a long way in progress and I am grateful, deeply so,...for your attitude wherein you are not defending any set of beliefs, but experimenting with all. (to Jim, from Chatham, ON, 1 April 1928)

After recovering from his illness Jim confided at length to Mary about what he would like to have said at his ordination examination: that he was entering the church because he believed "it did the most in the world for decency, kindness and peace," and that he had been led "to that feeling largely by the influence of his father." He would like to have explained how "Christianity is certainly a diamond buried in a slag heap." He also confessed that he now clearly understood, as he had not at the time, how his evasive answers to questions (Do you believe in the Virgin Birth?) preserved "all the old values," the "old dogmas" which he believed formed the "real framework of most of the closed minds...in the pew." He wrote out how he would have liked to have answered the Methodist fathers who interrogated him. To have explained, for example, why he rejected the divinity of Jesus but nonetheless "pledged [his] life to the 'beauty and honesty and simplicity of Jesus.'"

This letter was written on August 6, 1928, and because Mary would soon be boarding the train for Vancouver on her way back to China, Jim mailed it to Shanghai where it was waiting for her. For this reason there is no record of her response but undoubtedly she was deeply honoured he had written so freely to her and grateful that she and Jim were more on

the same theological wave length than even his Yangtze River letter had
suggested.

文月華

The "lonely way" up the Yangtze produced another confession relating to
his fleeting "intimate friendship" with another woman in Shanghai. Mary
had already written that she considered this "episode" to be a time when
"clouds hung over Eden," but Jim had not received that information when
he wrote to her. Although this particular letter is no longer extant, we
know of its existence from Mary's grateful reply:

> Jim! Sweetest of Men!
>
> The Most Discerning Of Women was frightfully thrilled by the four fat
> letters that came last Saturday....
>
> Your letters written on the river were so full of intimate personal things
> that it gave me quite an exciting morning reading them, and you may be
> sure they have been reread many times. I am so glad you let loose and wrote
> what you were thinking about, however intimate it was. There is nothing
> makes you seem more real and closer to me....
>
> Darling, you are so sweet to tell me how you feel about that affair last
> fall. It is one of your characteristics I admire most—that when you are con-
> vinced of error or persuaded by new ideas, you do admit it. I consider it is a
> source of strength in you, and makes your convictions all the stronger and
> more influential because you are open-minded. (to Jim, from Chatham, ON,
> 29 April 1928)

The dialogue on the "Shanghai episode" continued at some length mainly
because Mary thought it wise to tell Jim all the ideas the discussion brought
to mind lest she repress thoughts as she had done as a child. She believed
"that this was one place Miss Strong did [her] a very definite service."

The conversation culminated in the following letter from Jim:

> My Darling Mary,
>
> I treasure your comments on the episode in reply to mine of the 12th of
> May. I have long since come to realize that you were genuinely interested in
> it as a sort of commentary on life and an aid, perhaps, to clearer thinking.
> The way I have come to think of the situation gives me some cause for feel-
> ing happy but not the way I responded to it at the time. The only thing I
> really remember is that that was the only time in an intimate talk with you

文
月
華
的
中
國
日
記

文
月
華
的
中
國
日
記

I lost my temper. I don't remember how I lost it or why now. (from Chungking, 8 August 1928)

Apparently, then, it was because Jim lost his temper that "clouds hung over Eden" for Mary. The problem was not "intimate friendships" per se but the inability at the time to confide their feelings to each other. Obviously the discussions with friends in Shanghai on this issue had impressed Mary deeply. Perhaps, too, the long letter to Freda, confessing her perceived sexual transgressions (the kisses) before she met Jim, had been a real catharsis, paving the way for her receptiveness to the new ideas.

In any case, a year or so after returning to China, Mary herself twice had "little excursions into the much talked of freedom within married life." Although calling them "affairs," she made it clear that, while she was "deeply stirred," there was "nothing carnal" about them. In both cases she abandoned the emotional attachment when Jim confided it was adversely affecting their relationship. After that, the whole subject became a non-issue until the time of their prolonged separation during World War II.

文月華

Finally Jim raised some questions about their sex life. Some time that spring he apologized for what he called his "bunglings" as an inexperienced husband. Mary, who had been encouraged by her psychoanalyst, Dr. Strong, not to suppress thoughts or feelings, admitted to some disappointments, but went on to stress they had been a small part in the overall picture:

Dear Jim,

For the most part I have loved to watch your face with that light that never was on land or sea except in the arms of a true love, and the eagerness of your wooing. I have thrilled to it over and over, in experience and in memory....

If some of the differences were due to your bunglings as a husband, as you call them, I do more than forgive you, my dearest, because of your very sincere efforts to understand and to grow in grace. To that capacity in you is due the success of our marriage more than to anything else in either of us. And not all our excursions into psychoanalysis, or my desire to be frank at all costs, would avail if you did not possess that capacity. (from "Cobble Lodge," Erie Beach, 8 July 1928)

In spite of Mary's eloquent reassurances, the memories of those "bunglings" hung in a closed cupboard of Jim's mind. When the cupboard was finally opened years later, these recollections were like cobwebs, heavy with accumulated dust, grimy and disturbing.

A week later Mary had some more thoughts she hoped would be helpful:

> I still feel the urge to be pursued, so it would not solve the problem for you to leave things entirely to my initiative. There is a happy medium somewhere. I suspect you will have found some clues to it in your musings this spring. I know that part of the difficulty lies in the fact that I like some stimulation at times when I do not want complete satisfaction, whereas once roused you can hardly resist the impulse to be swept away. (to Jim, from "Cobble Lodge," Erie Beach, 13 July 1928)

She also took action on birth control. A visiting doctor friend offered to fit her up with the device called a Dutch cap. However, the one he had with him proved to be too large. He said he would cable for three smaller sizes. When the package came it proved to be an ordeal for Mary to put in place herself: Was the rim fitted as tightly as it should be? Mary persevered, even though the whole exercise was an emotionally draining experience. The best thing, she wrote Jim would be to have a doctor check it before she actually used it. The problem would be in finding a doctor who was experienced with such matters. The physician who fitted her originally was in Toronto, she did not think her family doctor in Chatham would be suitable and the only one she trusted in China would be far away.

Whether this experiment was a success or not is unknown. Perhaps they continued to use condoms, which Jim could easily order from Shanghai. "By the way," she wrote, "Did you get a supply?...I have hardly the nerve to walk into a store and ask for them, hardened modern as I am."

By August 18, she had received a letter in which (it seems) Jim jokingly confided a solution which he had briefly entertained then rejected:

> Dear Jim,
>
> I am glad you found [sublimation] unsatisfactory and I appreciate that you told me about it. The more we understand each other the better our chances for teamwork, don't you think? A judicious amount of comparing experiences with other people helps, too. Having talked with [the doctor's wife] was an asset, I think. She talked quite frankly not only of ways and means [but also] of times and places...little phrases about [her husband's]

文
月
華
的
中
國
日
記

reactions made me think of you. I asked her about their success in reaching the climax together and we had a good chat on that. They do achieve it, and have learned to wait for each other. (from "Cobble Lodge," Erie Beach, 18 August 1928)

For his part, having thrown sublimation out the window, Jim turned to the temporary alternative of fantasy:

Darling Mary,

All day today I have been having a feeling of great desire for you. I most certainly could fly up to the top of one of those pine-covered hills and dance out of pure physical exuberance with you. You know, I find on examining the dark cupboards of my mind that I am looking forward to a sort of second honey-moon when you come back. A joyful leap into ecstasy. But don't worry—I know in my rational mind that you will be tired out and probably nervously worn to a frazzle, and be needing a relief on the amah stint....

I have learned one or two things in this separation. I need you desperately if life is to be worth while, and all the sweet love that you have squandered on my useless self has not given me real satisfaction, except as I have felt in my inmost being that I have really stirred up the spirit within me and given you my best. (from Chungking, 6 August 1928)

文月華

Mary bought a gift for her husband to enrich their lives together—a violin, complete with a book of instructions—and took it back with her to China.

Jim mortgaged two months' salary and went to Shanghai to meet her.

9

Back to Chungking: Four Months in Purgatory

Mary was ambivalent about returning to China. She confessed to her father-in-law: "I rather dread some of the restrictions of life in China today, but as long as Jim feels this is his field of opportunity, I shall try to adjust myself to it." Her eight-month absence from the country had, of course, undermined her efforts to learn Chinese; when she returned in the fall of 1928, the two years for language study paid for by the Mission had elapsed. She knew the phrase for "foreign prostitute," however, and it was an epithet she often heard when out for a walk with Jim. Although there was less civil unrest than when she had left China, warlords were still fighting for territory, especially around the city of Chungking, the city in which Jim had been assigned to do pastoral work.

Looking back, she recalled both the joy of reunion and the pain of adjustments:

By the time we reached Japan I was worn out with the care of two lively children who kept waking by Canadian time. When we docked at Kobe they were waking at two A.M. Vancouver time. No word was ever more welcome than the cable from Jim stating he would meet me on the Shanghai docks. When the great day came I went to the deck with my heart pounding.

Sure enough, on a big red truck, appeared that dazzling ear-to-ear smile. Norman at two years and a half was full of excitement but could see nothing till a tall man put him on his shoulder and he saw the daddy he had heard about but forgotten. The reunion made the separation almost worthwhile.

On the river steamer Jim surprised me with the news that he had learned to dance. Two American girls staying at the Business Agency had convinced both Jim and Gordon Jones they were missing one of the joys of life and agreed to teach them both to dance before their wives got back from Chatham. To prove they had succeeded, Jim whistled or sang tunes from Gilbert and Sullivan's Gondoliers as we danced on the deck in the moonlight. Someone had lent the records to him during his convalescence from

文
月
華
的
中
國
日
記

typhus and he had practically memorized the complete score. I had always been fond of dancing but Jim was opposed to it on principle, a relic of Methodism. I had thought my dancing days were over so I was delighted to find he danced "so lightly and surely it is like dancing with the wind" as I wrote home to one of my girlfriends.

As we steamed into Chungking I was astonished at the affectionate reaction I felt towards the "Dirty old town" perched on its rocky citadel, rickety shacks along the shore, ragged coolies shouting hoarsely, and all the things that formerly had made me shrink. It was my home now and I was excited at the prospect of settling down at last.

Our house was on a street cut into the rock near the top of a high cliff. Jim had been to Chungchow and brought all our goods and chattels back by junk, [assisted by our house-coolie Lao Lew]....

One evening we celebrated the end of our second honeymoon by dancing in the flickering light of the fire and candles, which threw weird shadows round the walls of the long room. The dark royal blue of the chesterfield set and the matching curtains on the French doors were set off by the gold cushions and the oil paintings. All this was reflected in the long mirror in which we two—in our improvised filmy costumes—created the illusion of a fairy-tale ball. ("Life with Jim")

Her letters home at the time stressed the positive things. Jim began to play the violin a little every day. Norman made strange at first with the servants, but within a few weeks he warmed up to Lao Lew and played ball with him in their courtyard. Several times they had Chinese couples from the church in for supper: "We really had a very nice time, in spite of Jim having to do most of our side of the conversation. I find I can say a few little things to the women, but haven't enough for general conversation."

Looking back she felt free to recall the difficulties of living in the city of Chungking:

In the midst of our enjoyment at being reunited and putting down roots in our life's work, my roots would not go down. Symbolically, they could not, since the only open space, the courtyard at the front, was paved and behind the house was a sharp drop in the cliff. Not a square inch for a blade of grass or one struggling little flower. When you lifted your eyes to feast on the landscape, all you could see were the bare grey walls of other houses with a little patch of sky above. It kept reminding me of Oscar Wilde's "Reading Gaol."

I did not want to complain even to Jim because I had expected hardships but when I visited one of the Mission houses across the river, near the spot where we had originally lived in Chungking, I returned to our city home with the feeling of a condemned man to his cell.

To go for a walk was impossible, especially with Norman along, for he would be almost mobbed by friendly but inquisitive people who marvelled at his golden hair and rosy complexion and longed to touch him to see if he were real. Some of them were beggars with filthy diseased hands. On the few occasions when we tried it, Jim lifted him to his shoulders but the crowd pressed all the harder to see the little changeling. Jim said that I would get used to it and to pay no attention. ("Life with Jim")

Mary's anxieties centred on stammering. While in Canada in 1928 Mary had read—and accepted—an ominous warning in a book on child-psychology: *The appearance of a stammer is one symptom of an emotionally disturbed or mismanaged child.* On the trip back to China her worst dread materialized: two-year-old Norman began to stutter. Finally, she grew so worried she wrote a fifty-page report using the consultation form she found in the back of a child-training book from the University of Toronto. She decided not to edit and shorten it because she thought the first spontaneous draft might well reveal more of her nature than a polished report would: *"I suspect that the key to Norman's adjustments lies very largely in changes within myself"* (emphasis added).

Mary's anxieties at this time are revealed more candidly in this report to professionals than anywhere else. After giving the details of Norman's three major attacks of stammering on the trip across Canada to Vancouver, and several mild episodes coming up the Yangtze, she described the situation in Chungking:

The fourth "attack" came the first week after we reached our home in Chungking. I took the children with me in my sedan chair for a ride out to the country for tea with friends. It was the first time I had ever gone out any distance alone in the interior of China, but I did not think I would mind it, and overrode my husband's protests that I ought to give up the outing when he found he could not go. I thought the change and the country air would do the children good, as well as me. Going out was not so bad, although we had to go down a very steep hill, which is hard when you are hanging on to two children as well as the chair. Coming back, however, the dark came on the last 40 minutes.

文
月
華
的
中
國
日
記

Unless you have ridden in a sedan chair in the dimly lit streets of Chungking, with its crowds and its narrow streets, you can hardly appreciate the situation. I know very little Chinese and had forgotten most of that in the eight months' absence. I did not know the city and I began to surmise the chairmen were not quite sure of the way. Then we kept bunting people, as sedan chairs always do in a crowd. Once an old man who was bunted made us stop and started to beat the chairmen's legs. I felt powerless but a man on the street told them to get along and they did.

Again we bunted a woman who turned and looked at us. My hand flew out involuntarily and I tried to tell her I was sorry. By the time we were nearly home, I felt almost frantic and started to call out to find out the name of the street. It turned out to be our own and a woman recognized my foreign voice in the dark and told me our house was just a few doors on. When we arrived home, I felt quite limp, although I had worked very hard not to show anxiety in my voice or the tensions of my hand as we went along.

The children enjoyed the ride immensely, apparently, and the wee baby fell asleep the last half hour. Norman watched everything with interest and kept singing and calling out even when it was almost pitch dark. He was impressed by the woman being knocked, or perhaps more by the expression on my face, which he turned to look at.

He kept asking me over and over, both in the chair and the next day, why we hit that woman and I always answered very casually that it was because she didn't see us coming and the road was crowded and we didn't mean to.

The next day after that he began his fourth attack of stammering, more marked than before and lasting four to five days....

There were two more attacks during the next two months (November and December)—each time following a trip in the chair on the street although nothing unusual happened except that people always call out along the street, "See the foreign child!" and try to pat them or touch them when they can, and sometimes soldiers tease them. Norman never seemed to mind except to shrink back a little, and always spoke of riding in the chair with enthusiasm and kept begging to go again.

These attacks left me very depressed although I tried not to let that be betrayed in my manner at all. I tried reading rhymes to him and asking him to repeat them. He had learned to do this and loved it but at these times they would trip him up so I gave it up.

Since Blanton's *Speech Training for Children* arrived I have never taken the slightest notice when he has had difficulty in speaking—just waited for him

文
月
華
的
中
國
日
記

to finish and then repeated it smoothly whereupon he usually repeats it smoothly himself—though I never ask him to.

On such occasions I try to see that he gets a little more rest than usual if possible, although he is very regular, and I try to watch myself to keep my speaking as smooth as possible before him. I think he rarely hears me stammer except when speaking Chinese to the servants which often embarrasses me, partly because I am not very familiar with it, and partly because they are so often annoying and one longs to be able to tell them off or explain things to them at length and with fluency.

I have observed that Norman stammers a good deal when he tries to talk Chinese.

A few days before the seventh attack we had taken Norman shopping for the baby's birthday. It was only a few streets away so we thought he would like to walk....A crowd of children mostly pressing close behind him followed him. They were merely curious but he kept looking back at them rather anxiously. Then his father picked him up and carried him the rest of the way.

His father left for a six weeks trip up-country on January 8th. In the afternoon I took Norman to the country, he in his chair, I walking. Before this I had begun putting the rain-curtains down but this time I was persuaded by a neighbour to leave them up as it was quite warm and sunny and it seemed a pity to shut him in. I kept up close to him but on the country road some students poked at him and laughed loudly, almost thrusting their heads inside the chair. The next day he began to stammer badly and did so for a week. I noticed this time that he would stammer sometimes even when talking to himself, or saying the most routine things to me.

The next week some young doctors, Ed and Gladys Cunningham, were passing through and I talked the matter over with them. The severe stammering had passed off by then but they said they noticed he had difficulties when he was talking to them at first. They advised me to urge for a move across the river to the country, and suggested he probably caught a good deal of his super sensitiveness from me. (from Chungking, report to St. George's School for Child Study, 24 June 1929)

While Jim was at the annual Council meeting in Chengtu, the children came down with whooping cough. Mary had to attend to them three or four times during the night. The house was cold and damp; Mary had trouble convincing the servants to keep the fires going and, of course, as

文
月
華
的
中
國
日
記

she admitted, she "was a novice at stoking a stove herself." The Cunninghams wrote to Jim in Chengtu advising that he move his family across the
river "to better air and more freedom to move about." Within weeks Mary
and the children returned to the house at Duckling Pond—in the "Golden
Valley,"—where Norman had been born three years before.

Dear Family,

Here we are, back where we began!…

It seems like getting home, and it is great to look out of the window and
see the little fields and the hills in the distance, instead of the ugly gate-
house and the high stone walls and roofs on every side. I expect it will be
lonely, but I think it will be worth it….In the summer time [up at the hills]
we will be close to the Jones and Anderson families, and the rest of the community. (from Duckling Pond, Chungking, 3 March 1929)

She did find it lonely for Jim's work kept him in the city of Chungking
three or four nights a week and getting across the river was "the worst nuisance." However, Mary no longer feared the servants.

Canadian missionary group crossing the Yangtze River at Chungking by sampan in
the 1920s. Mary Endicott is in the front row, close to the shore, standing beside Jim.
"Getting across the river…is the worst nuisance."

Norman's stuttering did not disappear immediately. A severe episode
occurred just after the move to Duckling Pond. A dog living at the far end
of the compound jumped on him, knocking him over, in a friendly way,

but he screamed and turned pale with fear. Eventually a more congenial dog was found and, after careful conditioning for a day or two, Norman was at home with this one.

Still, several minor attacks followed this major one and Mary feared it was becoming a chronic condition. At the end of her Child Study report on Norman's stuttering she wrote:

> I have wondered whether the effect of my being with Norman is sufficiently serious that I ought to consider placing him in some other environment during his most impressionable years. It would, of course, spoil the family arrangements from the standpoint of his little brother who ought to benefit by being second, and brings up the point whether I ought to have the large family which it is my ambition and desire to have. The sacrifice in breaking up the family would be so great that one could only think of it as an extreme measure, especially since families living in the orient have to be broken up in the teens for educational reasons. However, if it were the only alternative to having the child unfairly handicapped, I would be willing to do it but I want to be assured there is no better way. (postscript, report to St. George's School for Child Study, 29 June 1929)

That she contemplated separation from her first child revealed her deep sense of stammering as a major physical handicap and of the heavy burden which the psychological wisdom of the day placed on her.

Mary said she would wait for a reply from the experts before thinking further along these lines. It is not known what the expert advice was, but fortunately, by the time it might have arrived, several months later, the problem had practically evaporated and disappeared entirely within a few weeks.

10

Golden Valley Scrapbook: 1930–33

Mary would later describe herself in the China years as a "little brown bird who sits at home on a nest." The image of passivity conveyed in that phrase, however, does not accurately reflect her life, even during the early years, as this "scrapbook" of anecdotes reveals.

While still in Canada, Mary had hatched a plan for her parents to be with her for the birth of her third child. The Austins came to China as part of a trip around the world (leaving Canada before the October 1929 stock market crash), arriving in Chungking just after Christmas. They stayed until late spring and assisted in the birth along with Jim. Shirley Jane arrived on April 19, 1930. She became the subject of intense scientific sibling interest:

> The two little boys were highly enchanted with the new baby. They had been told she was growing inside of mother. When their father brought them in to see the baby, Norman looked into the crib with its frilly curtain and hood and said, "Why! It's our baby!"
>
> He rushed over to my bed and asked excitedly how the baby got out. Since I was committed to the scientific approach in such matters, I said calmly, "Oh, she came out through a little hole." But that did not satisfy him.
>
> "Where is that little hole?" he demanded.
>
> "Well, it's between mommy's legs," I said off-handedly.
>
> "Let me see it," he persisted.
>
> "Oh, it's all closed up now and there's nothing left to see."
>
> And as quickly as possible I ordered them over to the Willmotts' house to spend the day that I might sleep. Earl sent back an amused note of the conversation when the children burst in on them at breakfast and Norman excitedly poured out all the details of the wonderful event. This experience caused me to indefinitely postpone the formal sex education of the other children as they came along. But I found that Norman kept them informed, as they were ready to receive further instruction. ("Life with Jim")

文
月
華
的
中
國
日
記

Indeed, Mary felt strongly that her children should not be taught any non-scientific ideas that they would later reject and resent having to discard. A good example is found in this 1931 letter to her friend Harold Robertson, then living in Chengtu:

I have a theory that it is good to have an embryonic conception of death while one is very young when one is shocked at nothing but full of wonder at everything. At present Norman is working out his own ideas because of [the death of a nurse] Miss McNaughton. Every little while he comes to me with an expansion of the idea that so and so will die some day. First it was our dog, then the kitty, then Stephen. A little while later I told him I was writing you. He began playing Mr. Robertson at once, and in a little while informed me that you were sick already, and in a few minutes that you were dead and there was no more Mr. Robertson.

He has quite often informed me that I was dead and there was no more mother but that they would get another one. I think this is the proper idea to have so I accept it without protest. I expect some people would think this was making the child hard but I am not a bit afraid of that, and in the meantime he may be all the more prepared to face this hardest-to-accept fact of existence. I don't mean that these rudimentary ideas in themselves are a preparation but that they are the basis of an attitude.

I have not said anything about a future life, and I don't intend to. I shall be interested to note when they first get it from some other source, but I would prefer them to first become accustomed to the idea that life as we know it ceases to be, so that if in later years they cannot hold the intellectual conception of immortality they will not feel they have been deprived of a prop which is essential to their peace of mind. I shall never tell them it does not exist, but only that we do not know, and that life should be lived from the standpoint of living and anything extra is a bonus....I think that the idea of immortality has done about as much harm as good in the world and is much better not to be regarded as a certainty.

文月華

In 1928 Mary had brought a violin as a present for Jim. Two years later he had become reasonably proficient when a fortuitous meeting occurred, fostering Mary's dream of family music-making:

文
月
華
的
中
國
日
記

Jim has made a friend among the steamer officers. He went down to meet the Rackhams and discovered that the Chief Officer, Mr. Donald Brotchie, has taught himself the violin for the last ten years. He has a beautiful instrument, much more valuable than Jim's, and does play exquisitely. He was eager to share all he knew with Jim, and copied down for him the points he had got from his teacher.

All the officers came up to the Andersons, the next Sunday, for the afternoon worship group and we had a nice orchestra beforehand. George Rackham is an old hand at the coronet and Andy got out his violin so it was quite a group. We asked Mr. Brotchie to come home with us for supper and had more music in the evening. (to family, 27 October 1930)

Whenever Captain Brotchie's steamer arrived in Chungking, he would give three toots on the ship's whistle to alert the Endicotts of his arrival. When the children were older an excited cry would go up: "Captain Brotchie is coming!" And soon he would arrive, violin in one hand, and fresh down-river fruit in the other. In the evenings Mary accompanied the violin duo of Jim and Captain Brotchie. The highest achievement of the trio was Purcell's "The Golden Sonata."

[*I was only five or perhaps six when this lovely melody filled our living room but every time I hear it, I literally relive the pleasure of those occasions. For all of us, I believe, it has come to stand for the happy times of our family life in The Golden Valley. SJE*]

文月華

The "Scrapbook" contains three reflections on social upheaval:

One wonders what the end of this terrific depression will be and feels that the whole capitalistic system may be tottering. If something approaching a sane socialism should be the outcome, I, for one, would be glad. A chance for the majority, at least to live in comfort, with enough excess for art and some pleasures, would be much better than luxury and swank for the few and being close to poverty for the most. Enlightened socialism would do much to bring it about, but it can never be accomplished until birth control becomes as well known and commonly practiced as smallpox vaccination, pure water supply and other basic elements of modern hygiene. (12 February 1931)

The cost of living is very high now and many are suffering. There are more beggars than usual on the streets, especially the steps to the city gates, and nearly always you see one lying there dead or just about expiring....When one sees these creatures dying thus one does not want to teach one's children too forcibly that God is a father who cares for all his children lest the idea strike them that so many of his family seem uncared for. (7 May 1931)

文月華的中國日記

Famine refugees in Chungking.

When I was laid up with my cold, I read a new book, which had just come to the book-club, *Education of a Princess*, a memoir by Maria, Grand duchess of Russia. It was intensely interesting....However much one deplores the tragedies of the days of the Revolution, one's sympathies go out to the struggling efforts to bring about a more equitable order of society. The grand Duchess' story vividly shows the artificialities and inequalities of the old days and the stubborn blindness of the ruling class to alter things. Under such conditions, the change could only come with violence....

One feels that nothing so stupendously violent and bloodcurdling could ever happen in the west, and yet, when one reflects on the differences between those rolling in the wealth of America and the increasing sufferings of the unemployed, one feels that anything might happen if the capitalistic order is not wise enough to forestall it by a sweeping change in industrial life. (4 October 1931)

文月華

In spite of the great sufferings around them, Mary's private world, her "Eden," was happier than ever. Her health was good and the dragged-out feeling that used to be common was now rare. She wondered to her

文月華的中國日記

mother "if many people at the same stage [of marriage] get as much sheer enjoyment out of each other's society....We never seem to get over the wonder of it ourselves" (March 1931).

Early in 1933, Jim had to go away on mission business for a few weeks. To cope with her loneliness, Mary sat down and spontaneously described her experience of joyous intimacy with her husband. Entitled "After Eight Years," it used extravagant phrases—*To lie within your arms encircled, as the saints have dreamed of God*—praising her husband as lover—when things were at their best. It became an important beacon of hope to return to when the relationship temporarily faltered.

文月華

Mary also described the beginning of an enduring friendship with Ola Dudley, an American teacher and widow who had been extremely happy in her marriage. When Ola came to visit with the Endicotts, Mary would sleep in the guest bedroom so that she could talk with her friend in private far into the night.

Early on Ola confided in Mary at length about her problematic engagement with a man who adored her but shared few of her interests. When baby Shirley was thirteen months old, Ola wrote a note saying that the engagement was ended. Mary reacted at once: "I felt I wanted to talk with her, so Shirley Jane and I bundled into a chair and went right out there."

"There" was a two-hour trip to the American mission compound in Chungking. Mary was about six weeks pregnant; the expedition involved being carried down 650 steps to the river, boarding a small sampan and crossing the treacherous Yangtze, being carried up 800 steps on the other side and then on through the teeming crowds of Chungking's narrow streets—all this with a thirteen-month old baby. Ola reported it was "one of the vivid moments of her life when the gateman announced a foreign woman had arrived, because she guessed it was us and why we had come."

文月華

Not long before the birth of their fourth child, Mary reported that Jim was seriously considering resigning from the ministry; he had become increasingly dissatisfied with Church creeds and felt like a hypocrite every time he went behind a pulpit. Some months later, however, he was reassigned to educational work and became free to work on a new way of teaching English— *The Direct Method* (see Appendix B, The Direct Method). Mary collaborated in this project, helping to write the required readers in simplified English. Jim's misgivings went into an inner cupboard where they festered—for years.

文月華

Mary had a knack for having her babies to suit her own schedule. Originally the Endicotts were due to go on furlough in the spring of 1932 so the fourth child had to arrive by late 1931. On Saturday, December 5, 1931, Jim informed Mary that he had arranged not to preach the next day and that it was the only day he could take off to have the baby.

Salts, quinine and a tramp up the hills were effective. After three hours of labour, Philip Michael was born at six minutes after midnight. Quota fulfilled. Jim, however, was not prepared to leave things to chance and arranged to have a vasectomy. Mary was horrified: "What if I die and you remarry?" Unruffled, he replied: "I'll never be able to afford more than four children."

文月華

As the summer of 1932 drew to a close, Jim urged Mary to take a break from child minding. They had been on holiday in a mountain resort; a few days before they were due to return to Chungking, there was an opportunity for her to go to Chengtu by bus, returning by junk, with escorts available both ways:

> We had planned to take a bus along the roughly constructed highway…to Chengtu but heavy rains had washed out the temporary bridges over the culverts. We were advised by an innkeeper not to wait for the bus as it might be delayed for several days, so we took rickshaws which could negotiate the bad roads by means of planks laid across the pot holes or wash-outs. We piled into these rickety vehicles, which jogged along with the rims of the wheels covered only by solid strips cut out from old rubber tires [and] lurched from one rut to another of the unsurfaced road.

After an uneventful overnight stay (on their camp cots in the ancestral hall of a wealthy family) the party set out the next day hoping to meet a bus:

> Sure enough in the afternoon when we came to the beginning of a gravel road, we heard a bus coming and hailed it joyfully! To our dismay, though it slowed down out of curiosity, it kept going. It was half-full of soldiers, which made us hesitate….Still we were anxious to get away from the dilap-

文月華的中國日記

文
月
華
的
中
國
日
記

idated rickshaws and avoid another night on the road so we ran after them waving frantically and shouting to them to wait. Mr. Starrett offered the driver a substantial payment so he agreed to let us on.

Now Mr. Starrett went off to pay the pullers and to his surprise a violent argument ensued. The spokesman for the pullers shouted and gesticulated, giving a story about his sick father and how he himself suffered from stomach trouble. Seeing the man's swollen abdomen and sickly pallor, Mr. Starrett was about to give in when the soldier next to me took out his gun and aimed at the rickshaw puller. For a moment I was frozen with fear, then snapping out of it I shouted: "Don't shoot!" "Don't shoot!" The solder was surprised and asked if we didn't want the man punished. The Starretts and I all shouted "No!" The surly soldier put his gun away. ("Life with Jim")

文月華

Missionaries were often asked to undertake special assignments. For Jim the most interesting one at this time was being asked to teach English to Communists in a Chungking prison. It turned out to be a venture in which Mary left "the nest" to take an active role. It was also the first face-to-face contact the Endicotts had with Communists and undoubtedly helped to neutralize their distrust of this revolutionary group:

On Sunday, Norman and I went to church with Daddy and later to the Communist prison where Jim teaches several times a week. It was about the neatest building I have struck in this country, though the sleeping quarters were very bare and unkempt. The prisoners were unkempt, too, but were very delighted to see us. They grinned all over, and kept watching us when Jim was trying to teach them. They asked me to make a speech, but I declined. Jim asked them if they would like me to come once a week and teach them music and they were delighted. It was really pathetic to see how excited they were....

We are going to try to get hold of a small organ, and have a try at teaching them to sing while I play. It will be something to brighten them, even if it isn't music. (to family, 9 November 1932)

Wednesday I had my first session in teaching music to the Communists. I was glad to find that a few were acquainted with foreign music, and surprised to see how quickly they got on to the ideas and how well they carried the tunes. Of course, the whole mob of over one hundred crowded into the lecture-hall, so one couldn't do much real teaching, but they seemed to get a lot of pleasure from the singing, especially, and that is the main thing. Their lives are drab enough, goodness knows....Some of their faces are so keen and bright that it is a pleasure to watch them. Of course, Jim translated into Chinese and did most of the actual teaching, but I directed him, playing the organ. (to family, 28 November 1932)

文月華的中國日記

11

"When Death Threw the Dice"

Eight years after Mary's first encounter with the wild Yeh Tan whirlpool, she and Jim returned to Canada for a year's furlough. This time the steamer would speed *down* the raging Yangtze Gorges, making this trip the most perilous of any Mary would experience in China.

For two weeks before they left, there had been no steamer coming up the Yangtze River. At low water times not even the smallest ship could make it safely up as far as Chungking. Finally the water began to rise, and the Endicotts moved over to the city and stayed for several days at the Agency waiting for a small British steamer to arrive. At five o'clock one afternoon, word came that the *King Wo* was anchored at the floating dock of the Jardine-Matheson Company and that all passengers should embark. In great excitement, Mary and Jim, with their four children—Norman (seven), Stephen (five), Shirley (almost three) and toddler Philip Michael—walked through the narrow, dimly lit corridors to the two small cabins reserved for them. "There were only three other first-class passengers as no Chinese were allowed to go first class on foreign steamers at that time," Mary recalled. The latter were "crowded together like sardines on the lower decks, scores of them sleeping on the deck."

> Before long a stranded steamer far above us on the shore loomed in sight, a reminder of an ill-fated encounter with an invisible shoal at high water. Looking up, "the boys," Norman and Stephen, shouted gleefully: "A shipwreck!" For miles the towering walls of granite held the river in a winding chasm, like a prehistoric monster twisting, turning, sprawling across the face of China. All day long we stood tensely on the foredeck as the small steamer ran through the first two gorges, two eyes painted on her prow in ancient Chinese fashion, to guide us by the hidden reefs.
>
> The day's excitement ebbed as the river broadened and the banks became less steep. Then, Death threw the dice for us.

文
月
華
的
中
國
日
記

Looking ahead, Jim pointed to the next bend in the river and called out: "Here we come to the Kung Ling Tan!" As the ship rounded the curve in the river he pointed to a large rock in the middle of the stream: "That's the Goose-Tail Rock...the pilot must steer between it and The Three Pearls, over there under the bubbling water." There would be only inches to spare in that channel now, he explained.

Brown waves in the narrow channel thrashed and churned like a wild beast spewing white curling foam from his mouth and snarling, "This is my lair! Beware!" The *King Wo* headed straight into the fierce jaws.

BUMP! BUMP! The beast had nipped at us.

I was stunned and incredulous but Jim bundled the baby under one arm and his small daughter under the other, made for the hurricane deck shouting to me to bring "the boys." As I pulled them up the steep narrow stairs, we met the First Mate running down who urged me to get them on top. Norman, of course, stopped, tugging on my sleeve, and asked, "Why?" By the time we reached the top deck the bow was visibly sinking and the land seemed out of reach. As the Captain rang "Full steam ahead!" the ship staggered in a death-defying frenzy to be freed from the clutches of the fierce onrushing current. Around a sharp bed the *King Wo* headed upstream towards a sandy beach.

Would we make it?

A shipwreck on the Yangtze River. A steamer, similar to the *King Wo*, is stranded on the shore.

Words from an ancient hymn flashed through my mind: "O God, our help in ages past, our hope for years to come." I looked down the side of the

文
月
華
的
中
國
日
記

ship and saw the heads crowding the rail below—scores of Chinese jammed into the lower deck. What chance for them if we didn't quite make it? What chance indeed for anyone?

No one screamed, or panicked as we watched and waited until the ship's nose grated on the beach, slanted at a dangerous angle. "You're lucky to be alive," the Captain said. "Eight ships have gone down like stones on that spot. It's one of the graveyards on the river."

Our small boys were radiant: "We've been shipwrecked! Hurrah! Hurrah!" (paraphrased from Mary's 1962 poem, "The Goose-Tail Rock")

During the Cuban Missile Crisis in October 1962, when the world came perilously close to nuclear war, Mary remembered the experience: "It was a week, when we stood on the deck of civilization and watched the bow sinking as we did on the little *King-Wo* nearly 30 years ago. It was the same feeling" (to Earl Willmott, January 1963).

Part 3

文月華的中國日記

12

Furlough: An Oasis of Opportunity

The Endicotts arrived home in the middle of the worst and most pro-longed economic depression in Canadian history. The salaries of all United Church missionaries had been cut in half, but the Mission Board provided a furnished apartment in Toronto, paid half the cost of medical and dental work and arranged for various "perks" such as free lessons at the Conservatory of Music. When the church did not pay for things, a life insurance policy provided collateral for making loans. When the Endicotts were unable to pay the premiums, Mary's father came to the rescue.

They hired a live-in maid and gratefully accepted the loan of a car from Father Austin. As soon as the opportunity arose Mary headed down to the University of Toronto to sign up for courses: a graduate seminar in Anthropology (complete with assignments and a final examination), a non-credit course in modern poetry with E.J. Pratt and another in group psychology with Dr. Kenneth Rogers. "Having been denied these things for eight years I was like a traveller reaching an oasis," she recalled. She and Jim also took in plays and concerts whenever possible.

One of the things she felt worth "mortgaging the future for" was enrolling three-year-old Shirley in the nursery school at the Institute for Child Study founded by Dr. W.E. Blatz at the University of Toronto. Blatz was well known for his progressive ideas on education: "kindling a fire instead of pouring water into a pot." His philosophy stressed giving children freedom within set limits, helping them be accountable for their actions without the threat of corporal punishment. In a society where the prevailing notion was "spare the rod and spoil the child," his ideas were controversial to many but attractive to Mary.

Her sixteen months in Canada were not without strain. Mother Austin, the capable woman who had helped at Shirley's birth just three years earlier, was now suffering from memory loss and showing signs of mental confusion. It was painful for Mary to realize that once she returned to Chungking she would never see her mother again.

文
月
華
的
中
國
日
記

Mary and Jim relax at "Cobble Lodge," the Austin cottage on Lake Erie, after arriving home to Canada on furlough, summer 1933.

On a more positive note, Mary felt she had an opportunity to dig deeper into the psychological cause of her stammering. During the winter of 1934 she asked Dr. Blatz for a personal consultation. He had a different analysis from that given by Dr. Strong in 1925. In Blatz's opinion, as a little girl, Mary had wanted to rebel against her mother, but because the latter was her primary parent and first source of affection, subconsciously she transferred these negative feelings towards her sister Jane—a safer target for the repressed anger. The stammering sprang from this buried emotional ambivalence and resulting "sister fixation." Mary accepted this explanation over that of Dr. Strong and, in time, it would increase her peace of mind.

文月華

At Easter 1934, a university friend persuaded Mary to go with her to a large conference sponsored by the "Oxford Group," held in the Chateau Frontenac in Quebec City. The Oxford Group was a popular religious movement whose members had a Quiet Time every day to listen to guidance from God. When the group met you shared your sins and your God-given guidance. The friend who urged her to go to Quebec City was a university professor who had found greater serenity in her life through the spiritual practices of this movement.

The Oxford Group emphasized "moral rearmament": the way to improve the world was through changing individuals, especially the leaders of society. Jim was strongly opposed to their approach because it did not promote changing the existing social and economic system. Mary agreed with this criticism, but that did not stop her from wanting to find out about the movement first hand. Thus, going to this conference was almost an act of defiance against Jim.

It was a large gathering which Mary experienced as a "mob atmosphere." Not until she was alone on the long train ride home was she able to have a meaningful Quiet Time experience. Why had she been unwilling to enter into the spirit of things at the conference? She had come with two blocks: her intellectual concept of God as "not interested in us as individuals" and "the possessive love" she felt for her husband, which made her "feel dependent upon him." In the solitude of the train journey it came to her that not only was she willing to give up both these blocks but that indeed she had already done so. "I felt no elation or radiance, but a sense of peace and of being gathered back into the security of my childhood. I remember thinking how nice it is to be back home with God again."

But back in Toronto she talked things over with friends—and Jim. He "had a violent reaction." She changed her mind—again—and decided she had not discarded the impersonal concept of God she had developed at age twenty-five—"a Power waiting to be understood and used by [people]." She wrote in a private document: "It was probably impossible for me to find some belief which combined the God of my childhood and of recent years."

What are we to make of this "on again-off again" account?

First of all, it was the methodology of the Oxford Group that attracted her. The fact that she attended the conference at all and had a subsequent epiphany on the train suggests she was open to a more personal, meditative spirituality. There is a difference between thinking about God and opening up yourself to a relationship with "the sacred," to connecting with the biblical "still small voice of calm," often called "the God within."

文
月
華
的
中
國
日
記

Twelve years later Mary recorded just such a moment. She was "jittery" about what to say in a speech:

> I was actually shivering with a chill before supper when I was lying down for a few minutes rest. Then I decided to listen for an inspiration from some inner source (God, to most people). Presently a memory of that first terrible raid on Chungking flashed into my mind as a pictorial representation of the world today. I made a few notes, rehearsed it to the children, and went calmly to the meeting. (to Jim and Norman, 23 January 1946)

Secondly, her intellectual beliefs notwithstanding, the personal God of her childhood emerged in times of crisis as we have already seen during the shipwreck on the Yangtze. It would do so again in the bombing attacks on Chungking.

Mary allowed her heart its voice when the circumstances called for it. In spite of her formal words, at some deep level, she rejected the *either/or* approach in favour of the God of childhood *and* maturity. It helped her in times of adversity.

Upon her return to Chungking she would often attend the Oxford Group that met weekly because it provided a much-needed opportunity to interact with adults. In time she would share several spiritual insights with them, although she never became a formal member or discarded her reservations about the organization.

文月華

Mary dreaded the isolation awaiting her in Chungking. The Great Depression had taken its toll: fewer missionaries were returning, especially to the Chungking area. Sometimes she wept at the thought of bringing up children in China: although the Endicotts would be living in her beloved Golden Valley, the Mission school at Duckling Pond, which Norman had attended, was to be closed for lack of students. There would be no nearby neighbours. The only available playmates for her children would be those in the American medical compound—a two-hour trip away from Duckling Pond and across the treacherous Yangtze River. In addition, she would have to be both mother and teacher.

These "bogeys," as she called them, plagued her throughout the winter and spring of 1934 as departure for China loomed closer. Dr. Blatz provided practical support. He helped her equip herself to teach her own children using the "kindling a fire" ideas practised in his school. He made it possible for Norman and Stephen to attend Windy Ridge School, at a reduced rate, beginning in March. They loved it, which bolstered Mary's confidence. Blatz also used his influence to allow Philip to join Shirley at the nursery school for the final six weeks of the term.

When the director of the nursery school suggested a week of observation, Mary did so with great enthusiasm. After that, Blatz arranged for her to observe at Windy Ridge for four weeks, to take notes and talk with the teachers. All this raised her self-confidence as she reported to her family:

> Dr. Blatz is quite anxious that I shall prepare to do a scientific job for the children which will give me an interest outside of my own children—that is, keeping records, reading books etc. and hoping to do some writings for good journals and magazines. He is quite ambitious for me, and it is just what I should like to do, if I can. The fact that he has become interested in the idea will mean a great deal in boosting me. (10 May 1934)

Also, Mary had to contend with Jim's own reservations about returning to China. He now knew for certain that he was unsuited for pastoral work, and theoretically it would be possible to continue working on his Direct Method English readers in Canada. Furthermore, the newly launched Co-operative Commonwealth Federation (CCF) offered possibilities for the type of political work that appealed to him. On the other hand, he felt a loyalty to the church, which had invested so much in his training, and that it would be wrong to leave just when he was able to make his best contribution. There were also the unspoken wishes of his father who would have been sorely disappointed if he did not continue the work in China.

To stay or return to China? The question haunted Jim even after their booking to Shanghai had been arranged. In Mary's mind, her responsibility was to walk with Jim in his chosen life's work, whatever and wherever that might be. But his indecision, coming on top of everything else, played havoc with her emotional equilibrium: "That last summer in Canada I felt tense and on edge all the time and I lost all the weight I had gained so that by the time I got back to China I was lower than before I left" (to Dr. Blatz, 22 October 1935).

Nevertheless, Mary's last letter from Canada was one of determined cheerfulness:

文
月
華
的
中
國
日
記

Dear Jane,

I must tell you a joke that Uncle Charlie is enjoying very much just now. A man heard that there was going to be a cyclone in his district. So he sent his three sons to stay with his brother. After a week, the brother sent the boys back with the request, "Send me the cyclone."...

Philip developed a rash and Jim took him to a doctor yesterday. While he and Philip were in the doctor's room, the other three children were in the outer office. The door was open and Jim heard snatches of their conversation with a charming English lady from the hotel. Norman was the chief entertainer, but the others chimed in occasionally. They related all their family history, with principal events in China and Canada.

One sentence amused Jim a lot. Norman confided to the lady, "My father quarrels with my mother sometimes but generally he is very fond of her, and he's always kissing her." At the end of the twenty minutes the lady told Jim what a good time she had had, and what intelligent children he had. (from Banff, 2 September 1934)

A week later, the Endicotts boarded the *Empress of Russia,* headed for Shanghai and up the Yangtze River—to Chungking.

13

A Greater Acceptance
of the Universe

As I stood on the deck of the steamer, which had brought us up through the gorges to Chungking, one of the Y.M.C.A. secretaries leaned his elbow on the railing beside me and said, "Tell me just how you feel as we come into Chungking."

There was a beautiful valley on the south side of the river where we would spend most of our time....But already I could feel the shadow of loneliness a foreigner feels out here. I looked at the teeming crowds of people on the streets and remembered the dirt and misery one must see every time one goes out. "Frankly speaking," I said, "I feel as if I were going in for a second sentence of seven years." He smiled and nodded. "I understand," he said.

The emotion evoked by the question of my fellow passenger was with me as I stepped off the gangplank and the ragged chair-carriers pushed and scrambled to get the fare. Each throwing his rope onto the baggage to mark his claim. The wife of a senior missionary became quite alarmed: "They are going to kill us!" she cried. It took considerable tact to remind her that this was the customary way for the carriers to establish their claims. In the midst of the crowd of chair-carriers and sampans I saw the stout figure of our Business Agent, Gordon Jones and his capable Chinese assistant. I realized this was an everyday situation for them and so there was nothing to fear.

When I got on shore, to my surprise I felt "I am coming home" and no longer saw myself as going into prison. ("Life with Jim")

The isolation was real. The Endicotts were now living in the former Mission school dormitory at the Duckling Pond compound where Norman was born. One room was set aside for school and she was both mother and teacher. The first few weeks were trying: Norman was miserable and quarrelled constantly with Stephen. It was one of the "bogeys" that had haunted her on furlough. Remembering Dr. Blatz's confidence in her, she set about dealing with it creatively:

文
月
華
的
中
國
日
記

We tried a new plan this week. I suggested to the boys, when some disputes arose which seemed difficult to settle, that we take them to a Family Conference. They liked the idea but we had to wait all week to get any time with Daddy. In the meantime, I noted down disputes as they arose, and made a list of the agenda to be dealt with, and also a list of suggestions which I would like us to talk over all together.

The plan worked like a charm. They were quite willing to drop a quarrel, once it was suggested it would be better to take it to the family conference. They kept asking when we were going to have it, and were quite impatient as it had to be postponed once or twice. Saturday evening, however, we took the pre-bedtime hour for it. I suggested Daddy as chairman and he taught the boys how to move and second, how to elect me as secretary and so on. I took notes of the resolutions, which were passed in formal fashion. The boys both loved it and agreed that the thing was settled when it was passed on. (to Jane, 25 November 1934)

The Family Conference, November 25, 1934

Meeting opened with Daddy in the chair. Moved by Norman, seconded by Stephen that Mother be the Secretary.

1. The Canal and Philip

Resolved that we put a fence around the canal and Philip only be allowed to go in when the boys are there.

Resolved that another old bathtub be fixed up for Philip's boats.

2. The Schoolroom and Shirley and Philip

Resolved that S.J. may come in during the free activity, but Philip may not. S.J. must go out for Arithmetic—may return later.

P.M. may not come in till after 10:00. They are allowed to stay only if quiet.

3. Question of Knives

Decided that the brown knife probably belongs to Stephen and therefore should be his. Norman applied to Daddy for a knife to replace the one Philip threw overboard. Granted.

4. The Workshop and Shirley

Resolved that Shirley have a place to keep her wood and that each person put away his own wood when finished working, and that a piece of wood be left in the vice for Philip to saw.

5. Replacement of things lost by Philip

Resolved that if Philip breaks or loses things and it is due to the boys' carelessness in not putting things away, they will have to stand the loss. Otherwise we will replace them.

The Family Conference worked like a charm for a while. After it lost momentum, Mary tried other ways to solve the problem of the quarrelling between Norman and Stephen. She reported these in detail to Dr. Blatz, who had asked her to keep records of her experiences with the children. Each one of these techniques was successful—for a time:

Whenever the boys had a serious conflict I asked them to come to me, one by one, and tell me exactly what happened. I typed out what they said, after the manner of court evidence, and they discovered how difficult it is to remember just what did happen even a few minutes after its occurrence.

I also found that nearly always before the story was typed, the angry feelings had dissipated in the interest of the story, and after the first time or two, when I asked leading questions, the child himself saw where the mistake had been made and admitted his part in it.

Never did I apply blame to them, but if they had been wrong I tried to show them why they acted in that way.

One day, I had another inspiration: I told the boys I was like the League of Nations and could apply sanctions (withdrawal of privileges) if reasonable arbitration did not work. It did. (to Dr. Blatz, 22 October 1935)

Although each one of Mary's ideas only worked for a while, she did not seem to have been overly discouraged by temporary setbacks. After eight months of trial and error she decided to give "the boys" a taste of regular school and sent them both to Chengtu for the month of June 1935. They stayed with the Cunninghams, a couple with no children, and attended the Canadian School each day. This experiment had a salutary effect: they found that "far-away fields look greenest" and when she began teaching them again in the fall they were both more content. This re-enforced her belief that Norman was too young to be sent away to boarding school and motivated her to keep finding new solutions:

The school problem seems to have been improved lately by the adoption of the scheme of letting each boy plan out his own day's work. They know now what they are supposed to do and they plan in what order they will do

文
月
華
的
中
國
日
記

it. It has acted like magic for the last couple of weeks—speeding up their work and doing away with the dawdling and the arguing which I found so tiresome, and is one of the worst pitfalls of a home school.

Funny! They do almost exactly the same work, and generally in the same order that they would do if I laid out the schedule for them, but because they feel they are running the show themselves they pass readily from one subject to the next. If they cover the ground extra quickly, they get through a little early.

Mary as mother and teacher, 1935, to Norman (front left), Shirley (on Mary's right), Stephen (beside Mary), and Philip Michael (with teddy bear). On the front steps at Duckling Pond home, squinting into the sun.

One of the difficulties is that Philip and Shirley get attacks of wanting to "work" in the schoolroom. Shirley can sit quietly and work at her reader and workbooks, with very few interruptions, but Philip, for all his pious resolves, is apt to get into something that is distracting to the rest, if not worse. Today they got a passion for sewing cards, which quite upset the day for me. Between finding suitable threads and needles, threading needles, making knots and steering Philip around his little pattern, with so many exclamations etc., the boys' arithmetic was dragged out to twice its length, and set the day by the ears.

Every once in a while we make a rule that the little children cannot come in until arithmetic is over, but after a long respecting of this law, they occasionally surprise us with such an enthusiasm that we are swept off our feet. The boys beg us to let them come and they promise to work quietly—and so on and so on. (to family, 25 February 1936)

Until Norman went to boarding school in 1937, keeping "the boys" contented became Mary's major concern. Extracurricular activities abounded: raising chickens, training homing pigeons, having a pig and rabbits, growing vegetables and collecting stamps. On weekends Norman and Stephen were taught to play bridge to create a family-centred interest for them.

文月華

Mary's epiphany—"I am coming home"—was more than a fleeting sensation as this letter demonstrates:

Dear Family,

It is one a.m. and, for once, we are still up. We have been pounding away at *Moby Dick* all evening. Jim is determined to finish the rough draft tonight. He has been working on it off and on for weeks, and is so near the end, it does seem a pity to stop. I have started to type the finished copy, making some slight changes as I go along. Now I have come to a weak spot in his draft, where I must refer to the book, and he is using it to finish the story.

As I am still very wide awake from the strong coffee we drank, I will start this now, as I want to go on with *Moby Dick* at the first opportunity....This will be the fourth supplementary book, which Jim has sent to the press in Shanghai since we arrived back in Chungking....

I did quite a bit of work on parts of two of them, but for the rest it has been more advisory and mechanical work, as on this one. I enjoy it but it's hard to find time in the evenings, with all the other things to be done....

Still wide awake, Mary went on to take stock of the fears and anxieties she had about returning to China:

文
月
華
的
中
國
日
記

Jim is finding it easier to stop using that uncompromising manner of his which annoys people so....

I, too, find that things do not get my goat as much as they used to. We both put these changes in ourselves down to the refreshing effect of having been home—and particularly to the help, which Dr. Blatz gave me directly—and indirectly, to Jim through me—in understanding ourselves.

I find that the sense of exile and isolation does not weigh upon me as it used to, even though I feared it would be worse after being home. I miss the things and people I had to leave but I don't seem to be depressed by being deprived of them. Of course, occasionally things sweep over me in waves, but I don't stay down long as I used to do. I have learned to accept the inevitable to a degree I never had before.

I can't explain just how Dr. Blatz helped me to do this; I just know he did.

I also find I don't have the sharp fears and gnawing worries I used to have, although the situation is not much different. I used to be terrified that Jim or the children would die, and was always conjuring up dangerous situations in which this would happen. Those possibilities still exist, but they don't haunt me.

I think one of my worst fears in this regard used to be that if anything like that did happen, I would not be strong enough to bear it, but would break down, be useless and make everybody else miserable, as well as myself. That sense of inadequacy is gone now. I have a calm confidence that I will be able to meet life's hard situations, when they come, with the fortitude that most people do.

I find, for instance, that I am not nervous about crossing this old river as I used to be. Of course, experience helps: your fears wear down after you have done a risky things many times safely.

But I think there is also an acceptance of the universe, which I didn't used to have. After all, it was foolish to let myself be worn out by fears of what might happen, when they didn't happen to most of the people I know.

I find, also, that the disorder and lack of cleanliness in China don't depress me as much as they used to, though I dislike them as much. There is a familiarity about things now that softens the shrinking I feel from them. The servants don't bother me as much, either. I've had to change cooks once already, but it didn't upset me, as it would have once.

The children, too, are getting along nicely. I don't feel so weighed down by them being cut off from a normal school and play life as I expected to feel. I think they are really as happy as any children are. They are always busy and complain the days go by too quickly, rather than drag along.

Perhaps you will be wondering what effect, if any, this changed attitude of mind has on my speech....For the most part I don't think of it at all. Perhaps that is because I don't have as many difficult situations to meet. However, a month ago I noticed the speech problem very markedly—just as I used to notice it most of the time. I wondered why, and began to think why I should be worried. I thought of several possibilities and talked them over with Jim, thus bringing to light the foolishness of them. I really haven't thought about it since then—until I started to write in this vein to you: a good indication of how things are.

I am learning to re-educate myself so that more and more things that caused the symptom of worry to appear will be settled by my realizing what is worrying me, and what I ought to do about it. I don't imagine the unsteadiness will ever disappear, but now that I know the cause of it, I can accept that, too, and that acceptance will lessen the strain and reduce the effects. (from Duckling Pond, 26 January 1935)

文月華

Evacuation of foreigners still loomed as a possibility but Mary now faced it with more assurance than she had nine years before.

Dear Family,

There is great interest in the present political situation. The Communist activities in the province have got the wind up of the local government, and the Central government has been asked to help. Troops from Nanking are arriving now....The streets are decorated, and there is more attempt to keep order in them than ever before. Special police are out, and the usual straggling unruly crowds are kept strictly to their own sides of the road. It is probably just a face-saving device to impress the big bugs, but it is interesting to watch. It is said that Chiang Kai shek himself will probably come up here before long to direct operations....

All this is very helpful for the ultimate establishment of a settled government here. This province has always been nominally under the central government, but has never had any financial connection, which is the real key to stabilization. If the local Communists frighten the local governments into union with the central government, they will have done something good for China, though by indirect method. In some places, once the initial

115

文
月
華
的
中
國
日
記

conquest was over, the Communists have actually improved local conditions and so have set up a standard which the government has to keep up if they are to win back the loyalty of the people....

There is no doubt but that the foreigners will evacuate, if the Communists come this way. This time there is no question as to whether to take the risk or not, if they come....But there is almost no probability of that at the present time [especially in Chungking]. I certainly hope it won't come for I've just got a settled-in feeling and it would be a great nuisance to have to pick up and become gypsies again. Still, what has been done can be done again, and this time there would be no small baby to be concerned about. (from Duckling Pond, 13 January 1935)

文月華

Back in 1927, when Freda Waldon suggested that her friend might benefit from an independent creative activity beyond her role as wife and mother, Mary disagreed. She felt no urge, and besides, being a mother was a full-time vocation. But Freda was right. Mary not only had a strong desire for her creative pursuits, she was empowered by accessing this inner source of strength. The night she was working with Jim on *Moby Dick*, for example, she had already co-authored with him a reader in which traditional Western fairy tales were written as plays.

That was the beginning. A year later, at her Duckling Pond School Christmas concert, Mary had the satisfaction of directing her play *Rumpel-stiltskin*. Many of the elaborate costumes were donated by the parents of Nina Morosoff, a girl about a year older than Norman who came to the school as a day pupil. The entire foreign community was invited—twelve children and forty adults—and loved it.

Another channel for Mary's writing ambitions opened up in 1935 when Jim was asked to be the Chungking correspondent for the Associated Press, an American news agency with an office in Shanghai. The articles were not signed so Mary also wrote. One of hers was an article describing the drilling of peasants to fight the Communists, likening the effort to that of the Saxon King Harold in 1066.

Affirmation for her creativity came that same year when a musician living in the missionary community in Chengtu asked if Mary had any poems that she might like set to music. Mary was delighted to be asked and submitted two: one about Easter ("Truth Cannot Die") and a another based on a prayer she composed after Norman's birth (see Appendix).

Rumpelstiltskin, written by Mary while on furlough in the summer of 1934 and performed as a Christmas play, 1935, by her Duckling Pond students. From left to right: Stephen as the lead character, Norman, Nina Morosoff, and Shirley as the nurse-maid, whose elaborate costume enchanted the audience.

Both songs were sung at recitals in Chengtu; Mary was thrilled to see her words in print when she received copies of the two programs.

文月華

The isolation of the few missionary families in and around Chungking encouraged occasional get-togethers. In 1935 someone organized a Valentine party for the children, and Mary ended up going on a wild "mother away" trip. While the adults had tea, Dr. Wallace Crawford, a Canadian, asked Mary if she wanted to send anything to Chengtu because he was going to drive the new Mission truck there in two day's time.

Chengtu! A university city where foreign neighbours were ten steps from each other and Mary's most congenial friends lived. Impulsively she replied: "I wish you could take me with you." Dr. Crawford thought it was a great idea; they would leave from the Agency at 5:00 o'clock Saturday morning.

In earlier years getting from Chungking to Chengtu took nine days of walking and being carried in a sedan chair. But by 1935 there was a bumpy road made by Chinese peasants chipping away at rocks with hammers, so the trip up by truck would only take a little over one day.

Mary decided to take Shirley with her because, of the four, she was the one most deprived of playmates.

文
月
華
的
中
國
日
記

Dear Jim,

Please note the date of this letter, and see if you get any palps.

All the way up here I tried to keep my mind off my troubles by thinking of the funny letter I was going to write you....

Well, it was a mad, mad trip—the maddest thing I've ever done, I think. There were three other passengers besides us—Mac [W.A. McCurdy, an American missionary], a Chinese nurse and a student. Mac had the sense to bring a reed chair and that helped a lot. Crawford had planned that Miss Lo and I would sit on some *pugais* on the floor of the truck. Somebody did have to sit on folded up *pugais* there, and we took turns and it was literally torment. It was bad enough on the front seat or in the chair but on the floor it was simply dreadful. Words cannot describe it.

The trouble was we had to put off our load. We were carrying a number of cases of gasoline; the tins began to break open with the jolting and there was gasoline flowing all over the place. We would stop and empty one into the gas tank as often as possible but after five hours Mac said he was terrified of a spark coming from somewhere and setting our gasoline-soaked truck on fire. So at the first place where he had a chapel we unloaded all the gasoline tanks.

Irrigating rice paddies, Szechwan, 1930s. The fields are carefully arranged to fit the contour of the land so that water distribution is by an intricate dependence on gravity.

Well, after we did that the truck simply bounced up and down like a wild chin. We all got pains in the abdomen, and I got them in the chest and head as well. Just shooting pains every time we hit a rut, which was about every minute or more often. After a long spell of this, when you felt human flesh could stand no more, there would be a short spell of just rough road but not so bumpy, and then you got strength to go on. Really, it was like having a baby. In fact, when I tumbled out of the truck here, into Bea's arms, I said I'd rather have six babies in succession than do that again. I think that remark has spread all over Chengtu!

Peasants use a waterwheel to bring water uphill to inaccessible fields.

Shirley stood it very well, looking mystified and complaining that her tummy ached and she wished we'd hurry up and get some place, but she didn't try to make any fuss. She actually slept a good deal of the first day, though I don't know how she could. Of course, we tried to give her the least awful seat but the second day, Mac held her in his arms, sitting in the chair, most of the way, and at least she had something soft to land on when she came down, which was more than the rest of us had.

We got to Szechow the first night. Shirley, Miss Lo and I took a room in the inn, and we had a good night….We were warm, and free of rats or bugs.

We had very little to eat. Just our dry sandwiches, which crumbled up, a few peanuts and some tangerines, but you don't seem to want to eat under such circumstances….

文
月
華
的
中
國
日
記

At breakfast that morning I said to Wally that I had been told he was a fast driver and that I must just commit my soul to God and say nothing. During the day, I wished to heaven I could commit my body as well as my soul to God.

I thought of the weirdest things, anything to try and keep sane. I thought of friends who had died young and how lucky they were. I thought of the men I might have married and hadn't and how foolish I had been. I thought of any poetry or rhymes or jingles that would come to mind, and only inane things came. I thought of a "bowl full of jelly" and wished my belly were like that instead of something that hurt so terribly. I thought of everything except my sins, [for I] decided none of them were so bad as to have brought me to this.

When Mac got to Chengtu and was asked why he came, he said, "To see what hell is like!" so you will know my account is not exaggerated. Even Wally admitted it was worse than he had expected.

Sunday morning, after three more hours of driving, Shirley had to *zo bodze*. Wally said it was providential because when he got out he discovered that the temporary floor of the truck had moved over four inches from where it should be, and would have inevitably collapsed over one side. It was made of poor wood, badly put together, and some of it was broken off in splinters. I had noticed the back of the front seat moving back and forth but thought it was the delusion of a disordered mind and said nothing. Wally and Mac tied us together with ropes and thus we came the rest of the way, arriving at 3:30 Sunday afternoon....

After dinner, a bath and a sleep I felt much better and by the next day quite restored except for a slight stiffness, so I suppose I shall soon forget it. I tried to be bright and amusing whenever I did say anything, because there was obviously no help for it, and no turning back, and I had chosen to come. Now that it's over, I'm glad I did come, though I am content to go back by plane. (from Chengtu, 19 February 1935)

The small airplane on which Mary and Shirley returned was a recent innovation in China. This particular one held ten passengers and flew at the incredible speed of 100 miles an hour.

文月華

Mary's introduction to the Oxford Group movement while on furlough paved the way for her to attend meetings of the Group in Chungking:

文
月
華
的
中
國
日
記

Dear Mother Father et al,

The Oxford Group activities out here are bringing out some very interesting things....It is amazing how many people are suffering in their personalities from things which can be traced back to a lack of knowledge on the part of somebody....The Oxford Group introspection and searching for honesty and restitution digs up many of these cankers in the souls, but one wonders how far [its] principles can repair the damage. Very often there is need for expert knowledge, rather than for a greater straining after the love of God and devotion to Christ. If I were living my life over again I would be a psychiatrist. I wish I were one now. A married woman with the skill and knowledge of psychiatry could be a great blessing in whatever environment she went to live with her husband. (from Duckling Pond, 3 February 1935)

Jim had no use for the Oxford Group. He felt introspection was a waste of time: the solution for personal problems was to immerse oneself in some useful project. For Mary, however, it was a place where she could confide some of her inner thoughts and, for the most part, provided a welcome opportunity for adult fellowship. One week—in the winter of 1935—she typed a reflection on old age and sent it over to the meeting in a letter:

Dear Fellow Groupers,

I shall not be able to be with you on Tuesday, but I am sending a note about some things on my mind....I came on...this prayer:

Though the world knows me not, may my thoughts and actions be such as will keep me friendly with myself. Lift my eyes from the earth, and let me not forget the uses of the stars....And though age and infirmity overtake me, and I come not within sight of the castle of my dreams, teach me still to be thankful for life, and for time's olden memories that are good and sweet, and may the evening's twilight find me serene and gracious.

I confess I changed the last few words to something that suited me better than the original. I have been thinking a lot the last few years about what I want to be like when I am old....

One of the few sermons I remember brought this out and gave a new interpretation to "Lay up for yourselves treasures in heaven." It said, in effect, "In youth, lay up treasures for old age, that it may be rich for you and a blessing to others."

One of my older friends once told me that when her own mother came to her old age and was beginning to be childish, she was constantly worry-

文
月
華
的
中
國
日
記

ing about the state of tidiness of her dresser drawers, and other petty matters. She said it reminded her of how fussy her mother had been about material things during those years when her children were growing up, and she had so little time and energy left to enjoy them, muddy feet and dirty towels and all. I resolved, if ever I had children, I would enjoy them first, and worry about them afterwards, if at all.

I don't think I *have* always remembered this, but it comes to me now as a standard of beauty...by which it might be well to measure my daily life. Am I living so that I, and my children, insofar as they can remember, will look back on these days and find them filled with "olden memories, good and sweet"? Will I, in my old age be a source of anxiety and worry to them because I feel that my day is done, and because they feel that I am still treating them as children? Will they come to me as a duty, or because I am, and have been, an inspiration to them?...

Taking time for some introspection in the midst of her busy life as mother and teacher gave a much-needed balance to Mary's life. Her personal connection with Dr. W.E. Blatz provided her with another confidante with whom she might "talk over" her inner concerns.

Dear Dr. Blatz,

It has been a happy year...in spite of no school, no neighbours, very few playmates seen occasionally and no really congenial friends of ours living in this place. Those were the bogeys I was worrying about last year, you remember....

You will want to know something about what has happened to me since I saw you last....I wish now that I had made a point of seeing you in Toronto before I left....

Why, when I see so plainly the reason for the situation, do I still have this emotional feeling about my sister? I still dream about her in ways that signify to me that I have not accepted her into my life. What is the missing link that will carry over into my feelings what my intellect understands and accepts?

I have read two interesting books that bear on that subject. *Freedom in the Modern World,* by John MacMurray, says we have freed the intellect but are still emotionally primitive. He shows how the emotions are the guiding factors of our lives whatever we may think....We used it for a discussion group at the mountains this summer and found it stimulating.

A Life Of One's Own, by Joanna Fields, the pseudonym of an English psychologist is on the same theme. She experimented with herself to find out how to be happy. She found it was the childishness of her "blind thinking" which kept her emotionally immature. By writing out her thoughts and other techniques she describes how she freed herself from this sense of inadequacy and general disappointment in life...I did get some relief from a certain tension that seemed to be "chattering" to me all the time by writing it out.

But it does not seem to be enough to rid me of this childhood emotion. What further steps in re-educating myself can I do? (22 October 1935)

文月華

In June 1935, while Norman and Stephen were in Chengtu to attend the Canadian School, Mary used the time to expand her intellectual horizons. She described her new insights enthusiastically in a letter home:

Dear Mother and Father and all,

Father, did you read the article entitled "God of Wrath" by Gregory Vlastos in the *Christian Century?* ...

[What he says] helps to unravel the mystery of evil and suffering in this world. For some years now something in me has revolted at the emphasis placed by the church on God as a God of love. That seemed all right for comfortable, sheltered people to believe in, but it became a mocking farce when one looked at the underprivileged and suffering....Yet I rebelled against the idea of the God of the Old Testament, the God of wrath and vengeance. It seemed incompatible with the God of Jesus....Vlastos shows how the two Gods are one and the same—"source of life to those who obey him, doom of death to those who leave him."..."Only the God of wrath can keep us from turning the God of love into an illusion and an escape."...

I like the way he deals with the suffering of innocents, those who have not...turned away from God, but who suffer the consequences of the sins of their fathers or the social sins of the society in which they live. It is because of our essential unity and interdependence: "One of the greatest expressions of God is...affirming in wrath what he cannot prove by love that, whether we like it or not, we are one."...

Of course...the scientist sees we are bound by the circumstances of our lives and upbringing....We are seldom good or evil by choice but are pushed to it by forces of which we are unconscious. However, consciousness does

文
月
華
的
中
國
日
記

come, unravelling slowly the mysteries of life. [This] is where the evolutionary process comes in, and in that lies the hope of mankind. It is now possible to fight evils which a century or more ago we were not aware of....So I would say that there is a God of struggle, of growth, another facet of the God of wrath and love.

Mary also described a book which excited her—*Through Literature to Life* by Ernest Raymond—sent by Miss Lafferty, her friend in the wheelchair:

He says that "a work of literature is not an idle tale to entertain and relieve the reader but, rather, the cry of a great soul at the spectacle of life he sees before him." Then he defines the kinds of "cry"—"a moan, the cry of pain; a laugh, the cry of amusement; and a cheer, the cry of excited approval."...

He points out why...it is not only the beautiful and comfortable that attracts us. We are fascinated by the ugly, the sordid and the tragic things of life when we are shown the *inner significance* of the situation which they portray....Each such experience, if apprehended, deepens our ability to understand and appreciate the lives of [people]...."Literature makes us not only feel about more things, but feel more about them. It not only makes us re-live past experiences of our own but it heightens our awareness of these experiences and that of others which we may meet at any time." (19 June 1935)

Mary went on to describe how one afternoon she had observed five-year-old Shirley "twirling around, half singing and half talking to herself, stringing daily happenings together like beads on a string." Inspired by the ideas of Raymond, she copied down the rhythmic words as examples of her daughter's first poetry. "It is like the modern way of teaching children to draw or paint. Give them a brush and let them slosh the colours on any way they like and say what it is."

文月華

June 19, 1935. It was now ten years since the fairy-tale wedding on the banks of the Thames River in Chatham, Ontario. The psychological consequences of Jim's unexamined desire to follow in his father's footsteps were taking their toll on his emotional well-being. Although now he was teaching full time and relieved to be away from "the prayer and word business," he was subject to "bad fits of the blues." Mary confided the situation to her friend Freda:

Jim has kept his head buried in work all year and needs a complete change badly. He is usually too tired at night to read, much less play the violin. It is partly this uneasy conscience that affects him so....Just between you and me he has bought some tickets in a big lottery here, and dreams of fortunes possible to be made. That will show you how low he has fallen. It...seems to assuage his desperate square-peg-in-a-round-hole feeling.

Jim had launched, an innovative extracurricular project, *The Gin I* (ee) *Middle School English Weekly.* The entire attic of the Endicotts' home at Duckling Pond was devoted to the production of this one-page newspaper. There, in his free time, he reproduced the drawings and printed the copy by hand with special ink suitable for lithography. The *Weekly* dealt with a wide range of topics ranging from "How Man Invented Fire" to current world news, as well as cartoons lampooning militarism. It became very popular: schools all over the province of Szechwan and beyond began subscribing to it.

This creative journalistic endeavour did not salve Jim's "uneasy conscience." By 1937, Mary would observe: "I have developed...a growing confidence in myself....He has gone through disillusionment and dissatisfactions with things he felt quite confident about earlier. The result is, I am the happier personality now, whereas he used to be" (archives document entitled "Extract from a letter to a friend in 1937 from Mary in China").

14

A Time of Transition

1937. A decade since Mary's year in Shanghai, when she made significant reassessments about her life. Now the ground began to shift again in a variety of ways.

Norman—her "first fledgling"—went away to the Mission boarding school in Chengtu. He was almost eleven years old and had gone as far in school as she could take him. She grieved being no longer essential to him and briefly "gnashed her teeth"—to Freda, the friend she trusted to receive any and all feelings. "I'm not going to nag about it," she wrote "just air a grouse now and then to keep me from bottling it up."

文月華

In mid-May Mary received the news of her mother's death.

[I remember the day the cable arrived. The sound of my mother sobbing, all alone in the dining room, her head cradled in her arms. That sound has never left me. SJE]

Mary found this grieving particularly difficult because letters giving all the details of the actual event took so long to arrive. What had the final days been like? How was the service, who attended, what had Father Endicott, who took the service, actually said? Eventually it was her long-time friend, Harold Brown, who gave her the kind of detailed information she craved. Mary, in turn, felt free to describe the painful feelings that needed to be expressed before healing from her loss could begin.

> Dear Harold,
>
> I can't tell you how frustrated I felt—and still do—that I could not be there during Mother's last illness, dreadful as it was—and to be with my family at her death. It was foolish but there was no use denying that I felt that way, though I didn't allow myself to brood over it. That feeling of being cut off—of having nothing to do to produce nature's balance after a vacuum—that was hardest to bear. I know everything was done for Mother but to think that it was possible there should be a time when I meant noth-

ing to her and yet she needed personal relationships as a child does—the world shut out—hurts me yet. Perhaps it is an unconscious desire to compensate her for all she did for me that makes it seem so poignant.

You know, that old jealousy of Jane has occurred to me these months. I believe my grief has been harder because deep in my heart I am annoyed that she should have been the one to minister to Mother at the last. Perhaps she has always been as fond of Mother as I was—no doubt she was—but my impression of the past is coloured by the way Jane and Mother used to rub each other the wrong way and by the greater companionship I had with her.

I expect it is all part of that old emotional conflict because I do know that in many ways Mother and I were not "eye to eye," as it were. Perhaps it is a good thing that Blatz brought the thing to the surface. He didn't make it vanish into nothingness, evidently, but at least I know it for what it is and not for a nameless unrest. (to Harold Brown, 1 November 1937)

文月華

Early in 1937 Mary's creative energies became focussed on what would be her most challenging assignment while in China—becoming a foster mother.

We've taken on a new experiment. For me it's branching out on my first intimate contact with Chinese life....We've taken a little boy, George Whang, into our home—and into my school. Soon we're to add another, his cousin, Gerald Chen....They will have a tutor for two hours in the afternoon so they don't get behind in their Chinese studies....

It came about because George's father had been here once or twice and was impressed with the atmosphere of our home. He wants his boy to be ready to get the most out of an education abroad. So he urged us to take him. I was quite staggered by the idea at first. I wasn't sure I could do it and feared for the effect on the family....

Mr. Whang wants to send George to West Point Military Academy. Jim warned him he would do everything he could to turn his son against the idea, and also that Christianity was said to be a contagious disease. Whang laughed and said to go ahead....

George is almost nine but not much bigger than Philip and accustomed to considering himself a young prince. The Whang's eldest grandson, he is the spoiled darling of a family of six adults, three other children, 28 servants and the terror of his school-teachers. He doesn't know a word of English and has been brought up by the servants to look upon foreigners as bogeys

文
月
華
的
中
國
日
記

whom they could use as threats when he was naughty.

It was cold plunge for the little chap, and he looked wistful, if not tearful, for several days. He held to Stephen as to one friendly item in an alien setting. Stephen was driven nearly crazy by having George stick to him like a leech and howling if he moved away. That is wearing off more all the time, and I think the second little boy will be a great help to George in adjusting himself....

It's two weeks since this experiment began and Gerald has arrived. He has just turned nine, and is taller than George but not so robust, and shyer. George is delighted to have his cousin come, and has been much gayer since his arrival. He initiated Gerald into all our customs, which will help him over the first bewildering weeks. Stephen seems to have a good time with both of them, and that former feeling of being a martyr to the cause has passed off. The three of them tussle and roll around like three puppies sometimes....(February 1937)

Both boys were asked to call their foster parents Aunt Mary and Uncle Jim. One of the strange customs was Uncle Jim's carving the chicken and making sure that everyone got their turn at having the drumsticks. Another was the necessity of saying "please" and "thank you" at the table.

It's now two months since I became a foster-mother. Today we had foreign guests for lunch....The children all seemed to get along all right and the little Chinese boys behaved properly and looked nice. I spent part of the morning shortening their trousers to a smart length, as I knew my guests would notice their appearance. Some of my friends think this whole idea is a crazy one, so I want them to get the best possible impression.

The spoiled prince, however, remained a formidable challenge for Mary:

When George first came he would cry every time he didn't get his own way. I explained to him in Chinese that since he was behaving like a small infant I would have to put him where infants spent most of their time, in bed. Or, I would tell him that he must be tired or he wouldn't cry and so he must rest awhile. After a few such occasions he decided there was nothing to be gained by crying and it decreased rapidly. Then he began to be bossy with the other children but this didn't achieve anything, as they would simply go on with their play. After some months the bossiness decreased; he became generally cooperative.

文
月
華
的
中
國
日
記

When he goes home for the weekends or holidays, at first he astonishes his relatives by his improvement. But, if he stays for more than a day or two, he reverts to his old ways and begins to make a nuisance of himself, grabbing at food, kicking the servants, whining and crying to his parents and grandparents for what he wants. For these reasons, he seldom goes home.

We can see it is not altogether George's fault that he acts up at home. There is almost no provision for active play for him and George is full of physical energy. He is expected to sit up late to amuse his grandfather and then to keep quiet until mid-day so that his grandfather can sleep. The result is demoralizing. I am hoping that gradually I can help George to realize that he himself must do something to adjust to this unfortunate environment. He must definitely plan for quiet ways of amusement for the days he is at home, and he must take responsibility for seeing he gets to bed at a decent hour.

One day we were talking about cooking, and the boys asked how various things were cooked. George said he sometimes tells the cook at his house to make certain things for him and he watches him do it. Then he added, quite naively, "If he doesn't do it right, I kick him." It didn't seem to be boasting, just a simple statement of fact. I showed I was shocked and Gerald told how George kicks everybody at home, even his parents and his little brother. George looked rather low by this time but he didn't deny it. I said I hoped he hadn't done anything like that lately; he agreed he wouldn't want them to be kicking him, and therefore, he ought not to kick them. Putting aside the attitude of blame, I asked him casually whom he had kicked the last time he was at home. He looked straight at me, a little ashamed, and said, nonchalantly, "Just the cook."

Jim says it is not surprising—that his father does it to the servants when he isn't pleased....

Last week I stayed overnight in the city....When I got home George confided: "Last night, at supper, I told the cook he was drunk, and he said, 'Well, don't you take wine?'" Then George said, "We're Christians. We don't drink wine."

I was surprised at this, for we have never discussed drinking since the boys have come—indeed, hardly ever in our own family. Also, I wasn't aware that George even knew the English name for Christians. He has often asked me questions about Jesus but I have never used any terms that I thought might prejudice or confuse him.

Afterwards, I asked Stephen how George knew that Christians don't take wine and he said he had told him. The most interesting part of all is

文
月
華
的
中
國
日
記

that George included himself in the family picture. Perhaps Christianity can be caught like a contagious disease, after all. Perhaps when George and Gerald get to the awareness of the teens they will find that they've been growing in the Kingdom of God for some time, too.

George is certainly nearer to it than when he came to us, if actions are any criteria. He is very much less like the spoiled princeling, better in games, less grasping, less touchy and more aware of ways in which he can do things for other people. It is a joy to watch the sweetness spreading in him and the other things growing less....

We were all startled one Sunday afternoon to discover that George was nowhere to be found. His family, and especially his grandparents, are very nervous lest he be kidnapped, and have urged us not to let him out of the compound without an adult. I had to remind him of this only that morning so I was doubly shocked when we could not find him. Just when we were beginning to run in circles, he turned up with his mother. He had run home alone to his grandmother's house, which is now on this side of the river, about half-an-hour's walk from here.

George was in tears as his mother brought him back for she was saying that Jim would wallop him.

Jim had no intention of doing so—though he felt like it I've no doubt. Rather we sent George upstairs to bed. Such a fuss as he put up—wailing for his mother and then to go home. It was really dreadful and made us feel he is not very far from the spoiled princeling that came to us a year ago. He had never made a big fuss like this before.

It was revealed that he and his cousin had a scrap at rest-time, and he had gone home claiming that Gerald and Stephen had beaten him till he was black and blue. He was yelling for his mother upstairs because he still believed Jim was going to beat him. I went up and talked to him, but I no sooner got him quieted than his mother came up, and he started all over again. I would get him quiet again, turn his mind to something else, and then she'd stir him all up by pointing out to him how kindly I was. I could have shaken her. No wonder he got in the habit of wailing and making a fuss.

I finally got him to undress and get into his bed, and left him there supplied with magazines for the rest of the afternoon and evening. His mother was so obviously upset—but helpless to know how to handle him—that it would have been funny if I didn't think what it meant to the child....

Gerald has had no emotional difficulties. He played happily and was liked by all the children from the first. The main trouble I have with Gerald is that he doesn't imitate the English he hears. He clings to the present tense of the verb on almost all occasions. He also forgets the "s" on plurals. George makes these mistakes to a certain extent, but Gerald makes them persistently. This is why the language used during playtime is so important.

When the boys first came they were allowed to speak Chinese in their playtime, and Stephen learned a tremendous amount of spoken Chinese from them. It was difficult to change them over to speaking English in playtime but until they did so, their ability to understand and converse rapidly did not progress fast. I tried nagging; SPEAK ENGLISH signs, slight punishments. Once I became angry and whacked each of them on the hand with a stiff hairbrush. Stephen went white with terror and resentment. The two Chinese boys smiled and didn't flick an eye-lid. So that was a complete failure and I apologized to them all in a few minutes, especially to Stephen whom I have only struck about twice before. I am always heartily ashamed when I resort to that kind of authority and so it has seldom occurred.

At last I struck on the idea of each boy keeping a chart of his days in regard to remembering to speak English at playtime. They took it up voluntarily and it worked like a charm. In a couple of weeks they had dropped all their Chinese at playtime and were going ahead rapidly with English.

I had just solved this problem when a cloud appeared on the horizon in the person of a third boy. (compiled from various 1937 letters to family and friends and a report on children to Dr. W. E. Blatz, October 1938)

文月華

The coming of Dick Dzen in 1938 precipitated a major crisis in Mary's life: "I came as near—or nearer to a breakdown of some kind as I ever want to be." The seeds of this outcome were sown outside the walls of the Endicotts' compound. When George and Gerald arrived in the spring of 1937, Jim was preoccupied with the discovery that the Chinese principal of the Gin I Middle School had embezzled school funds. Two of the teachers, also Chinese, had been particularly helpful in providing him with the necessary evidence so that the principal could be fired.

This situation touched off strong nationalistic feelings among some of the senior students, who went on strike. We get an important glimpse of the inflammatory atmosphere in a letter from Mary to her parents:

The principal left on Thursday and the whole school escorted him to the river, carrying banners and firing off firecrackers. We watched it from the

文
月
華
的
中
國
日
記

upper verandah where we do our lessons in fine weather. The ringleaders of the strikers are heavy-set boys and they evidently cowed the rest into following their lead. They had signs up and slogans at their meetings about not wanting any foreigners' running dogs—as they called the two teachers who helped Jim—and all the unsavoury talk of 1927....There were threats of beatings for these teachers—and I expect unspoken ones about Jim—but they've had two police on duty at the school for some months past so nothing has come to a head. (to the Austins, 18 April 1937)

The new principal, one Mr. Shiao, was both a friend of Dick Dzen's father and a neighbour of the Endicotts. When Mr. Dzen heard from him that the Endicotts had taken in two Chinese boys he was determined that his son should have the same benefits as George and Gerald.

However, since becoming a foster mother, Mary's personal life—and the world—had become much more stressful:

- Mary had begun her first solo try at professional writing—an article on Mount Omei, a sacred Buddhist mountain where the Endicotts spent their summers. Hoping that *National Geographic* would accept it, she revised it five times during the next six months.
- After her mother's death in May 1937, Mary grieved deeply for months.
- Less than two months later, on July 7, 1937, Japan invaded China. Soon Chungking became the wartime capital which meant a real possibility of air-raids.
- That fall Mary accepted an extra English-speaking boy, John Honnor, because Philip Michael needed a playmate. Both boys required a lot of attention in the classroom.
- January 1938 brought a "bombshell" from Canada: her father was planning to remarry—within six months. Jane was greatly agitated. Mary felt compelled to write—at length—to persuade her sister of the error of her ways, and to assure her father that she supported his plans.
- On February 19, 1938, Japanese bombers reached Chungking.
- In April, a little girl Shirley's age arrived with her missionary family in the "medical compound," about half an hour from Duckling Pond. Mary was delighted to have Margaret Allen join her school because Shirley had never had a playmate.

Thus, when Mr. Dzen asked the Endicotts to take his son, there were already seven students—and four different grade levels—in the Duckling Pond school, and Mary had been on an emotional roller coaster for some time. Although she felt she could not take in a third Chinese boy, Mr. Dzen would not take no for an answer. Knowing his friend, Mr. Shiao, lived next door to the Endicotts, he sent his son Dick to live there—with instructions to pressure the Endicotts into accepting him.

It must have seemed a daunting task to such a young boy away from his family. However, there were two students from the Gin I Middle School boarding at the Shiao residence. Undoubtedly Dick listened with great interest to their tales about the previous year's strike with its anti-foreign overtones. During playtime—unheard by Mary—he began to call out to George and Gerald over the low wall that separated the Shiao house from that of the Endicotts. "Why are you being running dogs of imperialism? How can you be so unpatriotic?" George and Gerald went over the wall—and spoke Chinese.

A compromise was made: Dick would continue to live with the Shiao family, but would spend the school hours with the Endicotts. This move escalated tensions; a virtual Battle of the Playground ensued:

Since the new boy, Dick Dzen, has been living at Mr. Shiao's and spending the school-hours with us, some new problems have arisen. George and Gerald have been very chummy with Dick and want to play with him all the time. That is natural, but it means they talk in Chinese in their playtime, which is a pity as they have made great strides in idiomatic English lately, since Chinese has been tabooed in the family. Also, a certain anti-foreign spirit has crept into their play. There are two teen-age boys at the Shiao's too, and the bunch of them have formed a clique and, not only won't play with our children but are very unpleasant to them whenever the latter come near. Our children are very much hurt as well as annoyed. Stephen is especially touched, for the two lads have been so near to him for so long that, as you know, he has considered them as brothers.

It is difficult to know how best to handle such a problem. I hate playing policeman but it has come almost to that. I have had to say that George and Gerald can not go down to Shiao's to play, but Dick can come up here. If the boys go without permission they have to go to bed early. This has happened two or three times....

133

文
月
華
的
中
國
日
記

Even when Dick comes up here to play, the three Chinese boys go off by themselves, and the delightful group they used to have has ceased. I've had to insist that they must add one of our family to their group when they play with Dick. This will ensure some English conversation, at any rate, and break down the race combination.

They have accepted that gracefully, and Philip was delighted to be chosen to be in their "company" today. However, they always accept my suggestions gracefully on the surface. It remains to be seen how they will continue to carry this one out.

I have one more plan, more drastic still. If this one does not work, after a week's trial, I shall have to say that Dick cannot play with them at all except in the group as a whole, and that they must tag around with Stephen as they did naturally when they first came. I hope this won't be necessary, for it will mean some enforcing, but I can't let the present situation go on. Dick will not be hearing English at all, and they will slip back in theirs. I won't try it this week, because Norman will be at home and I don't want Stephen to be restricted.

A few days later, however, Mary decided to take Dick into the family. Still, the problem of the Chinese boys ganging together and boycotting the Endicott children continued until she took an entirely different tack:

One day I had a quiet talk with George about it and asked him why he didn't want to speak English in playtime. He always said he forgot but I knew one doesn't forget what one wants to remember—not constantly. At last he admitted that Dick told them they were foreigners if they talked English and that Dick said that to the boys in the High School nearby where my husband teaches.

Light began to dawn upon me. I explained that we learned a foreign language, not to become foreigners, but to be able to be friendly with foreigners. I pointed out that "Uncle Jim," who speaks Chinese like a native, was able to be friendlier with them on that account but that it hadn't changed him into a Chinese.

Gerald at first denied and then admitted that what George had said was true. Then I saw clearly how all my efforts to make them speak English after Dick came had been futile. I told Stephen about it and he said, yes, he knew that was the reason, and that Dick also called them traitors when they spoke English. I don't know why Stephen had never mentioned these things to me himself. Perhaps he assumed I knew them.

文
月
華
的
中
國
日
記

Stephen also said that George teased Dick about having come to live in our house when we didn't want him—that his father had pushed him in. Then I understood why Dick was taking out his resentment by turning the other two boys against English. I had Jim explain to Dick, in Chinese, that we had nothing against him personally, that we had simply thought it unwise at first—because we thought it might be too much for me—but once we had decided to let him come, he was welcome, and we hoped he would soon feel a part of the family. Jim explained it also to Dick's family, and things began to improve at once.

I stopped nagging the boys about talking English. Instead, I asked each of them to help me teach Dick by giving him fifteen minutes of the oral work I had given them in the early months, before school started each day. They complied and the problem was soon solved.

During the summer holidays, all of the children, except Philip, gave Dick an oral lesson for fifteen minutes a day. He made excellent progress. By the end of the summer he was able to listen to and take part in conversations. Now, as we begin a new term, he talks English, as do the other boys, during play-time, and all the children play together happily as they used to do. Dick has enlarged our children's interests a great deal by the number of things he is always making out of paper or wood....

It is my hope that each of these Chinese boys will find a useful, if not leading place in Chinese society when they are grown and that their time here will prove to be a constructive factor in their lives as well as useful in enlarging the social experience of my own children. (report on children to Dr. W.E. Blatz, October 1938)

文月華

The three Chinese boys stayed until the Endicotts returned to Canada in the spring of 1941. They continued to refer my parents as Aunt Mary and Uncle Jim and to keep in touch with the family, even to this day. They did live useful lives and tried to be of service to the Chinese people. When the Communists were victorious in 1949, all three of Mary's foster children greeted this event with enthusiasm. The political climate of the times, however, was such that any Chinese who had had foreign connections was continually under suspicion.

Dick had not only lived in a foreign family, he had come to Canada to train as an engineer. When he returned to the People's Republic of China, it was with a Canadian bride. Although Ginny was half-Chinese, she

文
月
華
的
中
國
日
記

Mary's foster mother efforts to create harmony are successful. In the Duckling Pond compound, left to right: Stephen, George Whang, Gerald Chen, and Dick Dzen.

never escaped being defined as a foreigner. After five years, Dick felt he had no option but to turn his back on the land of his birth. His idealism shattered, he and his family came to the United States where he successfully opened an innovative and creative business.

Gerald, too, had come to Canada to attend university. Part of that time he lived with the Endicott family once again. When he returned to China, along with other intellectuals, his career as a bilingual journalist was disrupted many times. In addition, his foreign connections increased the burden of suspicion under which he lived. After the death of Chairman Mao, for the sake of his wife's peace of mind, he moved to Hong Kong, but continued to write for English-language, pro-China publications.

George, the "Prince" with whom Mary had struggled so valiantly, also threw his lot in with the Chinese Revolution. Like other intellectuals, he and his family were sent to the countryside for "rectification" during the Cultural Revolution. The spoiled little rich boy lived in a cave—and survived, though he believed the policy was madness. After he returned to Beijing to live, he eventually became a senior official in the Ministry of Coal, ending his career as Director of Finance. Because his command of English was so good, he often went with government delegations to negotiate foreign contracts.

文
月
華
的
中
國
日
記

15

Conquering Herself

The Battle of the Playground totally depleted Mary's already flagging energy. The following winter she described how her recovery had become a major turning point in her emotional and spiritual life.

> Last spring I came as near—or nearer to a breakdown of some kind as I ever want to be....The complete rest at Mount Omei and the chance to get a perspective on my life put me on me feet again, and there I hope to stay....Part of my recuperation last summer was due to the discovery of the psychotherapist Fritz Künkel. A friend recommended *Let's Be Normal* to me and it was so fascinating that I've re-read it several times, made voluminous notes and been quoting it ever since to all and sundry....
>
> His analysis of character is the most revealing thing I have ever read, and has awakened me to a new outlook on life, helping me to discover in myself blind spots of which I was only vaguely aware....It has done something to my inner life [and] has already brought me a new courage and a new peace. (circular letter, 19 February 1939)

According to Künkel, every individual begins life in a state of unconscious clarity before moving on to the egocentric, or self-centred, stage of childhood. The mature person, through growing awareness and effort, can change their personality to one that is genuinely other-centred. He believed it is possible for a person to be outwardly altruistic—always helping others—when the motivations are really "egocentric": to make him or her feel better about themselves. When this is the case, the person does not experience the sense of being fully alive, the life abundant. Irritability and depression are the two outstanding symptoms of egocentricity.

Returning from Mount Omei in the fall of 1938, Mary wrote an article about Künkel's ideas—"On Finding Life"—which she read at the weekly Oxford Group prayer meeting:

[Künkel] challenges us to experiment…with how we may change our personality from the self-centred to the outgoing type.…If we try to help others to find this abundant life, our success will depend on the degree to which we have changed our own egocentricity into [concern for others]. In every failure let us look for the cause in ourselves. But let us not be depressed by failure. One of the subtlest types of ego ideal is that which says: "I must not fail. I must not make a mistake." This leads to all kinds of cowardice, from blaming others to the refusal to act at all. Failure is inherent in experiment and only by experiment can we increase our skill in living.

Later that fall, Mary asked Jean Stewart from the Women's Missionary Society, who was living with the Endicotts at the time, to make a list of any signs of egocentricity she had discerned in Mary. The former was aghast, but finally agreed to the request.

Jean thought of three main points which she confided to me while we walked single-file on the narrow country paths between the rice fields around here. She walked behind me to give herself confidence.…

Her three points were:
1) self-satisfaction, tending towards social snobbishness because of an upbringing in more-or-less luxury;
2) intellectual pride;
3) a casualness in my personal relations which sometimes hurts people.…

I found an alibi rising to my lips for all of these but I did not feel either the resentment, and/or the desire to deny them outright, which I would have felt a few months ago, I am sure. I hope this is a sign that my egocentricity is less rigid than it was: Künkel says you can judge rigidity by the violence of the protest which a person makes when you happen to hit on their real ego ideal.…

I didn't comprehend exactly how these expressions were manifested in me—that may come with time—but as I thought each one over, I could see she might be right. It gave me rather a subdued feeling to see myself in such an unfavourable light, but it also gave me some release from a burden. I suppose if the ego can come to realize that the ends, which it has been seeking, do not actually fulfil the ultimate end—the finding of the happy and abundant life—it feels some release from a burden, which it was not aware of carrying.

Anyway, the last few weeks I do feel a certain lightness of spirit within me, which encourages me to believe something is happening. It is not

文
月
華
的
中
國
日
記

always with me—but I am sharply conscious when the feeling deserts me that I am concerned about myself more than about the other person or circumstance. This annoys or depresses me. As soon as *that* realization comes, I find the annoyance or depression lifting. I can hardly believe it. It is like watching the incredible mountain being removed....

If you are thinking that so much introspection is not healthy, I would like to add that I agree—if it ends in introspection. But if it is turned into constructive channels of action then it seems to me an eminently healthy thing to do.

Just such a constructive thing occurred on Tuesday when I attended the monthly meeting of our Local Committee. I have been vice-chairman for two years, but the only reason I let my name stand was because I never expected to have to act. I didn't like to admit I felt inadequate to doing it [because of my stammer]. Then, on Tuesday, Miss Wellwood, the chairman, was feeling so wretched with a broken wrist, that, as soon as I arrived, she asked me to take the chair.

For a fleeting moment I had a feeling of panic and thought I would ask Jim to do it for me. Then something new rose up in me and told the panic to sit down and be quiet, that there was no real reason why I should not be able to do it in this small group of people I know. I have never done it before, you see, unless in a group of children, and I wasn't sure I knew the right procedure, let alone the self-confidence to use it. However, it came to me that this was a good test as to whether I was thinking of myself—so afraid of making a mistake and risking criticism, if not ridicule—instead of concentrating on the thing to be done and on the people whom it would serve....

That calmed me and I was able to carry on the procedure without any trouble, and without any inward gritting of my teeth....The group, even Jim, seemed to take it for granted that it meant nothing unusual to me. This was, of course, the very best thing for me, but I found afterwards I longed for someone to pat me on the back and tell me I'd done it well. That showed me, more plainly than anything, how much the desire for praise enters into our egocentricity, how unfortunate it is if, as children, we learn to expect it, and to need it for our comfort and support. I think this viewpoint is an advance over assuming praise is a constructive thing. Interest and appreciation—yes—and thanks when due—but not praise. (to family, 20 November 1938)

Reading Künkel was a deeply spiritual experience for Mary. What she found there dovetailed with what she considered the central teaching of

Jesus: "Whosoever seeks to gain his life shall lose it; whosoever loses his life...shall gain it" (Luke 9:34). Künkel gave her the tools for reaching that goal. She also modified her theology:

> When I read Künkel's *Conquer Yourself* this winter I understood why I had been increasingly conscious of a desire to deepen my own religious life since I read that first book last summer. I don't know yet just what this will mean to me, or what form it will take. I only know that I feel a stronger desire to "know" God than heretofore; perhaps to be conscious of the reality of His presence is a better way to put it.
>
> It may have struck you that there are certain resemblances in all this to the Oxford Group experience. Jim and I were both struck by the same thing when reading and talking about Künkel last summer. Getting rid of egocentricity is like surrender; the productivity of being other-centred is like the creative energy, which is generated in some people through quiet times and guidance. The ability to help others through personal contact after one has set one's inner life in order is like the benefits claimed from sharing one's personal experiences. I believe the heightened realization of the presence of God, to which I have felt moved, is what Helen Bott felt had enriched her life through the Oxford Group.
>
> There are differences, however. Künkel pushes beyond the symptom to the cause—unlike the infallibility ascribed to guidance by many Groupers. Künkel says to try to cure jealousy or anger or alcoholism or any of the sins of the flesh by simply resolving not to indulge in them is like trying to treat scarlet fever by applying an ointment to the rash. One must go deeper; find what is the egocentric root that produces the symptom. Otherwise it will continue to break out in some other form. (circular letter, 19 February 1939)

文
月
華
的
中
國
日
記

16

Creative Writing

In the fall of 1938 Mary was given an opportunity to help produce a special Chungking issue of the *West China Missionary News*. She worked with two other women, one of whom suggested she contribute an original poem. Entitled "Vignettes of Chungking," the poem reflected her range of experiences on both sides of the Yangtze—in the city and across the river in Duckling Pond: "A city built upon a rock" that defied "the march of Time" was characterized by vibrant life—teeming crowds surging through the streets were "pressed by the panting coolies, bearing great loads upon their shoulders poles." But across the river, one may walk unhurriedly "in fertile valleys golden in the Spring" (see Appendix A). Perhaps it was her way of making peace with the place that had caused her so many traumas and where she had felt so lonely and isolated.

But surely the greatest satisfaction must have come when she wrote about her old nemesis—crossing the Yangtze River.

Coolie transporting bales of cotton, a common sight on the roads around Chungking.

Commuting from Chungking

文
月
華
的
中
國
日
記

After an afternoon in the city I often find it is too late to catch the last steam ferry to Dan Dz Sih, the town on the South Bank near where we live. In the gathering dusk I make my way through the alleys of the shack town, which springs up mushroom-like on the foreshore as soon as the autumn lower level of the river is reached.

If I am wearing a hat I carefully remove it, for once I had my hat nipped off my head in these very alleys. The riverside is jammed with junks and sampans, but by dint of some local shouting I find where the Dan Dz Sih sampans are located. If it is after dark I am greeted by too hearty a welcome by the boatmen, each of whom tries to persuade me to hire his boat, as night fares are few. If I make a wrong choice a bitter quarrel will ensue and I will have to scramble over several empty boats to find the one whose turn to go is next on the list. I can never disentangle this situation but have learned not to rail at the boatmen for the inconvenience they cause me. I accept my fate and go where the most insistent voices indicate.

Once settled in the boat my desire is to get them to push off before they overload it with other passengers...With a mighty heave of the bamboo pole we are off, but there are shouts of "Watch your head" as we back out between other small boats pressed behind us, whose huge rudders are swinging around idly. Out on the open water my ruffled feelings, if any, are smoothed away by the coolness and beauty of the river.

Strangers fear this mighty stream, which carries a little boat so swiftly down its course that one feels in the grip of some overwhelming and therefore sinister force. Those who frequently cross learn to have confidence in the skill of the boatmen, however rough or casual with the oar they seem to be. When one can glide unmoved by a whirlpool or find oneself rowed straight toward a purling rapid without forgetting that one will be turned away just in time, one enjoys the thrill of the river....

Sitting in the sampan in the middle of the river, I watch the shimmering reflection of lights in the water. I look back at the city, a great mound spangled with lights crowned by a modern red glow on a bank tower. On the southern shore I can pick out...a cluster of lights showing the position of the Canadian Hospital buildings.

Here and there, throughout shore villages and the hill-town of Dan Dz Sih, the darkness is pierced by lights on the streets and in the open-front shops. Everybody has electricity now except the smallest places where the

文
月
華
的
中
國
日
記

flare of a tiny earthenware lamp burning vegetable oil reproduces for the passer-by the atmosphere of a medieval painting in some humble shop. Kerosene, once popular as the *Oil for the Lamps of China* of Alice Hobart's novel, has become almost unobtainable since the war.

While I am trying to find some stars in the cloudy sky, I hear the request to pay up; the boatman at the prow lays his oar away and comes to collect. If I have not been perfectly clear in the arrangement there may be difficulty at this point, for he will hope I have forgotten the custom for hiring a boat to oneself, or, if he has not recognized me, he will try for the extortionate amount demanded of strangers.

The bow scrapes the rocky shore and I scramble out and begin to shout for my chairmen, fearing lest they may have given me up if I am long overdue. They are lounging by some food stalls on the foreshore and soon we are swinging up the thirty-minute climb.

Once in the heart of the town of Dan Dz Sih I am back in the old China of narrow streets. Steps have been cut into the solid rock all the way from the river to the top of the town several hundred feet above. Formerly, the shutters would have been going up on the open-front shops by this time, but electric lights have created a new night life and the streets are full of people....Tired, listless women watch the ever-present children who are not put to bed till they fall asleep in the endless occupation of watching the passing show....

The chairmen are shouting to clear the way in the crowd. They jostle someone who retaliates by cracking a long stick of sugar cane against the poles. The chair stops abruptly and the front man, enraged, engages in a verbal duel as to the deafness and blindness of some people and the dumbness of others. I tell him to forget it and move on, and he does so, grumbling audibly for a block....We are nearing the upper edge of the town, and the Mission School carpenter, tinsmith and barber hail us as we go by their shops. The word goes round that the missionary's wife is returning from the city.

We turn a corner and a cool wind from the fields blows upon us. The quiet of the country is before us for the last third of the journey. Like the river, the countryside soothes and rests one after the turmoil of urban streets. In the darkness I can distinguish a big banyan tree above the faint shimmer of flooded paddy fields. The light from the swinging chair lantern throws weird shadows along the footpath of uneven stones. We pass a farmer coaxing a reluctant pig to tomorrow's market by means of snatches of song and a tickling switch.

People walking in the "Golden Valley," just outside the Endicott compound at Duckling Pond, Chungking, circa 1926. Photo: J.G. Endicott. (*West China Missionary News,* May 1939

The chairmen shout to a string of pedestrians in a single file to keep to the inner side of the road. Some are carrying flaring torches of braided bamboo. In the light of my lantern they peer into my chair, then pass on, shouting to each other that it is a foreign woman.

Now the lights of the High Schools of the Canadian Mission make a brilliant display on the left and in the dim distance on the right I see a twinkle in the windows of the hill-top house whither I am bound. The chairmen step out more quickly—soon we are rounding the corner of our compound-wall and shouting for the gardener's wife to open the front gate. As she does so, the barking of the dogs, the staccato of the pups and the shouts of children who are playing Lions and Tigers on the dark verandah give me a welcome, which would warm the heart at any journey's end. (*West China Missionary News,* May 1939)

17

Wartime in Chungking

Dear Jane,

You will all be feeling as we did yesterday: "It's come at last" when you hear or read that Japanese bombers have reached Chungking. I hope you noticed they *bombed the military air-field only.* That is seven miles east of us, down the river. There's a range of hills between the airfield and us, so we didn't hear the bombs and knew nothing of it till the afternoon. At 9:30 a.m., nine planes circled the airfield, dropping eight bombs. One man killed.

We all looked at each other and soon began to smile and joke about it—children, servants and all. I suppose it was the feeling that the suspense was over—they could get this far, and earlier in the day than we expected. It was strange, too, to think it had happened—so long dreaded—and we had not even known. There was an air raid practice on at the time but we don't hear the signals from the city and don't know till we see the people running out of the suburb near us.

There have been several false alarms, with terrific panic jams, people killed in alleyways and in boats which were overcrowded, but I don't think it was generally known this time that it was not merely a practice, though they wondered why the All Clear signal did not come for two hours. I hear the recent practices have been more orderly and the streets are cleared in a few minutes. Everybody is made to go into the shops and the boards are put up. Rickshaw coolies reap a harvest holding up those who wish to flee from the city. Little boats—the *sampans*—crossing the river also put up their prices.

I was glad to find we could go on with our schoolwork after a few minutes talk about the news. We have put the last touches to the dugout, sandbags at the door, seats inside. I put some warm coats on the rack in the hall in the mornings. Jim and the children dug a shortcut path down the hillside this morning but I'm sure if I go that steep way I shall end by rolling in a lather of mud and ashes. (19 February 1938)

文
月
華
的
中
國
日
記

The first significant bombing of Chungking came a year later, early in January 1939. Afterwards Mary wrote a lengthy letter to her father, which included a glowing tribute to Madame Chiang Kai-shek. In view of how negatively the Endicotts later felt about the Nationalist government, this portrait is particularly interesting.

> I must tell you about the meeting of the Women's Club last Tuesday. Madame Chiang spoke, in English of course, and I was sitting in the second row so it seemed almost like a conversation. She is one of the most fascinating people I've ever seen or heard—perhaps the most fascinating when one considers her place in history. Part of her charm is her perfect naturalness, her simplicity, and her utter lack of any platform manner or grand style to impress people. I thought she was a splendid example of Künkel's objective person, one who is so interested in life around her and her responsibilities to it that she simply doesn't think of herself.
>
> If China survives this terrible invasion it will be, to no small extent, because of the type of personality she is. She is a queen in the best sense, not by birth nor by choice, but by her achievement. No wonder her people adore her....
>
> She told us of the work training young women in Hankow to do war work, and how they had enlisted the help of all the women they could reach. She said the women of the leisured classes were the hardest to interest. They lived in the French concession, and felt themselves safe so they said what does the war matter and went on with their majong.
>
> She urged those in the meeting who were teachers to go back to their schools and tell their girls about that and to be a different kind of *tai-tai* when they left school....
>
> Madame Chiang has invited Jim to join in the work of the New Life Movement, which is under her direction....When I think of his being away from home a great deal, especially in these days of bombing—and, of course, the Generalissimo's headquarters in Chungking is one of the prize targets of the enemy—my heart just sinks within me, for life just isn't life to me unless Jim is around. But when I think of China's plight and of the gifts Jim has which might be useful in this wider field, I can't find it in my heart to make any protest....

Charles Austin had the entire letter printed in *The Chatham News,* including this plea for political action:

文
月
華
的
中
國
日
記

It is up to the people at home to push to stop assisting Japan in any way. I wonder what Canada has done about nickel and scrap iron. It is ghastly to think that these bombs would not be possible without something from Canadian and American soil.

To all my friends in Canada I would like to say: Don't let your emotions find escape in useless worry, but turn them into constructive action. Push for action to wash Canada's hands clean from the guilt. (to Charles Austin, 15 January 1939)

文月華

A search for an adequate air-raid shelter began. First a cave (dugout) was carved about two metres out of the rocky hill in the compound at Duckling Pond. Sandbags were piled in front of benches. Soon Mary felt the need for a long tunnel with two exits and a room off to one side about half way in. George's father helped out with the expense, and by the fall of 1939 this room was equipped with bunk beds and benches. The two exits avoided the danger of concussion should a bomb explode nearby, and provided a way out if one exit got completely blocked. (This had happened in a government shelter in the city of Chungking with great loss of life.) Before the tunnel was completed, the family went to the basement during an air raid.

This was the situation when the first truly devastating fire-bomb raids occurred the first week of May 1939. Like a wartime journalist, Mary went to her typewriter at the first opportunity:

This has been an exciting and terrible week in the history of Chungking. It began well with the torch-lighting ceremony on Monday at which the Generalissimo inaugurated the Spiritual Mobilization Movement, which is to keep up the morale and resistance of the people. I wasn't able to go, but Jim said it was an impressive sight; the Generalissimo and Mme. Chiang looking so grave and determined as they spoke to the huge crowd before lighting the central fire from which a thousand torches were lit and carried in procession by groups representing all sections of the populace, singing the patriotic songs which are a new feature of Chinese life.

Jim felt it was an historic occasion, a pageant symbolizing the determination of a great people with their back to the wall receiving a baptism of fire to kindle their spirit against the crime against human freedom as well as their own sovereignty. Runners carried torches from the central fire to eight other big ceremonies in the city. The next night the fire ceremony was repeated on our mission school football field with over five hundred High School boys and girls participating.

Our children and I watched it from our balcony and were greatly thrilled. When the Chinese national anthem is sung well, there is something very noble but melancholy about it....

On May 3rd and 4th Chungking was given a baptism of fire which was realistic rather than symbolic and will always be a ghastly memory to those who witnessed it, and much more to those who experienced it....What you want to hear from me is what I went through and I'll try and give you that picture while it is fresh in my mind.

On Wednesday Clara Jones came over to give the children their music lessons. We had just finished lunch when the air raid signal sounded. We had been free of it for weeks and have had no air raids which came this far since the memorable one in January, but we knew the clear weather of spring would give the enemy the conditions they wanted. Still, we hoped it was a false alarm and watched the people running out of the suburb near us, and scurrying over the hilltops on the horizon until the emergency signal was given.

Then we took the children down to the basement, which we have decided is our safest place. There is a narrow alley between the tiny furnace room and the stone foundation of the house and Jim thinks this would probably hold up under anything but a direct hit by a demolition bomb over that very spot—a small chance. Clara suggested we play "Animal, Vegetable and Mineral" so we did and had quite a jolly time, almost forgetting to hear the different roar of the planes as the enemy planes arrived in the midst of the Chinese pursuits which always begin circling around as soon as the warning is given. We heard the deeper roar of the bombers but, in trying to keep the children's minds distracted, we did not hear the bombs fall and we hoped they had only fallen on the airfield or in the country.

When the drone of the planes had died away the servants ran in to say that two planes had fallen behind our High School. They had seen the trail of smoke and the pilots coming down with their parachutes. The Table Boy dashed off to see what had happened and didn't get back for hours, as it was a mile or two behind the school. Of course the children wanted to go too but I knew that would not do. We hoped they were Japanese planes but found out later they were not, although the pilot of one was conscious long enough to say that he was sure he had hit an enemy plane and perhaps it had come down farther away.

文
月
華
的
中
國
日
記

The Scoutmaster of our high school ran with the boys to get the pilots and carry them to the nearest doctor but both were badly burned and did not survive. The planes were a mass of black twisted steel.

Clara and I said to each other, "Well, those planes probably turned them back from the city, anyway," but when we got up to the verandah we saw huge columns of smoke rising from the city. There are hillocks between our place and the shore, so we ran up to the attic but even there we could not make out what sections of the city were affected, so I suggested that we run over to the highest hilltop and take the spyglasses.

At first Clara thought she'd rather not know until she got home whether there would be any home to go to or not, but when the children and I decided to go she went also and it was a good thing for we could see that, while one of the fires was on a street above the Agency it was not spreading down towards the Agency....We all wondered where Jim was but I knew he had plenty of time to get to a dugout and was probably all right. By the time we had looked our fill it was two p.m. so we settled down to the afternoon's school work and I am glad to say the children were able to do so without much effort.

Flames approach the Canadian West China Mission's Business Agency run by Gordon and Clara Jones, after the Japanese bombing, 4 May 1939.

None of them gets excited but one can see that Philip is deeply moved by fear. He remains quiet but he sticks to me like glue...is unable to eat much and looks rather feverish after a raid or even an alarm.

文
月
華
的
中
國
日
記

Greatly to our relief Jim arrived home about four....He wore a relief badge on his arm, which had enabled him to get through the streets to the hospital to see if they needed any help. The First Aid dressers had arrived and were attending to the wounded, about one hundred of whom were laid on the paved courtyard of the hospital. He didn't go into much detail about them but said it was very pitiful. One little ragged dirty girl about Shirley's age especially attracted his attention and he held her hand and rubbed her hair for a few moments while her pathetic eyes looked up at him as she lay dying from the shrapnel in her back....

We thought Wednesday, May 3, was bad enough, but Thursday was a lot worse. All day alarms kept sounding and planes wheeling overhead. The children insisted on going to the basement at each alarm but sometimes we sat on the verandah or lawn nearby, and in one spasm we had our daily reading—a loud class.

In the afternoon, when we have always felt the danger was over, an alarm came soon after five when Margaret Allen was just starting for home. She met Mrs. Campbell, a refugee from Ichang who is staying at their home, and the younger Allen girl who were coming over to call for Margaret, a short distance from our home, and the three of them ran panting to our compound, where we were already sitting in the coal room.

We waited a long time and then all was quiet so we came out and sat on the strip of garden lawn waiting for the all clear to go. Often it doesn't go at all, so at last Mrs. Campbell decided they had better leave or it would be dark before they got home. They had only got across the path between our house and a neighbouring farm house, two rice fields away, when the zoom of a squadron sent our children flying up from the lower garden where they had been playing and the Table Boy who is supposed to stay with us in the basement, came running up too, saying, "They're here! Get inside. Quick."

Gerald and Dick didn't come up with the others and for a moment I thought I ought to go and find them but the children said they had gone into the dugout in the lower garden where the neighbouring family goes. Dick's mother had been visiting them. Our servants prefer [our] dugout but, at present, I like the basement better....

No sooner were we seated on our little benches beside the furnace room, with a second exit at the other end, than we heard a rapid thud, thud, thud of bombs falling. The pursuit planes had been fooled or tired out and had gone down so that attack was a surprise one. It was all over in a few minutes—Jim says less than one—and when all was quiet we came out to see

文
月
華
的
中
國
日
記

great leaping flames coming up from the city. It was nearly dark—about 6:45 so the flames showed vividly, whereas at noon the day before only smoke had shown. We ran to the neighbouring hilltop again but in the darkness it was harder to make out which sections of the city were burning....

It was a strangely fascinating sight, and I recalled the fire ceremony on Monday night, and the one, which followed it here on Tuesday night when our 500 students lit torches from a central flame and marched around singing war songs on the football field below us.

Fire is such an amazingly beautiful thing when properly used, even beautiful when it is cruel, as on that awful night, but then its beauty is so sinister that it is just hard to believe that it is the planned result of man's greed and cruelty. How can those pilots remain sane when they fly off and see such glaring results of their work and know what unimaginable suffering they are causing to thousands of innocents?

I believe they found one plane brought down nearby and hanged the pilot to a tree, but first they ought to have taken him to walk through those tortured streets and made him listen and watched the wounded carried away. Then, if he had any humanity in him he should be willing to write a letter of protest to his people and his government.

Well, it was dreadful, and all of us were thinking of those we loved in that doomed city. It was just the time Jim would be coming home and I looked first to see if the wharf where he takes the ferry was going up in flames and was relieved to see it wasn't—or at least the spot where I thought it was, was dark. Gerald, George and Dick all felt sure their fathers' places were burning, but none of them got hysterical or lost control.

When we came home, I wondered if they would ever settle down to sleep that night, for I knew the fire would rage for hours. When we came in, the electric lights were off, which always makes a situation worse. We sat in the light of one candle in the living room while the cook was putting on the belated supper. I started to put on the gramophone, feeling it might be better than keeping on talking about the raid or sitting silent. Then I noticed someone was strumming on the piano and someone else singing a little so it occurred to me it would be better to make music rather than listen to it. I said, "Shall we sing, instead of having the gramophone on?" They all said "yes" and when I asked what we would sing Shirley said, "Hymns?"

I don't know whether it was just accidental or whether she realized they would be the most suitable, but all agreed, so we sang all the hymns we knew off by heart. It was easier than singing the joyous songs we learned last fall for our concert, but it was hard, too, in spots, for the hymns we have learned are ones of affirmation of the beauty and joy of life. I knew they would ask for "This Is My Father's World" for it is a favourite, and I wondered what was going through their little minds as we sang a third verse which is not in our hymnary but which I found in an American one. It goes:

> This is my Father's world,
> Oh let me ne'er forget,
> That though the wrong seems oft so strong,
> God is the Ruler yet.
> This is my Father's world,
> Why should my heart be sad?
> The Lord is King; let the heavens ring,
> God reigns: let earth be glad.

I was thankful the supper-bell rang before they had a chance to start the inevitable questions.

I wondered how we'd get through supper so I suggested we tell funny stories, not knowing whether it would fall flat or not. The Chinese boys took it up readily, and had a big fund of them and I was so interested in hearing them tell them freely in English that I managed to get through the meal. By this time they were all quietened down and I warned the older ones privately that they were not to speak of the fires again before the younger ones. Although it was very late, I helped the younger ones to have their baths, thinking it would soothe them, and they seemed to fall asleep the minute they touched the pillow.

I was dreading the long evening, for I knew Jim would be late coming home and, without light to read or write by, for our supply of candles and oil is limited and there is none for sale—I wondered how I should put in the time—no radio either, with the electricity off. There seemed nothing to do but sit on the upper verandah and watch the fires dying down, then flaring up worse than ever, in the city. Stephen wanted to stay out with me, so I let him, and the amah sat there too, and he chatted to her.

The electric lights did come on, but the neighbours were so nervous of a night raid that they asked us to keep them off, and the radio was so indistinct we couldn't hear it. At nine o'clock I wrote a letter over to our other Mission compound, a half hour away, on the possibility that they had any news of the city, but the messenger had hardly gone when I heard the dogs barking and then the gateman answering a shout at the gate and I tore down to see if it was Jim. It was, and I'm sure he thought I'd been a "weak

文
月
華
的
中
國
日
記

sister" all through for I almost broke down when I threw my arms around his neck. The relief to know that, for me, Chungking was not destroyed!

I soon heard a vivid account of it. Jim had been doing relief work all day for sufferers from the day before. As they were coming back from distributing the last box of food they noticed a fire flaring up again in one of the buildings that had been smouldering since the day before. They (the New Life Movement Workers) stopped to throw on some water and to organize a bucket brigade. Suddenly they heard a zoom and saw the squadron of 36 enemy planes flying overhead and then came the whistle of bombs through the air, dozens of them in quick succession, and within a few minutes the sky was red with reflection from fire all round, but none in the particular quarter in which Jim happened to be.

He made a tour of the various places belonging to the Mission and found that none were affected, but was not allowed to go into any of the dangerous areas. Clara and Gordon were not at home, as they had not returned from the weekly Missionary Prayer Meeting, which is in the American Mission property. Deciding there was nothing he could do, Jim went down to the riverside to come home but there was such a terrific crowd trying to get into the boats that he felt he might as well go back to the Agency and have supper and see if Clara and Gordon were back, as he had heard fires were raging in the neighbourhood of the American Mission.

Just as he was turning in to leave the foreshore a foreign woman grabbed his arm and said, "Don't leave me!" It was the wife of one of the American missionaries who had been bombed out of several places and she was just about hysterical. She and another foreign girl who lives on this side of the river...had been caught in the fire area at the American Mission but had escaped by some roundabout route. The boats were so overcrowded Jim did not want to go in them, but these people insisted on going and on taking him with them. They got out of one overloaded boat into another but it quickly filled up, and they came over with 40 in a boat that is supposed to hold sixteen.

He has promised me since that he won't do that again. I'd rather worry for several more hours than to have him leave a burning city and get swamped in an overloaded boat. He said the crowd were just frenzied and there was no way of controlling them.

After Jim had eaten a belated supper—we went to bed. At two-thirty we were wakened by the wail of the siren and little John Honnor saying, "Damn those Japs!" We wouldn't have wakened the children, but Shirley

154

was already at the door of our porch and John was awake so we thought perhaps we'd better get them all up.

I hated to disturb Philip but I wrapped him up and laid him in my lounge chair on the verandah and we all sat there and waited. Jim sat by Phil and said his arm was trembling, but he didn't say a word. We sat there for the best part of an hour and then went back to bed, though the all clear had not gone.

Whether that alarm had any basis or whether the signallers just got jittery we don't know, but it was a great mistake in many ways. Crowds tore out of the East Water Gate into the dugout in the rocky cliff there, and twenty, mostly children, were trampled to death....

Chungking, like Canton, is a much-overcrowded city. There are no open spaces for bombs to fall in by mistake or for the crowds to surge through in making their escape. The bombs blew up the water mains so the nice new water system of recent years was of very little avail....(circular letter, early May 1939)

18

Wedding Anniversary

When the bombings of May 1939 spread to Chengtu, the Mission decided to evacuate the Canadian School, where Norman boarded, to Mount Omei. Jim accompanied Mary and the children (including the three Chinese boys) up to their Omei bungalow and then returned to his war-relief work with the New Life Movement. John Honnor, the young English boy who had been a day pupil at Mary's International School, went with the Endicotts, along with his mother, Olive.

The evening of her fourteenth wedding anniversary Mary wrote a "stream-of-consciousness" letter to her husband:

Jim, my dear Love,

There are pink clouds over Mt. Omei, and across the years I see you smiling on the terrace as I raced down the lawn to you. This is a rotten kind of anniversary, in absentia, and yet I've had a good time all day remembering the little details of fourteen years ago....

I remember how tired Mother looked when she came to kiss me, sitting all in my veil and surprisingly calm and detached, and said she hadn't had time to wash her face, but she looked so happy and satisfied that I knew it didn't matter. I hope I can feel as pleased when I launch Shirley out. Actually, I suppose she'll be in Canada and I'll be in China, and I'll have to take it all out in letters.

Even so, with you beside me, growing old happily with me, I'll be able to be happy. How difficult it must be for those wives whose husbands look back yearningly towards youth and turn back, as Faust did, to recapture what is out of reach for her who has shared with him the first raptures and the heat of life's long day. That got a bit mixed in the writing but you know what I mean. There again, I imagine that the Faust motif is one of the surest signs of egocentricity—a demand that life give to one an end, which is unreal because it is turned inward.

This morning when I opened my poetry book I turned to "Tam in the Kirk." Do you remember my quoting it to you and how my paraphrase of it had been running through my head after your first visit to Chatham—or was it after Washington? [How he cannot sing the psalms "for a voice within is crying the name of his beloved?"] That's the way it is with me still, even as it was when I thought you would be a dream, to be remembered but never realized. And here all these fourteen years I've had you beside me, still I feel only half alive, in some ways, when you are not here.

In some ways only, for it is true that at times, when I am with you, I do not seem to be myself at all. I am someone suppressed, incapable of doing anything right and fearful of creating a situation when you will be obviously either disgusted or impatient with me. Sometimes I see quickly that I had misinterpreted something and then I just feel a fool.

Sometimes I know deeply that I am right but I have to be prodded hard by duty or necessity, or fear, to make myself preserve my self-respect and insist on carrying something through. I am not sure but I think that more and more I have learned to stifle my tastes and opinions and even my convictions of right in order not to prolong that tone and look, which I dread.

I'm putting this down to try to clarify it in my own mind as well as yours, for I'm not sure about it. Sometimes I know I have been a fool and I think you have helped me to slough off a lot of foolish fears and fussy ways, which I recall vividly in Mother and Jane. Actually, when you are not here I do control myself better with the servants.

When you are around I think I vent some of my irritability against you on them because I often feel that you could avoid difficult situations if you only would explain things for me when I ask and what I ask. This is a form of dependence, of course—and if I could have seen what it would mean I'd have studied Chinese someway, babies or not babies—but I confess it is a tremendous relief to me when I can ask Stephen to interpret for me and I know he will do it...and get across what I have in mind rather than what he thinks, and that he will never show to the servants that he doesn't agree with me. Then I can give my whole mind to listening to what the servants say and thinking what is the best thing to do.

Often they do know best what to do but I see it more clearly if they tell me rather than if someone scolds me for not seeing it. Even the Chinese boys are a comfort, but they are more mechanical as they don't always grasp the exact meaning, or the inner significance of what I want to get across.

Shortly after you went away, while I was still under a sort of cloud, feeling that life with me had lost its flavour for you in some indefinable way, it came to me that as a general formula it might be sound if we decided that

文
月
華
的
中
國
日
記

on small issues the person making a request should be given careful consideration as he has probably thought it out more than the other person who has a snap reaction to it which may be dependent on his digestion or any other physical or irrelevant factor.

In big questions these difficulties do not tend to arise. Actually, in big questions I think you tend to have the clearer and farther-sighted vision, or at least have it more quickly. My inclination to timidity slows up my reactions towards anything adventurous, but I have learned that it is usually safe to trust to your judgment, at least enough to experiment. In small practical details you tend to be so impatient of precision and precaution that you overlook many things that would ultimately meet with your approval if someone else carried them through without bothering you about it. Am I right?

I am not well developed in practical efficiency but I think I have a right instinct that it pays to observe the ways of others who are more efficient and to incorporate what you find useful. It actually makes me feel fussier about things when you want to pass over some suggestion of mine with a *carte blanche* dismissal. To people who are not practically-minded, like ourselves, joint efforts to experiment or to discuss practical ways and means ought to be of great benefit, instead of one person doing what occurs to him without consulting the other, or the other person feeling that she may make a mistake and land in hot water because she dare not consult her partner.

Do you see what is in my mind, dear? Do you ever realize that if you want to do some little thing you just go ahead and do it, and I can like it or not, but, because of the peculiar circumstances of this country and language, I do have to consult you about many little things and also because of my temperament I like it better to consult you and am not contented in the transaction if it does not at least meet with your approval, much less your cooperation?

This is particularly true where the spending of money is concerned. I find that I react more negatively to the spending of money than I used to do because I have the opportunity to spend so little on my own initiative and because I feel that you don't feel urged to consult me about most of your spending, with the result that I have no part in it. It isn't that you ever refuse me money—you hand it out lavishly, but it is the lack of thought in it, almost the feeling that I am spending your money and seldom that we are spending our money that has had an effect upon me....

Olive is the only person to whom I've talked today about it being our anniversary. This morning while dressing we exchanged reminiscences of

文
月
華
的
中
國
日
記

our weddings after the manner of new acquaintances in that field. Otherwise it has given me a secret pleasure to think that all day no one knew the
fun I was having in recalling that occasion. I was tempted to mention it this
afternoon when I [went to visit] Constance [Walmsley] for tea and found
several there, including Katharine [Willmott]....But I didn't want their
banal comments. They would not feed my secret joy nor assuage the accom-
panying feeling of loneliness. Yesterday, after writing to the family, the visu-
alization of what life would be like without you, and the vividness of the
risks you are now under—some of them voluntarily, or rather unnecessarily,
I fear—made me feel quite low.

Olive and I talked till quite late after we were in our beds about what we
would do if we were to get word any day that our husbands were gone. She
would pack up the next day and beat it for England. At first I felt I'd do the
same, but the difficulties of the trip appal me, and I might cling to the
known for a while until I had adjusted myself, or perhaps till the immediate
dangers of this country were over. I wondered if I wouldn't rather risk staying with the group here till the end of the war than travelling out alone in
the middle of it.

However, as I talked it over I remembered that probably some man
would be detailed to escort us out by truck and that we could, if necessary,
stay on the Chungking hills and just pick up the two packed trunks and a
few things and abandon the house as it is. After that I felt better, but I had
a lump of lead in my stomach even before I went to sleep instead of getting
it when waking up during the night.

Would you like to tell me what seems to you would be the wisest thing
for us to do under such circumstances? This is one of the big questions,
which I cannot contemplate without wanting to know what you would
think, though it's a queer sort of situation for you to be in.

This is a strange letter—not particularly what I planned to write, and all
day I've been promising myself an evening of quiet leisure with you. Yet I
don't think I need to apologize for opening my heart to you in more ways
than one. If I didn't love you tremendously and have lots of faith in your
flexibility I wouldn't be bothered to do it, even if I dared, and I need both
the above things to make me dare.

Darling, can you and will you analyse wherein I fail you? I know that I
do, and I still can hardly believe that you mean the sweet tender things you
write to me, even after all these years. I know I must not be concerned about
my lacks for my own sake, that is pride and vanity and other disagreeable

文
月
華
的
中
國
日
記

Mary with Shirley, May 1939. Mary is showing the strain of living across the river from Chungking, wartime capital of China. Shirley, now nine years old, is aware of her mother's terror, but also senses Mary's deep, quiet, rocklike strength.

things—but for your sake I'd like to see more clearly wherein I do fail you, so long as it is in places that I can do something about. No use in saying you don't like shuffling, if shuffle I must.

Hark! I hear a rat. I must stop and go to bed before I knock the lamp off this small table. It is 10:45 anyway, and Olive has been in bed for ages....

When? When shall it be, darling, that I shall lie within your arms again or secretly watch you as the day goes by, the turn of head, the expressive hands, the smile that lights your face, even the laugh that sometimes sounds a bit boastful or sneering.

Yours forever,

Mary (from Omei, at sunset, 19 June 1939)

19

Wartime Diary: 1939-41

It was assumed that the mountain paradise of Omei was far enough in the interior to be safe from air raids. John Honnor's father flew a small plane and promised that when he came up that way he would swoop low to signal "Hello." One day an aircraft came flying in and everyone rushed to get sheets to wave at the pilot, who may or may not have tipped his wings before heading away. The children were still standing on the lawn, sheets in hand, when suddenly thirty-six enemy planes came flying in formation overhead and several bombs exploded on the plain below. "Then we looked at the horizon," wrote Mary, "and saw columns of smoke rising from Kiating (Ja-ding) 30 miles away. The older children, especially those like Norman, who hadn't been in any raids... got a great kick out of this, but the rest of us felt somewhat shaken to find the security of our mountain fastness had been threatened."

[I, Shirley, think "somewhat shaken" is an understatement, to say the least. My memory is of a mother shouting in alarm: "Everyone under the dining room table!" I recall one of the older boys joking: "Maybe we'll be tried as spies for signalling an enemy plane." As I crouched under the table, I got no comfort from treating the event as an adventure. The sudden switch from shaking sheets at a friendly plane to witnessing an air raid was truly unnerving. SJE]

Jim immediately flew from Chungking to help organize relief work in the stricken city of Kiating. He sent word to Mary that when he had things organized the family was to go home with him by junk as he would not be able to come up again to escort them home.

She must have quailed at the prospect, for the intention had been to stay at Omei until the September moon was over and the work on the air raid shelter completed. When the family arrived back in Duckling Pond, the men were still working by hand from both ends of the tunnel in the hillside. The workers could shout to each other, but the opening was so small Mary believed everyone would have been flattened by concussion had a bomb fallen in the Duckling Pond compound.

文
月
華
的
中
國
日
記

To make things worse, nine-year-old Shirley contracted a dangerous form of dysentery on the trip home; her parents feared they might lose her. Mary never forgot the first moonlit trek to the unfinished air raid shelter that September, but it would be nine years before she wrote about the depth of fear evoked by this and the other Chungking air raids:

On the first moonlight raid Jim had to remain in the city. Our Chinese cook carried her to the dugout because she had a high temperature. As she lay there holding my hand, she said, "I feel so queer, Mum" and I reached for the pitcher of water I had had the sense to take down with us. The noise of the air raid reverberated through our tunnel as if the bombs were falling close by. I fanned her vigorously because my own legs were shaking and I felt a bit queer....

Before every raid in Chungking...I used to pray: "If only I could do something, anything, to stop it." As I gathered rugs and flashlights and marched the children to the dugout in orderly fashion my heart was beating fast to the tune of: "Don't let it happen to us, God. Oh, don't let the bombs drop in the section of the city where Jim is!"

I couldn't help it. I had been brought up on Psalm 91:

He shall deliver thee...

He shall cover thee with...his wings...

Thou shalt not be afraid for the terror by night,

nor for the arrow that flieth by day...

A thousand shall fall at thy side...

but it shall not come nigh thee.

Of course, I had long learned to spiritualise these truths but the early literal impressions remained and floated to the surface in the time of crisis. But my mind could not rest there; it always leaped on to the words of Jesus: "He maketh his rain to fall on the just and the unjust."...

As we would walk down the hilly garden path, and the drone of Chinese planes going out to meet the enemy faded into that awful lull before the boom of the invading squadron, my mind would turn to the prayer of Jesus in the garden: "If it be Thy will, take this cup from me."

It is natural for every one of us, even the greatest, to pray like this, but we know that the cup was not taken from Jesus, and that goodness will not save us from physical destruction. Inside the dug-out I would encourage the children in singing or telling jokes and in my heart I would be praying, "If it is to come, give me the courage to face it, and the wisdom to know what to do for them."

That kept me steady in the hundreds of raids that followed. (from "One Mother Speaks Out," draft of unpublished article on war, 1948)

Mary's 1939 Christmas letter to family and friends stressed how safe the dugout was now that both entrances were finished, how everyone had learned to sleep through the moonlight raids, the encouraging war news:

I wonder if your papers have space for even the outstanding news from China now; the great victory at Changsha with the resultant rise in Chinese morale; the change in trying to defend the country under modern methods of warfare (big guns and mechanized units)...to guerilla warfare on all fronts. The broad new highways are being ploughed into fields, tunnels and bridges blown up. China's modern transportation is set back to where she was a few years ago. What a waste, but the enemy must be held up by any means at hand....

The future is uncertain but there is a peculiar thrill to being among people with their back to the wall and knowing that the international friendship which we are here to express means more than ever in this dark hour when international strife is ever increasing. (circular letter, 25 November 1939)

文月華

Early in 1940, the Mission offered Jim a position in the university English department to replace someone going on furlough. He was becoming disenchanted with the New Life Movement and decided to accept the position.

At the end of April, in the midst of complicated packing, the Endicotts received a visit from Agnes Smedley, an American who had lived in China for years, worked with the Chinese communists and was presently with the Chinese Red Cross. Mary described Smedley as being all worked up "that sometimes a battle is lost through lack of food and warm garments while the old militarists live in luxury. It is terrible to think of, and one wonders if there will not be a rising of the people, some day" (to family, 29 April 1940).

[I remember sitting in the living room at Duckling Pond, utterly fascinated, watching Agnes Smedley talking so intensely—wearing khaki pants and jacket. I also recall the awe I felt—at a gala Christmas party in a grand new hotel-club for foreigners—when Madame Chiang, dressed like a queen, shook hands with me. I

文
月
華
的
中
國
日
記

had no way of knowing then that Smedley foreshadowed the future—both for China and my parents—and the "queen" would be swept aside. SJE]

文月華

The Endicotts were due for furlough in July 1941. The family returned briefly to Chungking where they endured severe air attacks before boarding a plane that took them through the night sky to Hong Kong. While they were waiting for a ship, Norman came down with measles. Jim stayed behind with him while Mary and the other three children found passage on a small Norwegian freighter bound for Los Angeles. After a week at sea, she wrote an unidentified friend:

> The captain says he doesn't think the ship would be attacked even if an enemy sighted her, because ships are too valuable now. He says we would just be taken off and we all have jokes about what we would do on a Japanese island, or even on a desert island, or what work we would be set to do in Germany. One of our passengers told of a party of English who were kept on a German raider for nine months, with the men kept below decks except for 10 minutes a day, while the women and children slept on the decks...until they were boarded by the British and transferred. We are just hoping not to have an adventure of that kind. The sea is all right when you are comfortable but.... (3 August 1941)

文月華

The Austins welcomed Stephen, Shirley, Philip and Mary at the train station in Windsor on August 22. Jim and Norman arrived two weeks later, three months before the Japanese surprise attack on Pearl Harbour, December 7, 1941.

Missionaries were not allowed to return to China until 1944. Jim spent his extended furlough speaking and preaching about his wartime experiences, exhorting the Canadian public to support the gallant struggle of the Chinese people to defeat the Japanese.

As for Mary, a surprising new chapter was about to begin.

Part 4

文月華的中國日記

20

The Little Brown Bird Takes Flight

When Mary returned to Canada in 1941, she did not seem aware of how much she had grown during her fifteen years in China. Her first public speech as a returned missionary, for example, began with these words: "I sometimes tell my friends that my husband is the one who does the noble deeds and has exciting adventures, and I am the little brown bird who sits at home on the nest." During the next five years "the little brown bird" not only flew into the wind but gradually came to appreciate her own strengths and dare to name them.

She returned to the Women's Missionary Society (WMS), where she had done volunteer work before she met Jim, writing for WMS publications intended for teenagers, especially the popular church-affiliated Canadian Girls in Training (CGIT). She began with stories based on her China experience: "An International Family" described her one-room schoolhouse in Chungking and the coming of the three Chinese boys; "Five Children In China," about a Chinese Christian who adopted five orphans, made both the horrors of the war and the humanitarian work of church people come alive for younger girls and boys. Madame Chiang and her "warphans" came to life in five articles. One ran under the headline "Today's Most Famous Woman." Mary believed in taking a stand for truth as you understood it at the time and being willing to change when new truths became available. Thus, when her understanding about the Nationalist Party changed, she did not expend any energy whipping herself for her 1941-42 commendations of Madame Chiang.

Later she would branch out into other topics. Her 1945 sixty-page booklet, *Spotlight on Africa*, geared for an adolescent audience, provided her "with the greatest thrill of creativeness yet." After that, came a booklet about labour unions and why they had to resort to strikes to obtain their basic needs—also designed for church youth. This required research into previously unknown areas.

文月華

文
月
華
的
中
國
日
記

After her beloved nephew, Austin Wright, was killed on a bombing mission in Europe, Mary delivered an impassioned plea for peace during a WMS meeting in the spring of 1944:

> It remains for the living to see that their sacrifice and our grief are not in vain. To do that the years of peace will need as courageous and continuing action as the years of war, and none of us is too humble or too lacking in talent, to contribute to that end.
>
> Just as the men cannot fly without the service of the humblest member of the ground crew and those who feed and shelter them all, so the big things of peace cannot come to pass without the efforts of every one of us who feels herself part of the great community of human beings all over the world—groping for a better world and willing to face anything, even death, to forward its coming.

She described how it felt to speak out like this to her sister Jane, Austin's mother:

> I spoke twice last Friday at the WMS Board—once the speech I had prepared and another spontaneously, and the women were thrilled. They said they were simply brilliant speeches, and when I think how ill-prepared I am to make a speech and how much I dread it and shrink from doing it whenever I can, I realize how much could be done by people who are not so handicapped.
>
> The seriousness of the challenge does give me strength, and I have very little actual difficulty in doing it, but it takes a lot out of me, both before and afterwards. However, when I think of how Austin performed his duty in spite of shrinking ahead of time, and the price he paid for it, I feel that if the way opens up before me to do this difficult business, I must do it. (7 June 1944)

文月華

Mary had been in favour of "a sane socialism" for many years. In 1943 she joined her local branch of the Co-operative Commonwealth Federation (CCF):

> I had been to only a few club meetings in the riding when they asked me to stand for Board of Education. I tried to convince my nominators they were under the illusion I was a counterpart of Jim, but they insisted I was the right person for the job....The local teachers' organizations also put

pressure on me and these two groups did all the publicity and bore the expense of my campaign.

I was scared to death and hardly lifted a finger to get elected, almost hoping I wouldn't. But I did. I lost six pounds the first month or two, but found I got less and less scared as the Board meetings came along. I discovered I could express myself on issues and stand alone, if necessary, and hold my own in debate....

Mary and Jim at the Sharman study seminar at Camp Minnesing, Algonquin Park, 1943. Photo: Alex Grant.

The first weeks were particularly full of tension and the meetings lasted until midnight. Among people with whom I had no common bond I had to stand out on a minority vote on a highly controversial question much misunderstood by the public. [The principal of Runnymede Collegiate had been dismissed. Many members of the community wanted him reinstated, but the teachers were opposed.] I read all the evidence carefully and the seriousness of the situation gave me courage but it was heavy going to have to make my first speech on that subject and before a throng of assembled citizens. I found I could do it and that certain people were very grateful for my stand.

文
月
華
的
中
國
日
記

> I managed to speak frankly without incurring any personal antagonism from Mr. Clarke or his supporters. I tried hard for that end, and felt that I really attained it, and it has stood the test of time.

The first time she actually spoke on the controversy was on February 14 when the Clarke issue was discussed in front of a delegation of ratepayers who, according to the minutes, created "considerable disturbance" throughout. The woman who had once thought she could not hold a job because of her stuttering, was heckled the first time she spoke at a Board meeting.

> A more congenial but prolonged fight came in the estimates for Teachers' salaries, much in need of adjustment. I was the only trustee who approached the problem by asking: "Are their requests fair? If so, can we grant them? If not, let us be frank with them and say why not." The others bargained as they do with Labour and my sympathies with the latter increased. The teachers and I persisted and eventually, after months of meetings, we have obtained a large percentage of their requests.
>
> Two of them met me on the street and said, "If it weren't so public we'd like to throw our arms around you." I said, "Go ahead," and they did. (They were women.) In general, the teachers regard me as their special representative and consult me on many things and I enjoy that relationship very much....
>
> Right from the beginning I determined to lay a friendly basis with my colleagues and I have succeeded in doing so. Within three months they became most cordial to me....I have taken special pains to establish a friendly relation [with] one of the rudest and most unreasonable men I've ever met, albeit he has some good qualities. A little subtle flattery and judicious "kidding" go further with him than stubborn resistance and he has actually moved certain things in the end which I have been advocating for weeks but which he had opposed....

By her second term, 1945, Mary was a seasoned veteran:

> Sometimes when I'm battling on the Board of Education, I remind myself of Mother. I feel myself saying things and doing things like her, and think how proud she would be of me if she could know how I have ventured forth....
>
> Last night I fought a hard battle against the chairman. The Elementary School teachers are well pleased with the victory I won for them a week ago when I got their adjustments that they've been asking for, and on the basis

父
月
華
的
中
國
日
記

they asked—that is, that each should be on the schedule, something the Board has never been willing to grant before. They don't mind being asked for a raise and giving it, makes them feel generous, though, of course, they bargain it down as to size, but they resent the teachers suggesting what they should do or what they should not have done in the past....

Well, the High School teachers weren't at all pleased that their maxima were just shoved up $200 for each group instead of re-arranging the ratio between the groups so that there is only a gap of $100 between Heads and Specialists and between Specialists and non-specialists....Last night they came back to ask *why*. Before they came in the chairman tried to bind us to no discussion in the presence of the teachers but I said I didn't agree: that if there were questions to be asked or points to be cleared up that was the time to do it. The chairman kept trying to shut me up but I hung on like a bull-dog and urged that they be asked to re-state their case. At last the others murmured agreement with me and he had to give in. As a result when the teachers went out, the Board was ready to re-consider these gaps—for the first time seriously....

[One] night I had a terrific session on the Board—fighting for the married women to have their salaries kept at the same level after they marry, but I couldn't make a dint in them! I felt like saying that they penalize women four or five hundred dollars a year just because she makes a social contract to live with one man. Most of the husbands in question are overseas, so it isn't the general question of taking women out of the home but the prejudice is related to that, of course.

I said they would wait till every country in the world and every other municipality had recognized the principle of paying for value received and not looking for a cheap labour market. Someone mentioned Germany and I said, "Well, if you want to be like Germany, the thing to do is to send the women back to the kitchen and keep them there." The chairman looked at me with a bit of a twinkle and said, "There's other women, not mentioning names, that we'd like to send back to the kitchen," and we all laughed.

However, the High School teachers did win a victory that night, and while I didn't make the motion they knew who had laid the foundations and called me afterwards to say so. It was one a.m. before we got home on Monday....

The Board gave me a pleasant surprise last night by accepting my motion that a young Japanese-Canadian girl, who has been brought here from B.C. to get her senior matriculation, should be allowed to attend Vaughan Rd. without paying fees....She had been refused because she was not the daugh-

文
月
華
的
中
國
日
記

ter of a taxpayer....Knowing our Board I was doubtful if they would let her come in...they were in a good mood and when I made my speech with my motion they asked very few questions and passed it unanimously.

By 1945 Mary has gained self-confidence, but is lonely for Jim who returned to China the previous year (chap. 21). Photo: Vida Peene, Toronto.

Perhaps my efforts to get a Japanese-Canadian teacher on the staff a year ago did something to pave the way. I went after them hard at that time on the grounds that the educated and Christian Chinese had not gone after us when there was popular feeling against us because of the actions of our nationals, and that it was a pity Christians in this country hadn't done as much for the Japanese-Canadians now. They said then that after the war, when criticism had died down, they would be glad to have such a person. Perhaps some of them remembered that last night and didn't dare raise a prejudice.

I've learned one thing—to speak up immediately with a definite motion the minute a question is raised rather than give somebody a chance to get started on the opposite side of the question and so influence the neutrals first. (excerpts from circular letter, 22 April 1944, and five letters to various friends and family members, winter/spring 1945)

文月華

Early in 1945 Mary joined a group of citizens concerned about the plan of George Drew's Conservative government to introduce compulsory religious—Christian—training in the high schools of Ontario. She had a long telephone conversation with Mr. George Evans, principal of Vaughan Road Collegiate.

文
月
華
的
中
國
日
記

> At first he was quite hostile, and on the defensive, but as we went on, frank but friendly, his tone changed.
>
> He said he thought the Jews were intolerant, that they ought to want to hear the Christian position just as he would like to hear theirs and was indignant that churches invited rabbis to preach. He said people were there to hear about Christianity. I reminded him that members were invited to the Temple and asked mildly if he didn't think that attitude was somewhat intolerant. He said, well, maybe it was.
>
> I said if he really wanted that he could go to their church just as they go to ours but did that make it right to have one side presented in a state institution. He said they were careful what they read so I reminded him that the day I happened to be at the Assembly last fall when the Rugby cup was presented, he had read the story of the Ascension. I asked if he thought that wouldn't be offensive to the Jews. I'm sure he really had never thought about it before. He said they didn't have to be present, that they could come into assembly or class after the devotions. I asked him if he thought any student wanted to be that conspicuous, wouldn't that just accentuate the most harmful aspect of the whole thing. He hadn't thought of that either but agreed.
>
> I suggested that it might be wise now, till the matter is carefully reviewed to stick to readings from the Old Testament, or those from the New Testament which were teachings of Jesus and not about him. We also discussed The Lord's Prayer every morning and whether it wouldn't be better to vary it with other prayers so that it didn't become a routine matter. There are several alternatives in the Departmental regulations and some are not bad. He agreed, and also they ought to be watched for things offensive to the Jews. (to Jim, 24 January 1945)

Later Mr. Evans invited a rabbi to speak to a Vaughan Road Collegiate assembly.

文月華

文
月
華
的
中
國
日
記

During most of her China years, Mary held the conventional negative views of the time about Communists. The Soviet Union had given up the ideals of the revolution and was a dictatorship. The Chinese Communists' trek across Szechwan in 1935 was a potential "invasion"—posing a threat to foreigners of another evacuation. In Mary's case, the change in attitude for which the Endicotts became famous took place in phases. By the time they returned to Canada in 1941, they understood that the trek of 30,000 Communists to North China was not an invasion but a retreat—the historic Long March—to the caves of Yenan. One of Jim's responsibilities in the New Life Movement had been to act as "leaven" between the Communists and the Kuomingtang, for officially there was a united front between the two groups to resist the Japanese. Several of the young men Jim had taught in the prison for Communists had gone to join their comrades in Yenan and from them Jim received direct information on the Party's practices. For example, Communist officers were paid almost the same as the rank and file in contrast to the KMT practices. Agnes Smedley's 1940 visit to Duckling Pond provided more information from direct contact. A high regard for the egalitarian practices and simple lifestyle of Chinese Communist leaders existed in the Endicott home for almost two years before they returned to Canada.

The second phase was the adoption of a completely different view about the Soviet Union. This occurred after coming back to Canada and played a large part in her eventual decision to resign from the CCF. Like many people during World War II she believed the heroic resistance of the Russian people against the invasion by Nazi Germany was based on their appreciation of the benefits of Stalin's socialism, not just a sense of patriotism. By this time, there were favourable accounts of life in the Soviet Union written by Westerners, and Mary read any that came her way. For example, she was deeply moved by *Wild River*, a novel by Anna Louise Strong, an American who lived there for many years. The story told of the difficulties of cultivating selflessness and a collective spirit in the early years and the struggles to build a dam on a turbulent river. Finally the dam is built—only to be blown up as the Nazi invaders approached. The story ends with its hero, Stepan, saying: "No, we're not back where we started. We're two hundred million life-times ahead. We not only built the Red Dawn Farm and the Dnieper Dam. We built the people that burned the farm and blew up the dam in the war to save the world from the Nazis."

文
月
華
的
中
國
日
記

By the summer of 1944, as all the Allied armies inched towards victory over Nazi Germany, the fear among left-wing political circles was that after World War II, the "red bogey" would once more raise its head and direct its venom towards the war-devastated Soviet Union. For the sake of world peace after the war ended, friendship with Russia was essential. Mary confided her concerns to Freda Waldon:

> The burden on my soul this year is the need for deepening and making more widespread our understanding of the USSR, if we are to avert another disaster. A barrage is already being launched in subtle ways, as you are no doubt aware....Professor Somerville of Hunter's College recently emphasized that there is no hope of averting war a generation hence unless the present teenagers are soundly informed about the Soviet Union *within three years....*
>
> Therefore my Christmas gift this year is two booklets by Rose Maurer whom I heard at a luncheon at the Canadian-Soviet Friendship Council. These [describe] the changed lives of women and children,...the vitality of women [who are] integral parts of the motherland. (18 December 1944)

The third phase—working with Canadian Communists—came later, after Jim had returned to China.

21

Eden Rent Asunder

Toronto, early July, 1944

Jim was supposed to have returned to his mission post in the summer of 1942, but conditions became too dangerous because, without warning, on December 7, 1941, Japanese bombers attacked American naval ships at Pearl Harbour, Hawaii. World War II extended to the Pacific. He used his lengthy furlough to generate support for the War of Resistance in China against Japan. His mixed feelings about being a missionary became acute during this time. In 1943, he was offered a job as a full-time CCF secretary in Toronto, but the West China Mission wanted his return because of his language skills and wide connections with different groups of Chinese. His father, of course, wanted him to go back. Permission to return—alone— came early in 1944 but he had to wait three months for a passage from New York City to India, from where he flew over the hazardous "Himalayan hump" to Chengtu.

[*The memory of the night my father left has never faded. After supper, as we waited for the time to take him to the train station, he stretched out on the couch. My mother lay on top of him, clinging, as if by the sheer weight of her body she could prevent his departure. My anxiety mounted: this could be no ordinary wartime separation but, at age fourteen, I was totally ignorant of why this would be so. SJE]*

Misunderstandings began right away. The night Jim arrived in New York, Mary thought he would call at midnight to get the cheap rates so she went to a "stupid hen-party" and left at 11:30 to arrive home in good time. To her dismay his call had already come. "I might have known you would do things differently," she wrote, "and should not have gone out at all....Shirley enjoyed the conversation...but you know how disappointed I would be. I nearly called you back, but thought you would think that too silly." She hadn't realized the American discount rate began at 10:30 p.m. and, of course, it never occurred to Jim that she would not be home.

Most of Mary's letters during this separation were written from the Endicotts' three-storey home at 134 Glenholme Avenue, Toronto, bought early in 1944. A wartime censor read all letters to and from Jim. He spoke in vague terms and shrunk "from pouring out too much personal stuff." He claimed to have evidence "that some other people's personal and even intimate things get back to the embassies in Chungking to be bandied around as a joke."

Letters often took months to arrive at their destination. The intimate dialogues that had been characteristic of their 1928 separation were not possible.

Mary would experience the two-and-a-half-year separation as "a long black tunnel in which we call to meet each other but cannot meet, a tunnel in which hurt and bitter aches banged back and forth between the walls." From the beginning she felt she had been swept aside. A cable arrived announcing the Mission's agreement for Jim to go on a war assignment. He was to be a liaison officer with the American General Joseph Stilwell, an adviser to Chiang Kai-shek who wanted to provide the Chinese Communists with arms from the United States to assist the war against Japan.

Dear Jim,

When the cable came I couldn't help feeling dislodged again—not knowing where you would be, whereas it was so delightful to have you placed in a familiar setting once more. I called your father and he was quite disturbed about your dashing off to a war job. He hoped it wouldn't be long before you settled down to preaching the good old gospel. (from Toronto, 12 October 1944)

Within days Mary heard from Jim who said: "I miss you a lot but do wonder if this is really the place you should come to."

He was waiting in Chengtu to go on his war assignment and had been reading *Wild River*, Anna Louise Strong's idealized story about life in the Soviet Union:

"Wild River" is making quite an impression here. It is really stirring in its implications and may have something, more than a little, to do with my finally taking the step I am taking....

One sentence in Janet Kilborn's last letter to the Spooners has borne out Norman's analysis of you and me in China. She wrote, "The vigour that Mary has in Canada is amazing. It has taken ten years off her age." (from Chengtu, 10 October 1944)

文
月
華
的
中
國
日
記

Mary's mixed feelings continued. Watching the play *Rebecca*, she thought of how Max de Winter could have helped his young, naive second wife, "if he had been thinking imaginatively of what it all meant to her":

Then, oddly enough my mind jumped to my discouragement over the Chinese language and the times when I had asked you to give me a hand with it by taking a few minutes at it with me every day. Sometimes you said, yes, you would and then never implemented it....

I suppose there was something about all this that I was wrong about, but it was a no-man's land in our relationship, which I could never comprehend. It always left me frustrated...feeling myself pushed down a black hole each time.

All this swept over me yesterday and I found the tears raining down, not only—or not at all—for the young woman in the play. When she stood by the window on the precipice and Danvers tried to persuade her to escape from a hopeless situation, I saw instead a cliff in the Chungchow hills and a cistern at Omei, and relived the times when I felt I was not going to satisfy your needs or fill the place I had so joyously accepted.

Künkel has made me realize why people come to such a low point, and I suppose I must relate the whole problem of my frustration over the language to his explanation. If it were not for my egocentricity I would have been able to find a way out of it myself—for it is the only thing, so far as I am aware, which I have ever found difficulty in learning or remembering. (to Jim, 11 November 1944)

Suddenly in mid-October, at the insistence of Chiang Kai-shek, President Roosevelt recalled Joseph Stilwell home and Jim's plan to go north was cancelled. Within several weeks, he became deeply depressed. His November letters, all written before receiving Mary's "Rebecca Reflection," revealed feelings of desperation. In February of 1945 Jim reported that he was beginning to regain thirty-five lost pounds. Perhaps this dramatic weight loss was already in progress in November.

He had begun an agonizing struggle to bring himself to resign from the ministry; his theology no longer had any significance for his life.

Dear Mary,

I believe that Stepan in *Wild River* is really like me and that religion obviously has not done for me what social living did for him....

I have been reading over some of our old letters and am dismayed that the effect of them on me is a depressing one. When I relax and try to drift off to sleep, a whole series of pictures floats through my mind and they are all the mistakes, failures, and clumsy blunders. I listed them in my mind this morning [and later wrote them down]. You really ought to have married some kind of creative artist instead of an immature, half-shell-shocked, neurotic with a father [fixation] plus egocentric stardom complex...

P.S. Your poem "After Eight Years" gives me the lift I need. (from Chengtu, 5 November 1944)

A week later he referred to "a great cleavage in my soul" and said "the struggles in my head are eating up considerable energy." The final November letter was even more despairing:

I have a sense of inner defeat about so much in my own way of life. I have tried hard to see the best in the church and to hold to a belief in it, but the effort has cost me too much in rationalizing. Please don't discuss this with anyone. I really didn't get any education for life that was especially helpful from it. It didn't give me any real understanding of the forces of evil that made it necessary for me to go to war. It certainly didn't give me any courageous or realistic or even honest teaching on sex....(from Chengtu, 26 November 1944)

Jim's last two November letters came speedily, and Mary was able to speak directly to his concerns in her weekly letter:

Dearest Jim,

This morning early I dreamed you had come home, looking very sad and forlorn. And then, I couldn't find you around the house; I got tangled up with a lot of people, and couldn't find my clothes. After that our old servants, even the cook seemed to be part of the household....

Your letters of November 19th and 26th arrived just now....You and I seem to have been going through a slough of despondency in October and November. I trust my letters begin to get more cheerful after that for I see they aren't the right things for you. You need to be bucked up and when I wrote you with tears—as I did several times—it just washed you deeper into the mire of despair. I wish I could be with you in this trying time when you feel so frustrated and torn....

My moods of depression have left me. I hope yours have too. I miss you lots but the moods no longer get me dissolved....(from Toronto, 17 December 1944)

文
月
華
的
中
國
日
記

[My parents were simultaneously in gloomy moods that fall of 1944 but there the similarity ended. My mother wept as she relived past grievances—her letters were a form of journaling and appeared to have been cathartic. Furthermore, she was living in a lively, optimistic household: The Swanns (with whom the Endicotts lived those first months in China) and three of their four children were living at 134 Glenholme for a year. The "Swanncott" co-op, necessitated by the wartime housing shortage, created a buoyancy that was supportive of my mother in her loneliness.

But out in China, where Chiang Kai-shek's government was becoming increasingly corrupt and repressive, the "black dogs of depression" were sinking their teeth into my father's neck and injecting self-loathing into his mind, body and soul. All through the separation, apparently, my mother was unaware of the perilous condition of my father's emotional health. SJE]

文月華

As 1945 began the war in Europe was progressing favourably for the Allies. In the Pacific the struggle against the Japanese Empire still looked bleak. In Chengtu a long-time friend informed Mary that the morale in the missionary community was low, Jim was pessimistic and distinctly unsettled about what he was going to do.

From Toronto, Mary concentrated on writing newsy cheerful letters to her husband. How, looking at his smiling photographs, she seemed to hear him tell her that she must get over being frightened of speech-making and of the thunderous applause she got that night. And Shirley's first prom, tottering around the house in her first pair of high-heeled shoes.

Soon Mary received four disturbing letters from Jim. They emphasized his growing desire to leave the church and ideas of pursuing plans in China, which would prevent Mary from coming out. He reiterated that his outward appearance was a facade covering a sense of inner defeat going back to his childhood frustrations and fear of his father. He was having a difficult time and feeling the need for warm human fellowship.

Norman, now in the air force, happened to be home on leave when these letters arrived; he and Stephen (joined later by Phillip) gathered in her study to hear the news. Shirley was away for the weekend so she heard the news by herself later. Mary took several days to type her reply:

Dear Jim,

Your hints at a decision involving indefinite separation have lain like a lump within me for these three months but when I'd talked them out with the boys they became real; at the moment they completely darken my landscape.

The boys say they understand your point of view and Norman, at least, thinks it is the only one for you to take, much as he admits it is grim for *me*....He thinks it would be impossible for me to live in China in the new regime, that I would be too dependent while there to carve out a life for myself, that I am really a career woman, that I could not "take" the reduced comforts, that it would mean cutting myself off from the children permanently and that I would not be willing to accept that....

[When Shirl came home Sunday evening I read it all over again.] When I came to the part where you felt you would have to leave the church I saw her face quiver, and then a tear or two stole down her cheek. At the end she threw herself on the couch and sobbed, "I wish Daddy were here. I wish he had never gone back to China. I want him right now. Why, we'll hardly ever see him again."

Poor darling, I hated to see the burden coming down upon her, especially as it is all in the future and still speculation, but it released some tension in me, too, to find another whose reaction was like my own. The boys had been so stoical about it though I could tell Steve was feeling it inside and understood my reaction. He even went so far as to refute Norman's idea that I couldn't adapt myself to the new life you contemplated. He agreed that I'd never done anything like it, but he said, "Mom could change." I blessed him for it....

I hope you won't mind that I talked it all out with the children. I felt it had to be done sometime and probably Norman will not get home again for ages. I looked to him as a bulwark, and in many ways he was, but oh, how hard he seems, how uncaring, how critical of anything less than stoicism. Perhaps that hurt me a lot, too, and altogether the impact of [your news and his hard-heartedness] was devastating. (from Toronto, 10 February 1945)

Within a week Mary received a total of eight letters from Jim. She responded by defending the church:

It has come to me that I have more real understanding of the church than you have—a strange reversal of former roles. I have come to this through my participation in the inside workings of the WMS organization. I have enjoyed that more than any other contact with the church, and I have not been irritated by it for almost the first time. I think it is because it is not talk, but action. I see the work of the World Church constantly in review,

文
月
華
的
中
國
日
記

I share in the planning for it, I am free to criticize that planning as vigor-ously as I like—indeed, my criticisms are welcomed even when they stir up discussion.

There is little to do with theology and a great deal to do with people, cooperation with people, creative activities among them, help for them in their difficulties. I find it inspiring. I don't feel hampered by it in expressing what is vital....I have said and written what I believed. On every occasion where there is any point to it, I have presented the Social Gospel viewpoint. I find it comes into all sorts of places, into prayers, into criticisms of reports and policies, into every page of the Monthly, which I write, and into most of the letters. I'm sure that some of my hearers and readers have been criti-cal but none of them have made me feel that I didn't have just as good a right to express those views as they do to express theirs.

Moreover, a large number come to me frequently, or mention it in writing, how very grateful they are to me for bringing into the open thoughts which are in their minds. Many middle class church people think and say what they do because a more enlightened point of view not been presented to them in a way to catch their attention. Ranting repulses them; they listen when the way is prepared and the case is stated. (from Toronto, 16 February 1945)

文月華

While Mary was writing her defence of the church, Jim's thoughts were going in the opposite direction. He awoke early one February morning, after many sleepless nights, and typed out his resignation from the min-istry of the United Church. He sent it to Mary asking her to hold it until the annual meeting of Toronto Conference, the body that had ordained him in 1925, and began to gain back the thirty-five pounds he had lost.

Soon, however, deeper wounds surfaced to torment him:

Dear Mary,

Your cable ["February 19th forever"] came on Sat. 17. Thank you for sending it....

I brought over the trunk [of letters] from Spooners' attic after getting your cable and that night explored it until 1:00 a.m....One of the first things I came across was the broadcast to America I gave from Chungking in 1939. It gives me a dismal feeling, all those eulogies of the leaders. How blind I was to the implications of the killings of 1927. It seems to me that all my life I have been trying to hold on to something emotionally...that down deep in

文
月
華
的
中
國
日
記

my mind I knew was indefensible from the point of view of clear analysis and reason.

Well, the 19th really brought forth a sense of failure in me. I was really a coward at that time. And the "chattering" has gone on my mind for years. Without ever saying anything to you at all, I ought to have gone to Belleville and cleared the situation. Instead of that, if I couldn't have the first best, I was going to take the second best. It is that fundamental weakness of character that up to now I have not done much about that gives rise to so much evasion and irresponsibility in me. The plain truth is I don't like myself.

I always reacted emotionally to your questioning, as if it might become a personal insult, do you remember? I was afraid that I might have to admit what I didn't want to admit became of emotional things having to do with my father, and probably the social security of the church. Do you remember how once I bought a lottery ticket as a gesture of a desire to be "free." That was a hell of a cowardly way to be "free"....(Chengtu, 19 February 1945)

Mary received this letter along with two others describing the situation in the mission in graphically negative terms. Although overwhelmed with the "disturbing nature" of all three letters, she sat down to type a reply that same day—March 19, 1945. Her letter revealed conflicting feelings: an unwillingness to believe Jim might be in the clutches of a serious depression, and a fear that it might be so.

She began by saying that although Jim's ideas were no longer new "they burst like fresh bombs every time you state them. You shoot them off with such vehemence and bitterness that they explode afresh." She reminded him of Fritz Künkel's ideas and that "the effect on your life of the conditions you now face depends to a considerable degree what you do about them....[Perhaps you] are seeking to escape from something for which you ought to be living to change." From there she went on to recall his long-term tendency to exaggerate and his love of the dramatic, relating it in part to his difficulties with his father as a child. "If I did not recognize this love of the dramatic in you I would be more alarmed than I am at the note of terrific implications in your letters this year. The trouble is, I can never be sure that it is just your exaggerating complex."

Only then did she address the issue of his despair:

Darling, I don't want all this analysing to increase your "dislike of yourself."...Just remember, for antidote, that for twenty years I have regarded

文
月
華
的
中
國
日
記

you as very little lower than the angels, and much preferable to anything I have heard about them....

When people in Canada, or in China, are drawn to you strongly on meeting or hearing you, it is not alone by what you say but by the real You they sense behind the words. In fact, some of them love you in spite of words which they do not understand you saying....I can just imagine how much your mother must have loved that real you when you were growing up. (Toronto, 19 March 1945)

Jim would not receive this mixed message of admonition and comfort for months. His emotional state worsened even as he was doing what he could to assist the growing resistance to the Nationalist Government. He had trouble sleeping in spite of having talked long and intimately with his friend Fritz Kobler, a psychoanalyst. His letters now made Mary feel "like the kind of nightmare where you hold out your arms to a person and they keep fading farther and farther away."

During that winter of 1944-45, Jim made frequent references to his friendship with Hilde Kiang. Reading between the lines, Mary painfully guessed he was having an affair; she willed herself to feel glad he was finding comfort in his distress. As part of this process, she wrote a poem pledging that when he returned she would not ask "what joy gave you blue skies when clouds hung low." (See Appendix A.)

22

Deciding to Work with Communists

Although Mary-as-wife felt trapped in a long tunnel that winter of 1945, Mary-the-rebel was expanding her horizons. When her son Norman joined the Communist, or Labour Progressive Party in 1943, she was disturbed. But she read the Party pamphlets he sent her with care and interest. Wanting to be even more informed, she attended LPP events and met a number of its leaders. She wrote her long-time friend, Earl Willmott, that a whole new world opened up as she got to know their stories:

> [I spent an evening] at the home of Annie Buller, one of the pioneer communists in Canada...It was fascinating. I just wish I could have written it all down, especially her experiences in prison in the 1930s. What struck me most forcibly was that we must be near the same age, but when she was in the earliest labour movements in Canada, as a buyer for the garment industry, I was a young college graduate with a smattering of culture and no purpose beyond a mild interest in the religious approach to a better life for man. (22 May 1945)

She was especially impressed with the LPP national leader, Tim Buck. After hearing him speak several times, she seriously contemplated resigning from the CCF to co-operate publicly with Communists. She felt a need to confide these thoughts to her father:

> I'm not declaring myself a Communist, because I don't know enough about it. There may be things about it to which I could not commit myself. All I know now is that I am willing to work with Communists for the things for which they are working....
>
> The question of my influence in the church will concern you most deeply. I have come to have quite a place of my own in the Women's Missionary Society and many are grateful for the push, which I give there to

文
月
華
的
中
國
日
記

progressive thought. Whether I should, by being a labour sympathizer only, keep on with the role I have had in the church until they shun me is a question. You see it isn't just a matter of political differences. I have very grave disagreements with the church in theological matters. I am convinced the church is holding back the spread of the Kingdom of God because she…keeps on clothing her appeal for it in Paul's thoughts.

I am for the Kingdom of God—now and always. I see it as a simple, profound but demanding way of life….I see where I shall have to be explaining it on all sides from now on…since I shall be accused of deserting religion. But that is what I see happening in the life of Jesus—a constant effort to clarify, to re-interpret and put richer content into the religion in which he had been brought up….

The boys feel you will be very disturbed to find the family all becoming so radical, but I have assured them that you will be able "to take it" in your stride….This is another adventure of the spirit, one of the most far-reaching we have ever made. (to Charles Austin, 14 February 1945)

She asked if she could be a visitor at the LPP Ontario convention. In a joint letter to Jim and Norman (now overseas), she described how Tim Buck had won her heart:

He spoke on Sunday morning and it was really magnificent…. You feel he is just himself, so full of his subject that he is just pouring out his soul to you…. I suppose Norman will laugh here, but the fact is that Tim reminded me of you, Jim, in your best moments. He has the same apparently unstudied flow of language with tremendous driving force behind it…. I would be willing to work to get him into the House no matter what party I belonged to. We need men like that badly. He is head and shoulders above any other political speaker that I have heard. (to Jim, 25 March 1945)

Two months later, Mary mailed her resignation to the South York CCF Association. Her main rationale: fear of Bolshevism had been one of the main causes of the war; it alarmed her that some members of the CCF were again expressing that attitude. After resigning, Mary felt free to become a self-declared Communist "sympathizer" and offered to help in any way she could. There were numerous opportunities that spring because LPP candidates were running in two elections—provincial and federal—which took place about a month apart.

文月華

The Ontario election in the spring of 1945 was one of the most dramatic ever. Two weeks before voting day the Ontario CCF leader, Ted Jolliffe, charged that the Conservative government of George Drew maintained a secret police that had drawn up a blacklist of 10,000 citizens. Mary made enquiries and believed the charges were true but, like many others, was dismayed there was not enough time for them to be fully aired. The Conservative Party won a landslide victory—sixty-six seats—while the CCF was reduced from thirty-two to six seats. The day after this fiasco, Annie Buller telephoned Mary to ask if she would write a letter to be used as a leaflet urging all progressive people to vote for Tim Buck in the upcoming federal election. She agreed.

MARY ENDICOTT, SCHOOL TRUSTEE
York Township

June 5, 1945

To the Electors of Trinity:

What did you say to yourself when you heard the results of the Ontario election? I have heard of several who said, "If there is anything I could do to make sure of the election of one progressive candidate in the Federal House, I am going to do it." The words recalled a remark I made after hearing Tim Buck address an audience this spring. I said at that time, "I'd like to work for that man to get in, no matter what party he belongs to. We need men like him in the House of Commons."

There are many progressive candidates running in Toronto, but...they will not be elected unless there is concentration of effort. Therefore, for strategy's sake, and with no intention to disparage other worthy candidates, I hope that the utmost effort will be made to secure all the votes of progressive electors for outstanding labour leaders in the ridings where labour is a predominating element. Tim Buck, because he is well known in labour ridings, probably has the best chance *if* everybody who cares does what he can. Those who live in Trinity can do most by telephoning and making as many calls as possible....

I am not a resident of Trinity, nor a member of the party, which Tim Buck represents, but I believe he will raise a clear and persistent voice in parliament to promote legislation for the welfare of those in whom I am deeply

文
月
華
的
中
國
日
記

interested. These include not only my children and friends, but those I meet in church work...and educational circles in York Township in which I am a School Trustee. They are wage earners and salaried workers, owners of homes and shops, homemakers and their children. Any not mentioned will have plenty of other representatives in the House. We all want jobs for the breadwinners, security against the misfortunes of life, opportunities accessible to all for skill training and a broader cultural basis for living.

Until recently I had never seen nor heard Tim Buck and would have had no grounds for writing this letter. Then it dawned upon me that I knew almost nothing of labour movements from the inside. I began to go to meetings where I saw their speakers advertised, both union and political meetings. The first was a meeting of the Union of Electrical Workers, where I heard a report from a delegate to the World Labour Conference in London. That brought me in touch with labour movements all over the world, including China, my second homeland, where so much remains to be done for the welfare of the average person.

In the labour meetings I attended, I found many things that reminded me of the deep convictions of religious people and the concern of educational people. "We ought all to be working together," I said to myself. "We have much in common."

Each time I heard Tim Buck speak the impression has been renewed: "Here is a great Canadian, one who knows the outlook of the humblest because he is one of them, one who has suffered in their cause, one who has the insight and mind of a leader. Here is one who ought to be supported by a broad cross-section of our society just as Roosevelt was supported in his later days."

I was particularly struck with the quietness of Tim Buck's manner of speaking on political themes. His listeners are impressed by the clarity and earnestness of his presentation, and there is no need for resounding phrases. Anyway, they would be out of place from him. He is too unassuming, too uninterested in himself as a performer. They would not suit his style. He is even able to admit naturally that his judgment has been mistaken.

After one public address, I heard someone from the floor ask him whether religion hinders progressive action. The questioner expected the answer yes, but Tim Buck said he did not think that was always true, that he himself had changed his mind on it since he had observed that people in religious groups could see the need for progressive action and would act upon it. He added, "It is not the task of labour movements to oppose religion. We have made mistakes on this in the past. Labour movements have responsibility to fight for social reform, and not to mix in with the faiths of individuals."

As I listened, on this and other occasions, I became convinced that Tim Buck was a leader whose experience and passionate purpose is expressed through a personality that is highly gifted and has dynamic driving-force. As such, he should be in the House of Commons to speak for the common people. Progressive electors of any party would do well to ensure his presence in parliament by voting for him on June 11th.

Yours sincerely,
(Mrs. J.G.) Mary A. Endicott

Mrs. Endicott's husband has returned to their home in Chengtu, West China, to continue missionary work for the United Church of Canada there. Mrs. Endicott is in…the Women's Missionary Society of the United Church of Canada.…For two years she has been a member of the Board of Education for York Township. She has four children, one of whom is on his way to the Pacific front in the Air Force.

文月華

Annie Buller thought the letter was "a honey," although she suggested removing the comments about religion. Mary balked as she considered them to be the most influential part of the letter. She did agree, however, to revise her original statement which said, "It is not the task of Labour movements to…mix in with philosophies and opinions or faiths of individuals." Annie said it was not Marxian to say they were not out to change philosophies so Mary removed the words "philosophies, and opinions."

The afternoon of the day she took it down to the riding office, Tim called her up on the phone. She confided her feelings to Jim:

He said he was embarrassed but he wanted to thank me for my beautiful letter, and to tell me how much he appreciated my writing it.…I appreciated his phoning and asked him if it was O.K. to put in the quote re religion and he said yes, he was especially glad of that, he was always glad when that question was asked at a meeting.…I must say I've never got more satisfaction out of anything than coming out strong for Tim. There's something real about it when the person comes up to par as well as the ideas.…

文
月
華
的
中
國
日
記

With all this excitement I'm feeling on top of the world and did I enjoy your letter of May 14th, which came today. I felt outside of that tunnel I wrote about in my last letter....(to Jim, 7 June 1945)

Tim Buck missed getting elected by eight hundred votes.

23

Two Solitudes

The "War in the Pacific" ended shortly after the Americans dropped two atomic bombs—on Hiroshima and Nagasaki, August 6 and 9, 1945.

Jim cabled Mary mid-August: he would return home February 1946. Soon, however, he was having second thoughts about leaving China.

In September 1945, Mary and a male colleague on the Board of Education agreed, on her initiative, to get better acquainted. She believed this was in keeping with the philosophy of extramarital "intimate friendships" she and Jim discussed in 1927-28. According to this theory, the marriage would be enriched by such relationships and if sexual feelings arose no one should feel guilty.

It is not clear whether Mary actually disclosed her decision to embark on this "intimate friendship" to Jim. She discussed it with a friend who had just returned from Chengtu; the latter advised against being candid with Jim because things might be misunderstood 5,000 miles away. Mary typed up the details but it seems likely she did not mail that particular letter.

Soon the special friendship escalated to a full-blown secret affair.

文月華

Jim was painting a vivid picture of the growing corruption, inflation and political repression in China. The sight of starving conscripts in the university football stadium sickened him. He felt his fellow missionaries were like those in the parable of the Good Samaritan who passed by on the other side.

He asked Mary to hold on to his resignation from the ministry for a year. He was still a missionary but becoming increasingly involved in Chinese politics. The climax of his new political consciousness came in early December 1945. A movement had been growing to stop the civil war between Communist and Nationalist forces. During a protest in the city of Kunming, police killed four students. In Chengtu, Chinese students asked him to address a mass rally protesting the Kunming killings. Under

文
月
華
的
中
國
日
記

cover of darkness Communist students told him they had reliable information that Nationalist plainclothes police would shoot any Chinese who spoke at the rally. They thought that Jim, as a foreigner, missionary and former advisor to Chiang Kai-shek, might get away with it.

Addressing the rally was a watershed in Jim's life: "I have inner peace in my soul because I am not only now fully committed to do the truth as I see it, but I am not afraid of the truth." The night before the day of the rally he wrote a letter to Mary in case anything should happen to him:

Pictures have been racing through my mind. A little black squirrel in the park at Washington. A car waiting for an already departed train. Norman's first cry in the grey dawn of March. Your arms thrown round my neck at midnight when I came back from that first terrible bombing in Chungking. (8 December 1945)

Later, however, he told Mary he was glad she was not with him when he accepted the invitation to speak at the demonstration because he believed she would not have been willing. She was upset at his underestimation of her courage and her understanding of what it means to lay down one's life for a cause. In fact, she wrote him, she felt it was the only thing he could have done.

In May 1946, Jim finally left for Canada, but history intervened. On his way down the Yangtze, changing steamers at Nanking, he met with Chou En-lai, a leader of the Chinese Communist Party. Chou pleaded with Jim to stay in Shanghai to do publicity for the Communists, who were having trouble getting the Western world to hear about their accomplishments. By now Jim was desperate to get back to Canada, but had been told that returning to China might be impossible since he would no longer be a missionary. If he left knowing he would not be allowed back, he told Mary, he would feel like a deserter.

June 1946: Mary prepared herself mentally for a longer separation and/or the possibility of living in Shanghai with Jim. She was deeply disappointed that Jim had as yet given her no clear indication he wanted her.

September 6, 1946: Finally, Mary received a cable from Jim: PLEASE COME EARLIEST SAILING: "That cable put me into a sort of exaltation in which I lived for days—feeling myself en route to Shanghai. The kids get a kick out of it. 'You're having almost as much fun as getting married, aren't you, Mum?'"

The long painful separation would soon be over. When Mary tendered her resignation from the Board of Education, Superintendent H.A. Griffin sent a warm letter of appreciation. It said, in part: "Nothing stimulates progress quite as much as genuine interest. Due to your untiring efforts, I can state quite frankly that our system has benefited tremendously. Our teachers have reason to feel happier and in turn, this is reflected in our work....[You] have exhibited a happy combination of tolerance, tenacity and vision."

Mr. Evans, the principal of Vaughan Road Collegiate, asked Mary to come to the Remembrance Day Service at the school and say goodbye to the students.

> I spoke to each of them, junior and senior, for about fifteen minutes on China today. I wasn't a bit nervous and my voice was low and steady and Shirl said it was really good, and much better than anything she'd heard me do before. She hadn't wanted me to speak at all, but...I somehow feel inspired to want to speak about China—now, of all times, when opportunities are few—but such as they are they count a lot. (to Jim, 12 November 1946)

At her final WMS meeting, her fifteen colleagues each wrote an unsigned note on a small slip of paper: "Things we like about Mary Endicott":

- I admire Mrs. E's ability to see two sides of a question—thus being fair.
- I love Mary Endicott for her deep concern for the best and because she's such a good sport in any concern.
- Mary Endicott impresses me with her intensity of enthusiasm; putting her *all* in and behind everything she attempts.
- The mischievous look in her eyes.

Dorothy Young, a United Church staff person in youth work wrote to say: "I have never failed to be inspired when meeting with you by your sincerity, your impatience with sham and your originality."

These testimonials boosted Mary's morale enormously, helping her to cope with the difficulties that awaited her in Shanghai.

Part 5

文月華的中國日記

24

Heaven and Hell in Shanghai, 1947

We had more of heaven and more of hell in the first six weeks after my return than we had ever expected to experience; the heaven came from a deeper realization of the meaning of our love because of the suffering in our separation, and the hell from the terrible periods of despair into which Jim would be plunged every few days, sometimes lasting for a few hours, sometimes most of the night. We suppose it would be called a nervous breakdown, or the verge of one, and there were moments when I felt terrified and desperately alone. (to Earl and Katherine Willmott, 12 March 1947)

A report had come to Mary in Canada, from fellow missionary Dr. Robert McClure, emphasizing Jim's impaired health. Only two ships were taking passengers to China in 1946: it might be months before she could get a passage. Desperate to join her husband as soon as possible, she wrote to Secretary of State for External Affairs, Lester B. Pearson, for help. Pearson had been a friend of Mary's in her youth; he and Jim had been tennis partners at Victoria College. Now he arranged for Mary to go to China with the new Canadian ambassador, Chester Ronning; she was listed as nursemaid to the Ronning children.

Dr. McClure had a reputation for exaggeration, but when Mary arrived she found his assessment of Jim's health was accurate.

Jim's life in Shanghai was extremely pressured—hazardous for someone coping with depression and nervous exhaustion. He led what he called "a double life"—a "white" and a "red" one. The "white" one was a facade to cover his real purposes—to help the Chinese communist movement—and included revising his English Readers, working on a government commission for the reform of English teaching in middle schools, and a half-time teaching position at St. John's University. The "red" life was producing the weekly *Shanghai Newsletter*, to publicize the gains being made by the communist forces and news of the increasingly repressive measures of the Nationalists. There was a cloak-and-dagger element to *The Shanghai*

文
月
華
的
中
國
日
記

Newsletter: ways had to be found to mail it without having to pass the KMT censor and material had to be gathered from a variety of sources without Jim bringing attention to himself. It was an intense and risky assignment.

Before he was asked to undertake this assignment, Jim had felt desperate to get back to Canada for a reunion with his family. He had been living this high-intensity life for six months before Mary was able to arrive in Shanghai. The toll on his nervous system was enormous.

In spite of Dr. McClure's warning about Jim's health, Mary was not prepared for how he looked: anxious wrinkles in his face, his voice and manner often jerky and quite different from what they used to be. She conveyed these details to her father:

> Every few days the strain welled up into an emotional crisis where he could not sleep, his head felt full of tight knots that nearly drove him frantic, with the result that he became deeply depressed and lost all interest in life and all confidence in himself....
>
> Fortunately for us both, the change that Jim observed in me was of just the opposite nature. He was amazed at the difference in my self-confidence, my quiet independent poise and the lack of the old strains that he remembered used to make me took so tired. (to Charles Austin, 30 January 1947)

Their home was a small two-room flat on the campus of St. John's University, where they cooked on a little coal-oil stove, ate mostly canned goods and kept boiled hot water in thermos bottles on hand. The bedroom was perpetually cold, but three or four hot water bottles warmed the bed. They lived in the kitchen-dining area, which had a large chair—"a chesterfield cut in half." There they sat, cuddled—and wrestled with Jim's inner demons.

He had been running away from Mary when he left Canada. In a letter to Stephen, which he showed to Mary, he confessed his ambivalence was present even on the day he sent her the cable asking her to come as soon as possible: "I both wanted her and was afraid of her coming. I was afraid because I knew dimly...I would have to be frank and tell her that in my effort to protect myself from giving up my egocentricity and my desire to 'star' I had been running from her and had planned to go off to the north to join in the revolutionary war" (Shanghai, 29 January 1947).

He had been having a series of "nervous breakdowns" ever since he returned to China—in spite of a brave exterior, his cheerful and aggressive front.

Twice he had contemplated suicide—"due," he said, "to a hard core of pride of what Künkel calls egocentricity"—once in the fall of 1944 and again at a later date.

Painful buried childhood memories had surfaced. Mary described these to her sister, Jane:

> His father was very severe with his children because he believed that was the way to make them good. He used to whip them when they were naughty and Jim, at least, was terrified of him and would lie to him and do anything to avoid being found out. This made him feel guilty and ashamed. At the same time, he admired and loved his father more than most children because his father was an overwhelming personality. This made Jim want to follow in his father's footsteps. (Shanghai, 25 March 1947)

As soon as a temporary improvement in Jim's mood occurred, Mary wrote her children a long letter:

> Darlings, Dad is really a changed person—much happier than he used to be. But he has gone through deep waters, which have threatened to engulf him at times. Ever since I came there have been two or three crises which have almost frightened me—times when he was terribly shaken by remorse for his mistakes in the past.
>
> I was puzzled as well as startled to see him in this new role...lacking self-confidence...to a degree I have never witnessed in anyone. I was afraid lest I would not have the skill or the wisdom to help him and thus might say or do the wrong thing and thus push him nearer to the precipice of a complete breakdown.
>
> It was terrible to be alone at those moments—and they always came so unexpectedly and suddenly I wouldn't be prepared—but I just prayed hard to be shown what to do and the answer seemed to be just to be myself and to be honest as well as calm. And then the mood would pass and he would be all smiles and full of restored faith in himself and able to sleep.
>
> This breaking down of his egocentricity—which is the real explanation of what has happened—is part of the story of his life, and especially those two years in which his suffering has brought him to a new clarification. These are terms, which Künkel uses and I hardly know how else to express it....
>
> Dad's egocentricity was bound up with his worship and fear of his father so that he grew up without finding his real self at all—but dramatizing what he thought he wanted to be....

文
月
華
的
中
國
日
記

It was I who first criticised the Church and he resented that but gradually saw I was right. However, no Ego as strong as Dad's ever gives up without a tremendous battle and a long-drawn-out one at that. Knowing that I was the enemy which dared to show him up, his Ego caused Dad to regard me in a dual light; his real self loved me as devotedly as ever but his Ego resented me and magnified my defects and blamed all his troubles on me.

This was all subconscious, of course, but the effect on me was to confuse me; consciously I was aware of his love and happy in it, but subconsciously I felt insecure and lacking in confidence, which was just what *my* Ego wanted, for it had early chosen the pattern of the defeated person, the martyr perhaps.

My success as a mother and foster-mother prevented me from becoming neurotic and did much to break down the power of my defeatist ego, but the latter kept reminding me that I couldn't learn Chinese and therefore would never be much use to Dad in China and therefore was dragging him down in his career. How I used to wish that Dad would take half an hour a day with me to teach me Chinese in his clever way and have fun about doing it, but he never would, and I understand now why—his Ego didn't want me to get adjusted to China because my lack of adjustment was a convenient prop on which to hang all Dad's own failures in China....

Well, his real Self has emerged and oh, how I love him, and how secure I feel in his love....One by-product is that he is no longer afraid to go home and face his father and his father's church....

And so, you can think of us now as laughing and enjoying life together, reading when we have time, meeting friends together, separating for a few hours to realize again how wonderful it is to be in the same place—and, in general, behaving much like we did twenty-two years ago when the miracle of love was fresh and almost incredibly joyous.

P.S. During our separation, when I wrote to Dad about discovering a strength within the Church, [this] bolstered the theory which his Ego was promoting—namely that I was identified with the past from which he had to break. (17 January 1947)

At the end of January, Mary sent a second letter, reassuring her children that Jim's breakdown had been serious but "now it is *over*."

It was not true, but that was all she wanted everyone but Stephen to know. Philip and Shirley were too young and Mary did not want to burden Norman with further information because she felt he had enough on his plate as a young husband. Stephen, of course, had been particularly close to his mother for years—cheerfully translating her desires to the servants, keeping watch with her on the upper verandah the night of that ghastly first fire-bombing of Chungking. He had been to Sharman's Camp Minnesing with Mary just after Jim returned to China the summer of 1944. One evening they'd discussed Karl Marx while out in the canoe!

In that harrowing winter of 1947, Stephen became to Mary what Freda had been twenty years earlier—someone to whom she could speak frankly. "We wanted to get the record home to the family lest something happen before we can tell you verbally, and you seemed to be the logical person to whom to address it." However, as the other family members were never shown this "record," it does seem that what Mary really needed was a sympathetic confidante, a role Stephen would retain for the rest of his mother's life. Mary's confidences included details of extramarital relationships on both sides.

While in Canada Mary had surmised the truth about Jim having an affair, but had decided she would not ask any questions. But now, Jim needed to confess. Before he left for China, Mary had asked for a pact setting limits to any extramarital friendships. Jim remembered this and felt great guilt about his liaison with Hilde Kiang. Furthermore, as he had previously confessed in a letter to Mary, Hilde had criticized him: "Unless I can 'star'...I prefer to retire into the blackout of my own thoughts." Remorse compounded.

In the bitter pain of the long separation and trying not to think of his affair, Mary had forgotten about the pact. Now she revealed her own extramarital excursion—and that it had been a good experience for her. Jim was devastated.

More distressing information came out:

Mary told of paying Hilde a visit in Chicago on the way to her sailing in San Francisco. (Jim had sent the address in order to have some documents forwarded.) During the visit Hilde commented: "Jim doesn't love anybody but himself."

Jim disclosed that among Mary's papers he had found a note she wrote in Chungking which said: "There are times when Jim is a stranger to me and I think he does not love anybody but himself." The same phrase from two different women stung; he was unable to get past the pain.

Already brooding on his mistakes of the past, Jim plunged into the vortex of despair. In mid-February, Mary woke one night to find him on the

文
月
華
的
中
國
日
記

verge of taking his life. Several days later, Jim's friend from Chengtu, Fritz Kobler, a psychoanalyst, happened to be in Shanghai briefly and spent five hours with the Endicotts. Two weeks later, Mary, in acute pain with a sinus cold, wrote Stephen a lengthy report "to get the record home":

[The] suffering is still taking its toll of him and the result is wearing me out....O Steve, when these moods are on I wonder how many more I can stand, but the thought of you dear children keeps me from giving up hope. I can especially see and hear you saying to me, "Cheer up, Mum he doesn't really mean it. It will be all right again in a little while." And then afterwards the realization of how he has hurt and frightened me tortures him, though I think he forgets some of the things he says....

Dad still has some deep resentments, which he accepts rationally but evidently has not fully accepted deep down, or these moods would not continue....When a person is suffering [like this, it] interferes with what he wants to do externally as well as with his personal contentment. As a result he forgets to carry out things he promised, and even when he is speaking or writing something important, he feels his heart is no longer in it.

These things...cause him to be convinced he is never going to be effective again; a fear of premature age sets in—along with this resentment about the lost years when he didn't know what was wrong with him and I didn't know what was wrong with me, and both of us felt frustrated.

Fritz Kobler helped us a lot....Not that the suffering has been less since Fritz was here; in some ways it has been more often acute and up to the surface—that is, his remorse has given way to accusation of me. Fritz pointed out that his remorse...was really a veiled form of accusation which patients frequently take, so I suppose it is better that it has passed into a more open phase but it is harder for me to take....The repetitions every few days have used up a lot of the reserve I had when I returned. Dad has lost weight, too, and now looks thin, even in the suit I brought out to him.

Fritz says this kind of suffering and urge for clarification is typical of the forties and fifties if there are causes of frustration, which have not been cleared earlier. (from Shanghai, 28 February 1947)

Mary went on to explain how Jim forgot the happy times and brooded on the failures and mistakes, including his early "bunglings" as a husband, to use his 1928 phrase. All the long-time hurts to his inmost self, which had surfaced during his soul-searching in Chengtu, returned again to torture him.

Fritz Kobler was a Freudian, and his main contribution during his five-hour visit was to offer an unexpected analysis of the dynamics of the Endicott marriage:

Dad and I both wanted to tell him about the difficulties Jim had been having since my return. Each of us, in the few minutes we were alone with Fritz, told him about the one most terrible night [here] when Jim actually contemplated taking his life....

Well, after we'd told Fritz separately and then together about Jim's black moods since my return, I described a vivid dream which I had the morning after this contemplated suicide of Jim's. Mother and I were dressed as blue nuns and she was making faces at father through the window. Then I saw father sitting with his head on the table as if in despair. I was very angry with Mother, whose face looked hideous to me, and I pulled off our blue veils crying, "I hate nuns. They don't have babies." O yes, I also said to her at the window, "You can't do that to father."

At the time Mary felt the dream related to the sexual inhibitions her mother put on her as a child. Fritz Kobler had a different view:

He said quietly, "That's a perfect dream for a psycho-analyst. If you were a patient I wouldn't tell you my interpretation but try to get you to find it out for yourself." I asked him not to stand on such ceremony....

"Well," he said, "you know what the Electra complex is?"

"Yes," I said, "It's the opposite of the Oedipus complex, and it means a fixation of sex desire on the parent of the opposite sex."

He said my dream was a perfect revelation of that complex in me. "The reason it was not veiled, as is usually the case in dreams, is that Jim's recovery from the desire to suicide was a great triumph for you, and so the censor was lifted and your dream revealed clearly the desire repressed when you were an infant, or probably between the ages of three and five."

It seemed as if the lid had been taken off a box and a whole flood of evidence flew out at me....It was plain as day that was what had happened to me. The results showed in all the places which I had ascribed to egocentricity of defeatism—my sense of inadequacy, of half-paralysis in so many of the ordinary things of life—both wanting to do a thing and not wanting to do it, and so, ending up by half doing it, or at half-speed.

My speech difficulty is one of the most outstanding symptoms, confirmed by what I had told Fritz about my [former] panic at using my mar-

文
月
華
的
中
國
日
記

ried surname. He said it was because it represented the most painful break with my father—namely, marriage—it substituted another in my father's place, as it were, and I had a bloc or hysteria about it.

The reason Mary had thrived in her affair was now "obvious": the stranger did not threaten her unconscious tie with her father; she wasn't thinking of marrying him, or going to a far country with him.

Moreover, there were deeper reasons. Fritz asked me suddenly,

"What did you resent about marrying Jim?" I looked astounded and said, "Did I?" for I always thought it was *the* great triumph and fulfilled desire of my life. Then one of us said, "He was different from the father image," and I said yes....

All of a sudden it struck me—why, Mr. X was dark, a conservative, a businessman, not impulsive—all ways in which he was like my father where Jim is not.

Fritz looked triumphant that his theory had worked out so well....

Jim could not accept it at first and even yet, when the black mood gets him, he does not want to accept it, he just wants to rail against everything that hasn't gone according to his desires in all his life, and chiefly now when he feels frustrated by...the uncertainty about his future work, and so on....

The effect of all this has been to take off some of the rested confident look I had when I returned, and he feels he has done it, and rails against that, too. Then, when the mask-look drops from his face his eyes and mouth smile at me again he knows that the past is all gone and all we have to do is to enjoy the present and the future, and make the most of the very creative part of our lives that are still left to us. As I said to him, "Think if this hadn't happened to us until we were 70! (to Stephen, 28 February 1947)

Mary was anxious to set the past aside and move ahead, even though her supposed Electra complex diverted attention away from Jim's difficulties with his own identity and his "running away" from her.

Then, too, having the focus put on a childhood situation for which no one was to blame might well have reduced Mary's fears of Jim succumbing to yet another suicidal bout.

Stephen Sends a Healing Letter

文
月
華
的
中
國
日
記

Dearest Dad and Mother,

Equinox has come and spring is here! Snow is melting and water lies soaking the back yards. From my grime besmeared windows everything looks drab and inert, after winter's desolation. Even the trees are gaunt and grey; everything is still save the chirping of some birds. Yet the trees bear life concealed, on their uplifted branches sit buds soon to spring forth in radiant bloom. I shall be glad when the world is clothed in green....

It is nearly a week since I got that long letter from Mother. I have not yet shown it to anyone....I find it difficult to write this letter to two people, so from now on I shall...write as if I were writing to you alone, Dad....[It] saddened me to hear, of the intense personal struggle that you are having. I can almost feel your deep suffering. Then the things which I had never known before...about your early marriage relationship, [including] certain of its shortcomings, and now the things that have happened since you and Mother have been separated these last three years, of which I had some knowledge....

Your marriage, as I have seen it worked out [has] great meaning to me, despite the blowups and the weepy spells (which were better than repressions and sullenness) which seem to tax the meaning of love. I have seen a deep central understanding and love between you and Mother which neither of you could probably have found as well in somebody else. A "deep central love enables one to go out and be in unconfused relation to all things else," says a certain writer....In this respect, I do not believe...that the relationships you have had in each other's absence is in opposition to true love and therefore bad. The only thing bad is if it leaves you with a guilt complex....As [someone else] has written, if people are "perfectly secure in their love, their companionship, their home and children, the 'felt values'...they have no fear of losing them and so can happily have intercourse with other human beings freely."...

Dad...I have always had complete confidence in you and still have. When my college friends ask me about you...I always refer to you as you have been and are to me, an interested sympathetic father, very sincere and with integrity, one who will always do what he thinks right, a man who uses his rather remarkable speaking power to fight for [the common people], and one who, above all, has a brimming-over sense of humour....

I ran across this poem the other day....It is called Rock Bottom:

父
月
華
的
中
國
日
記

I have been defeated again and again
But there is something within one
That is never defeated,
And I am full of new beginnings,
My blood shall drink iron of the spears that pierce me,
And my lips shall make laughter of the bitterness of any cup
And out of despair I shall make a song.

And Dad, sometimes when things look grim and you are tempted to take the short way out, please remember me, and all of us to whom you are so dear as a person that we cannot bear the thought of being without you. I have always admired your intellectual ability, what you lacked in objectivity sometimes...you always made up for in enthusiasm....

As I sit here all sorts of pictures flash before my eyes about my boyhood—the interest you showed in us as kids, in Chungking, with the chickens. I'm sure they would all have died of thirst six times over if you hadn't come to the rescue....Then again at Humewood when we played hockey on the little back rink and tried to slam pucks behind your big crepe-soled shoes....You and Mother have been wonderful parents. Come on home and continue. (from Toronto, 23 March 1947)

Dear Stephen,

Your long letter of your reactions to Mother's long one about our personal states, arrived yesterday. We were just on our way to get registered at the police station for residence permits and all other such appurtenances of a police state, but we lay down on the couch and read it at once. Steve, you can probably never know how deeply we were moved by it. You have written so well, shown such maturity of understanding and judgment. Mary wept silent tears of gratitude and love....

I accept that when people have long separations some compensations may take place...but when two people are in love with each other, and the expression of it and the living together are sufficiently satisfactory, I have a strong feeling they will not want other intense experiences; in fact, they will have neither time nor energy for them....

Anyway, everything is all right now and we are very happy and *I have learned to accept the explanation of the whole thing as Fritz Kobler has helped us to see it....* (Emphasis added.)

Yesterday Mary and I went pedi-cabbing all over the place, dropping a few Newsletters here and there in the various post-boxes and hoping the watchful eye of the censor will not get them all.

Asking Mary to come out here and see the work and get the feeling about what it is all about was the wisest decision that I ever made and it will ensure our mutual understanding and happiness no matter where we are or go.

In the meantime we are going June 19—home to you all.

With much love and great gratitude for your letter which was really a noble effort,

Dad (from Shanghai, 8 April 1947)

文
月
華
的
中
國
日
記

25

Life—in the Cold War—with Jim

By April 1947, Mary and Jim had found "safe ground." The harrowing winter in Shanghai—Electra complex and all—became a crucible for a strong partnership that would weather over a decade of severe political persecution back in Canada. In June they sailed for Canada with no plans. The entire family, including Norman's warbride Kathleen and baby Suzanne Michelle, spent the summer building a log cabin on Beaver Lake in the Kiwartha Lake district, north east of Toronto. In her book *Five Stars over China*, Mary described the process by which she forged a partnership with Jim in his second career:

> On our return [from Shanghai] Jim lectured across [Canada] on the upheaval in China, interpreting it as the final stage of a grass-roots revolution begun a hundred years ago in the Taiping Rebellion. The people in one form or another, he believed, would have continued this struggle against internal and external oppression, even if they had never heard of Marx. He reported on why the Chinese Communists were gaining the support of the people and his conviction that they would carry out their promise to set up a coalition government.
>
> Few believed this, and fewer still believed the evidence he presented of the corruption and incompetence of the Chiang regime and of its eventual downfall in spite of American backing. In these speeches, my husband called for organized protests to our government against sending any more arms and aid to Chiang to prolong the civil war....Even on this issue many well-meaning people were confused and divided.
>
> Our friends worried about our practical personal problems. The four adolescent children cooperated loyally in our changed economic situation, which, fortunately, was not acute because of a modest inheritance, which came to me about that time. Our mothers were no longer living, but our fathers, both in their eighties, have been a source of deep comfort and opened their minds to understand our point of view.

Many of Mary's friends shunned her as a pariah at this time because she and Jim were defending the Chinese Revolution and willing to cooperate with Communists in Canada in the work for peace. It began with a "harsh and bitter" letter from a long-time friend in Windsor who declared they must never see each other again.

In dismay, Mary went to see another friend, someone she felt sure would be willing to continue her long-time relationship. Here she heard a stunning, unexpected explanation: her Windsor friend was really afraid of the Endicotts or afraid the police might shadow them and all their friends. "I gasped," she wrote, "wondering if I was back in Shanghai, or…dreaming of being in Germany ten years ago." Not everyone was that blunt but, over time, the invitations to visit simply no longer came. Mary developed new friends, but the loss of the ones who got all those circular letters from China was a deep blow. Freda Waldon, Mary's long-time confidante, did not turn her back on their friendship, although it was never as close as it had once had been—which might have happened anyway. Friendships do change over time. She was Norman's godmother and remained happy to see him when his law practice took him to her home city of Hamilton, Ontario.

In the United Church, although many church people ostracized Jim, not everyone disowned him. In Toronto, for example, several ministers actively supported the new peace movement. Reverend Crossley Hunter, a classmate of Jim's at Emmanuel, and now the minister at Trinity United Church, welcomed the Endicotts as members of his congregation.

Mary's creative energy now focussed on her partnership with Jim. In January 1948, the Endicotts initiated a monthly bulletin—the *Canadian Far Eastern Newsletter*, a continuation of Jim's *Shanghai Newsletter*—giving their interpretation of the rapid changes taking place in China. It began as a mimeographed report to friends, stuffed by hand into envelopes around the dining room table at 134 Glenholme Avenue, and grew from there. For Mary this was "a means of serving China and working for peace in a team with Jim:"

> Before long, this service to our friends became a monthly printed bulletin of news and views about Asia, read by thousands in several countries, and maintained by their subscriptions. It remained a non-profit venture in which I soon found myself spending my whole life, first in circulation, then in editing and in writing sections of it.

文
月
華
的
中
國
日
記

Occasionally, when Jim is on a long tour, I write all of it. A part-time office staff attends to circulation. It is a labour of love, reviled by some but regarded by many, even though they do not share all our views, as a "necessary and constructive corrective" to the commercial press....

Looking back one can see how close to the brink of war the Western world came in 1949. Anxiety over international tensions—the Berlin blockade (see Appendix B) and explosive Western reactions to the Chinese revolution—led to the formation of peace groups in many countries and under many auspices....

Late in the year a new door swung unexpectedly open before Jim. Since he was available they asked him to tour Canada, arouse people to action for peace and unite them to be effective. When we talked it over, the way ahead, though not seen far or very clearly, promised a means of continuing the work on which he had taken his stand in China, the necessity to end war.

I was happy when, in May 1949, Jim was elected chairman of the Canadian Peace Congress....This movement, as we hoped, has co-ordinated the peace councils, which sprang up in all the large centres of Canada, as well as reaching out to individuals in many small places. Jim's salary, when it comes, is raised by public meetings and various activities of the peace councils....For me, the outstanding opportunity was the Second World Peace Congress at Sheffield and Warsaw, an experience, which gave me such a deep realization of the solidarity of the common people all over the world for peace that I have never felt discouraged since that time, no matter what difficulties loomed before us. (*Five Stars over China*)

文月華

Returning from the 1950 Second World Peace Congress, Mary felt a need to publicize the epiphanies she had experienced on her trip. *My Journey for Peace* was a self-published twenty-four-page booklet, selling over 10,000 copies. Originally the Congress was to have been held in Sheffield, England, but as the date drew nearer the English government refused visas to more than half of the delegates. The gathering was moved to Warsaw, Poland, but not before Mary had taken notes about her own feelings and the grassroots enthusiasm for the peace movement in England:

I thought the English would be stand-offish with strangers but they were quite the opposite. They took us for Americans and became friendlier and more relaxed when they learned we were not. They said they were proud to

文月華的中國日記

have peacemakers coming to their city from all over the world. American peace delegates delighted them—a different brand from those who had already sent 16,000 troops to "occupy" England. On the train a British student mentioned that the Americans were building or enlarging many English airbases.

"Do the people resent them?" I asked.

"They don't have much to do with them," he said. "They don't mind troops around but they don't like them being Americans."

Then I asked, "Don't they realize all these bases for atomic bombers mean that this country is sure to be bombed if war comes?"

He said, "Yes, they do, but they think there's nothing they can do about it." When he got off he glanced at our Peace buttons and wished us a good trip.

On Sheffield streets we soon realized that foreigners, since it was off-season for tourists, meant delegates to the Peace Congress. We enjoyed Yorkshire friendliness. The sales-clerks, the taxi-driver, the old man at the newsstand, the waitresses—everybody—ended their remarks to us as they do to one another: "Here's y'r change, luv." "Post office? Round the corner, luv." "Jam sponge or apple tart, luv?" It's just an expression but they say it as if they enjoy it. When we told them why we had come they looked at us with warmth in their eyes and said, "Think of that! Bless y', luv!"

We had arrived several days before the Congress was to open. The first night we went for typical English entertainment in a music hall. To our minds the best gag was:

She: "I haven't been so insulted for a long time."

He: "You should get about more."

We felt like adding: "Try working for Peace."

All the delegates reported little ways by which the people tried to make up for the hostility and rudeness of their government to the Congress. People spoke to us on trams and in restaurants. For example: "I just want to you know, sir," an elderly clerk told Jim, "that the people of England are ashamed of the way our government has treated you people."

Mary met the beautiful white-haired Russian woman known as the Mother of Zoya:

She is a widow whose...daughter [Zoya] was captured among the Partisans and hanged by the Nazis. As she was driven naked through the woods to her death she called out to the villagers, "Do not despair; liberation will come!"

211

文
月
華
的
中
國
日
記

I had wanted to express to this mother the feeling of the women of Canada for what the women of Europe and Asia had gone through. I had no words, but there was no need. I asked for her autograph, then, impulsively, I laid before her the coloured photograph of my four children all about the ages of hers. I threw my arms about her and we wept together for a moment....I shall not forget how she trembled, nor will she, I think, ever doubt that I have dedicated myself, as she has done, to the preservation of human lives. ("My Journey for Peace," winter 1951)

文月華

In the spring of 1950 the first worldwide "Ban-the-Bomb" petition (the Stockholm Appeal) was circulated. In a letter to Stephen, Mary caught the climate of the times in this anecdote about Norman's wife:

Kathy and a friend were doing opposite sides of a street collecting Peace signatures when a man in one house got terribly excited and started yelling to the neighbours, "The Reds are here!" A few minutes later when Kathy was signing up a man at his door, a police cruiser drew up at the house. She said to the man: "I see I have some friends here. If they say anything to me, will you testify that I have come here to ask you quietly and have not put any pressure on you to sign?"

He said, of course he would. She walked down the sidewalk in dignity but I expect with her heart hammering a bit. The police said they wanted to speak to her. She showed them the petition and explained it a bit. Just then their station radioed them: "Have you found that woman who was making the trouble?" They said yes, and read the petition over the radio-telephone to their chief. He said, "Nothing wrong with that. Just tell her it's getting late and she better go home."

Kathy replied, "If you think it's getting late for me to be out (it was 9 p.m.), I'll go home now, but I'll be back again to get more names."

The police were quite impressed when they looked at the three sheets she was carrying, two of which were filled. They said: "So they really are signing it." She told how 200,000,000 had already signed it all over the world and how ministers, doctors and lawyers were signing it in Canada, as well as other people, and about the 79 municipal councils in Quebec who had signed it already.

They asked her, "But what would you think if the Russians dropped a bomb here?" She replied, "I don't think you read the petition carefully. You will see that it is addressed to all countries, and I can assure you that

100,000,000 Russians have already signed, including all the members of their government, so they have agreed that whoever drops an atomic bomb first is a war criminal. That shows they will not do it unless someone else drops one of them first."

Then they asked for her name and if she was related to James G. Endicott. She said proudly she was his daughter-in-law, he was a very good Christian and doing everything he could to keep bombs from dropping on Canada as well as the rest of the world....

By this time they were quite friendly, so she smiled at them as they pulled away and said, "It's too bad you couldn't take me for a ride, if only to please the neighbours." (from Toronto, 30 April 1950)

文月華

In early 1952 Mary revisited the country where she had lived for fifteen years amidst beggars, famines and the oppression of women. It was just two-and-a-half years since the victory of the Communist forces and the founding of the People's Republic of China. Upon her return to Canada, she began her greatest single labour of love: *Five Stars over China*—over four hundred pages of interviews, documents and experiences, again self-published.

Stephen, Shirley and Philip (Mike) had by now all left home, but Norman, Kathleen and their daughter, Sue, continued to live in the three-storey house at 134 Glenholme. Kathleen gradually assumed more responsibility in running the household, helping out with the *Canadian Far Eastern Newsletter* and making it possible for Mary to travel and write her book. Kathleen's role was an invaluable but unsung contribution to the Canadian peace movement of the 1950s. When boxes of *Five Stars over China* arrived in the Endicott's basement, she bore the brunt of wrapping and posting the 10,000 copies that were eventually sold.

The book was dedicated to "Green Jade," whose story, Mary believed, exemplified "the suffering, the heroism, the faith in the future which caused the pattern of Old China to give place to the New China we have seen."

Green Jade's Story

Like all Chinese girls, Lu Yü (Green Jade) was called Mei-mei, (Little Sister), by her family until the next daughter was born. Then, she became Big Sister and the others were Second Sister, Third Sister, and so on. The name chosen by her parents for formal use expressed qualities she hoped she would

文
月
華
的
中
國
日
記

develop. Those who saw her tested in the revolution would agree her name suits her, for she is modest, strong, and beautiful, like jade, the delicately coloured stone used for jewellery and precious ornaments in China since ancient times. Her cheeks are rosy and her face unlined. Her eyes shine with the joy of living; her ready smile and confident bearing betoken serenity and buoyancy of spirit. A casual observer would assume she had led a sheltered, uneventful life. At first glance, seeing braids of hair on her shoulders, I thought she was twenty or younger, and was astonished to learn that she is close to thirty and has borne five children. The story of her life proves her endurance is like that of jade; I refer not to her body, which reached it limits, but to her spirit which never faltered.

The direction of Green Jade's life was determined, in large measure, by her choice of a marriage partner. Their stories will show why people of different home backgrounds became Communists in old China.

Chang Lin was the son of a rich rice merchant in Tzeliutsing, famous for its salt wells from which the bureaucrats drew riches. But the poor, who worked long hours to produce the precious commodity, drew only a pittance and all the miseries resulting from underpaid, unprotected labour. It was not these conditions which made a revolutionary of the second son of the comfortable Chang family. The ugliness of the salt wells and the underfed miserable workers were familiar to him from birth, and might have been accepted as an inevitable part of the landscape.

In childhood his imagination was caught by the earnest, eager face of his mother's brother who visited them once overnight. He did not understand the conversation between the two in low tones, but his mother held him very tight when she tucked him in that night and a tear fell on his neck. He asked her what she was crying about, but she just kissed him again and said she would tell him when he was older. A few years later a letter came from his mother's home and she wept all day. His uncle, she told him, had been killed by the Kuomintang secret police because he was a Communist.

All the children were moved by their mother's grief, but Chang Lin asked her, again and again, to tell him about his uncle's life and what was in the little books he had given her. She dusted them off and read them, trying to understand why her brother had risked his life. She eased her grief by passing on to the eager boy her brother's stories of the heart-breaking oppression of the peasants by the feudal landlords. The lad was fascinated by his uncle's passionate belief that these problems could be solved. His father, kind-hearted as he was, said that life was like that, and that it must be that heaven willed it so.

As Chang Lin grew older he and his mother pored over "the little books."…As the years passed Chang Lin followed the Thought of Mao Tse-tung closely and eventually found kindred spirits [at] West China Union University. There he met Lu Yü, "Green Jade."

文
月
華
的
中
國
日
記

They met at a folk dance at the university. Green Jade had won a scholar-ship to study midwifery at one of the university hospitals.

Their friendship grew apace and Chang Lin persuaded her to read some of the works of Gorki and his famous counterpart in China, Lu Hsun. Tolstoi was also among the writers who stirred her young mind.…Chang Lin's zeal for social justice touched her and she was soon reading pamphlets issued by the Communist press in Chungking.…

By the time Chang Lin had graduated in Arts and was a lecturer at Nanking University (one of the refugee universities in Chengtu), Green Jade had completed her midwifery course and was working in a public health centre on the outskirts of Chengtu. She found herself explaining to patients, whenever she could, that their bitter poverty was due to the lack of democracy in the country and, above all, to the depletion of manpower because of conscription, which the Kuomingtang government continued even after the Japanese had been defeated. She told them about conditions in the training camps, where thousands of recruits starved to death because corrupt officers had sold their rations.

Green Jade's work was in a rural health centre. She helped in the general medical clinic and also took midwifery cases. She visited the poor farmers' homes and daily saw their misery. They had only small, throw-away sweet potatoes to eat. Each family possessed one bowl for all purposes, from cook-ing to bathing the baby. Their homes were straw shacks built over fertilizer pits, like her mother's childhood home.

The people confided in Green Jade. She saw men who had blinded an eye or cut off a finger to avoid conscription. They knew conditions in the train-ing camps were worse than in their shacks and that their families would starve to death if they were taken away. The men were usually roped together like criminals and dragged off to the camps.…

She was beginning to understand that the old system of doing things in China was no good and should be changed. She was beginning to realize, too, that in China, deep-rooted corruption in the Kuomingtang and landlord oppression gave little chance for democracy to develop.…

文
月
華
的
中
國
日
記

When she talked about these things with her father he spoke of the two philosophers who had influenced Chinese life most profoundly. (Both lived several centuries before the New Era which we call A.D.) Laotse had been concerned about the misery of the common people, under the heel of the landlords. He taught passive resistence, indifference and quietism, not revolution. From his teachings came the religion of Taoism. Confucius, on the other hand, had given his life to the purifying of society by teaching strict obedience to those in authority, in the family and in the state. This philosophy crystallized into an ethical system by which feudal society was justified as virtuous. The gulf between upper and lower classes was deep. From the "Book of Rites" her father quoted such sayings as: "Courtesy is not extended to commoners, and punishment is not applied to lords."

Green Jade began to think about the familiar background of Chinese history in the light of Chang Lin's talk about Marxism. She looked forward to asking him about it. She did not see Chang Lin often and his letters did not discuss these questions. Young professors caught expressing "subversive" thoughts were in danger of losing not only their positions but also their lives, even before the united front [between the Kuomintang and the Communists] melted away. As long as negotiations for a truce and a coalition lasted, she could buy the communist newspaper, *New China News*, at an obscure bookstore near the clinic. She found this paper always took sides with the poor and reported police brutality against peasants who couldn't pay the exorbitant rents or who tried to evade conscription. Her own experience confirmed the truth of these accounts and so, pressed by events to study political theory and policies, she began to believe that the Communists had solutions for the basic problems of the Chinese people....

She began to want to become a Communist herself. She no longer believed the stories that in the areas controlled by the Communists in the north, they killed the old who could not work, and that in the Kuomintang areas, they set fire to public buildings.

It was also common gossip at this time that Communists nationalized wealth and wives. She thought the part about wealth was good but believed the other was absurdly incredible.

Green Jade had found the Communists she met were people of good character and morals, contrary to what she had been told. She discussed these things with her father. He warned her to be careful....

Green Jade told him she met people who had gone to the Liberated Areas in the north and who had seen how the people lived under Communist control. "If you had a chance to go there and see for yourself, my father, how the poor are able to solve their economic problems," she had said to him, "you would feel as my friends do." She always took home a copy of *New China News* for him. He read it and began to be impressed by her words. Her young friends brought Marxist books to her home and they discussed them freely there. Her dad took the attitude, "Let them come. I don't know much about it, but they seem to be people of understanding and good character. Maybe the sooner we're communized the better!" (These bits of conversation are just as Green Jade told them to me.) Her mother said nothing. She left these things to her husband and her eldest daughter.

In the spring of 1945 Green Jade married Chang Lin and they went to live in Chungking where she found work in the clinic run by the *New China News*. Soon she was not only doing midwifery but pinch-hitting for the doctor who had left the clinic, getting by with only the basic courses in medicine she had taken in Chengtu. Soon she was elected organizer of the Women's Department of the community formed by the staff running the Communist newspaper. A good community creche enabled her to continue her work after the birth of her first baby: by adjusting her schedule she was able to feed him and enjoy taking care of him to some extent.

When her son was a year old, Green Jade and family had to flee to Yenan in Northern China as full-scale civil war broke out between the Kuomintang and the Communists.

Green Jade was thrilled by the atmosphere in Yenan. The simplicity and honesty of officials were reflected in the life of the whole town, where thousands lived in caves carved out of the yellow loess hills. She met young men and women from all over China who had risked their lives to come there to study at the Revolutionary University....

Green Jade also wanted to study Marxism-Leninism and other subjects she had long desired to explore. But here, as everywhere in China, there was an acute shortage of medical workers so she could not refuse to continue her midwifery and do the best she could to look after sick people.

In the winter of 1947 Yenan was bombed daily by Kuomintang planes. The people were constantly moving from place to place in the hill villages. The villagers took the revolutionists into their homes. Green Jade was amazed at the way the people adjusted themselves to overcrowded and

文
月
華
的
中
國
日
記

primitive conditions, grumbling only against the guns which strafed them in the fields or on the roads.

By the spring a Kuomintang army was approaching Yenan. The Communist community packed up and melted away into the mountains of Shensi Province.

Thus began an epic period when for two years several tens of thousands of people trekked across the barren north country, with thousands of camels, horses and ponies to carry their necessities. The children rode in baskets hung over the backs of ponies. The sick women rode also, but the men and all women in good health walked. Green Jade walked with the pregnant women and delivered babies as the Communist families moved from one Liberated Area to another....

Green Jade does not remember now how many refugee babies she delivered under these precarious conditions. She estimates there were about thirty, and three of them were very serious cases where she had to use instruments. These she can never forget. All were delivered without anaesthetics, for drugs were scarce....

Despite the lack of drugs, Green Jade did not lose one mother or baby in her care. Whenever possible, the most serious cases were taken to places where fully-trained doctors were in charge. There were not enough doctors available for so many people, scattered as they were by the necessities of their march. At times Green Jade was called back to deliver a baby in a unit other than her own. Afterward, she would hurry to catch up with her own unit where her family was—and also, her ration of food supplies.

During these two years Green Jade herself bore two more babies. As she told her story she did not stress her own difficulties excepting as part of the total picture. The women helped one another to look after the children, and the fathers, also, took responsibility. Chang Lin often helped Green Jade in her medical work. For a difficult birth, four strong men had to hold the patient still so that Green Jade could use instruments or perform repair work without anaesthetics....

Green Jade told us of the difficulties of finding fuel in the north; how she used to scramble up the sandy hillsides to find twigs and dry grass for cooking supper for her little family. I could visualize the scene. I remembered the women and children in Szechwan walking along the narrow paths which used to be the only roadways, searching for fallen twigs and dead leaves to fill baskets slung on their backs. It was much harder to find them in the bare northern hills.

Finally Green Jade and the others were no longer refugees fleeing enemy armies. After two years their side was clearly winning and they were safe in a countryside where railways were being repaired and land reform being organized.

But as is often the case when excessive strain is lifted, Green Jade's strength waned. Reluctantly she agreed to take a long rest in the Bethune Hospital at Shih-chia-chuang. Her third child was only a few weeks old but she was too ill to look after him. The women in her group offered to care for her children in an improvised creche but a childless friend looked wistfully at the new baby when Green Jade was leaving for hospital. "I would gladly look after him as I would my own that cannot come to me," she said. Green Jade was moved with sympathy for her friend. In the hospital she and Chang Lin decided to give their youngest to this childless couple to bring up and keep as their son. Green Jade smiled as she told me but from the way she spoke of her children I knew it had not been an easy decision.

For months Green Jade was in the hospital, stricken with an enlarged heart and abnormal blood pressure. She was thin and worn after the three most strenuous of her twenty-four years. [Her] enforced rest lasted a year and a half.

When Mary met Green Jade she was living in Peking, teaching psychology at one university while her husband taught Marxist philosophy at another. They only saw each other and their children on weekends. Mary exclaimed on the sacrifice they had to make.

"Our country is vast, and there is so much to be done in a short time," Green Jade said, in reply to my exclamation of astonishment.

Her vivid face was lighted by an inner radiance hard to describe as she prepared to say good-bye to us. "Sitting here this afternoon," she said, "it seems to me as if I've been telling you about another world from the one in which we now live. But, you know, when you are engaged in the struggle, especially in such conditions as a military situation brings, your spirits rise to it and you feel exhilarated and able to endure what sounds almost impossible to someone who only hears about it."...

文
月
華
的
中
國
日
記

When the time came for farewell, I wished that Peking were closer to Canada so that we might hope to see our young friends more often. Of all those we met in China they symbolize most vividly the joyous selflessness of those who have transformed this ancient land. The word sacrifice slipped out again as I was bidding them good-bye: "You two who have sacrificed so much make me ashamed of the little I've done to help the world," I said.

Green Jade took both my hands and held them tight. Smiling, but in earnest tones she said: "No, no, we have not sacrificed; we have been most fortunate. The hardships we met are nothing compared to the price paid by those who have not lived to see this day—those who longed for it as we used to—people like Chang Lin's uncle who was killed in the revolution twenty years ago. *He* sacrificed, not we."

"We're fortunate that we understand what all the suffering has been for," Chang Lin added. "Not everyone in China is so confident about the future, because some do not yet fully appreciate what the revolution has brought. They grumble or even run away, thinking to find a more comfortable life. But the people know—our hundreds of millions of peasants, our workers building our new industries—*they* know! And they will guard the fruits of the revolution. To see our children deprived of those fruits—*that* would be a sacrifice. To avoid such a sacrifice, nothing is too hard to do!"

文月華

The biggest crisis in Mary's life was triggered by something that happened at the end of that 1952 trip to the People's Republic of China. Eleven years later her "Life with Jim" memoirs began with a prelude pointing toward what she believed was the severest threat she and Jim had faced together.

Crisis

At three o'clock of an April morning in 1952, the night porter in the old-fashioned Royal Hotel in Great Russell Street, London, knocked on our bed-room door.

"Telephone call for you—trunk call, sir," and added apologetically, "sorry to disturb you, sir, it's from Canada."

We were still making up the sleep lost on the flight from China across Siberia on our return from a first visit since the Communist Revolution. The porter had to repeat his message before we responded clearly.

"It must be a death in the family," I thought, throwing on a dressing gown and pattering after my husband through the silent corridor to the left, down to the office and the phone booths. No. It was not from the family. It was a member of our Canadian Peace Congress executive calling from the emergency meeting (at 10 p.m. their time) to urge Jim to get as early a booking for the home flight as possible. I heard snatches of the conversation in which Jim said:

"I can't leave tomorrow; I preach in two churches here. But I will try for passage on Monday....Yes, I've been interviewed by some London papers and by the Canadian Press....No, I didn't say anything about Korea, only China....Oh, the Maple Leaf Gardens? Do they think there is that much interest?...Well, our thanks to the Executive for their faith in me. We'll cable flight arrival. Good night."

It was the time of the Korean War. That three a.m. call was how we first learned of the great cry that had arisen against Jim because he had alleged the Americans were using germ warfare. The Opposition in Parliament was demanding indictment for sedition, some of the press were hinting at treason, with ghoulish headlines as to the fate of the traveller not yet contacted: "Endicott Faces Jail."

Mary and Jim are greeted by their granddaughter Suzanne Michelle as they return to "Endicott Faces Jail" headlines in May 1952.

Our Executive had decided to meet the attack head-on by a grand rally in the hockey stadium on May 11th at which Jim would make his report to

文
月
華
的
中
國
日
記

the people. What he would say they had no idea, but they knew Jim. They wanted him home as soon as possible to prepare for the rally and to stop the wild rumours that he was in hiding.

I had often wondered how we would meet such a crisis....Jim's favourite pulpit text for years had been the answer of Jesus to the young lawyer: "This *do* and thou shalt live" (Luke 10:28).

While in China, old friends, now carrying heavy responsibilities came to ask him to go to Northwest China to look at the evidence. We knew if he did so, he would have to report his findings on germ warfare. If nil, it would greatly displease his Chinese friends who were greatly agitated about the question. If true it might alter our future uncomfortably and embarrass the peace movement to which we were dedicated. But we could not consult anyone.

Jim said, "I will be sure to be asked at home what I think is true about this hot question. I can hardly plead indifference."

I had nodded and said, "If it is the right course to take you will have to take it regardless of the cost." And so it was settled....

These thoughts ran through my head as we prepared to renew our broken rest. In less than half an hour Jim was sleeping soundly and, before long, so was I. "So this is what a crisis is like!" was my last waking thought as I drifted off in a confused medley of courts, prisons and...I woke with a start and found myself trembling just a little. My mind began to go all over it but I knew this meant no more sleep so I switched to an old game of recapturing moments of our life together, for nearly thirty years, and soon it was morning.

They arrived home to hysterical headlines in the press, one newspaper calling Jim "Public Enemy Number One." The plan was for him to say nothing to reporters—he would divulge his evidence at the Maple Leaf Gardens meeting, one week after Mary and Jim arrived in Canada.

The days leading up to the rally were tense. The Endicott family vividly remembered ominous events that had occurred during the past year: howling crowds, blockading a peace meeting at Toronto's Massey Hall, while singing the Nazi song "Horst Wessel," and carrying an effigy of Jim hanging from a scaffold. The time rotten eggs were thrown at the enclosed front porch at 134 Glenholme where Jim and Mary lived along with Norman, his wife Kathleen and their young daughter Suzanne. The evening someone tried to set the house on fire: a burning incendiary device was

文
月
華
的
中
國
日
記

placed just outside the front door and another on the landing of the side entrance. (Kathleen has never forgotten how grateful she was there was a third exit to the back yard: "Burn marks remained for years.")

Now, during the tense time before the 1952 Maple Leaf Gardens rally, the Peace Congress arranged for a bodyguard to be in the Endicott home. A big burly former seaman slept at nights on the chesterfield at 134 Glenholme Avenue. When finally it was the evening of May 11, the huge hockey palace was surrounded by hundreds of hostile, noisy protestors. Security was a major concern for Peace Congress officials. Everyone entering the building was frisked, including Jim's sixteen-year-old nephew, Giles, who had been playing in a park and arrived at the Gardens with a tennis ball in his pocket. It was removed. Inside, five hundred volunteers from unions and other peace supporters supplemented the regular security officials. About fifty young men sat on three sides of the podium to protect the platform guests, which included Jim's elderly father who had asked to introduce his son.

[My job was to sit with my grandfather in a dressing room until it was time for him to go to the podium. Soon my parents joined us and then the two men were escorted to the platform at one end of the rink. My mother and I had seats reserved for us close to the face-off line. As Grandfather Endicott rose to speak, we held hands. It was one of his finest speeches and a hush filled the huge arena. As my father stood up, noisy heckling broke out and our grasp tightened. My mother did not speak—her hand clenching mine said it all: "Keep him safe. Don't let him stray from his carefully prepared speech. Keep him safe." SJE]

Although the Canadian government said it was considering charging Jim with treason over his germ warfare charges, no legal action was taken. (The law had been changed the previous year, expanding the definition of this crime to giving aid or comfort to the enemy *whether or not a state of war existed*—to cover situations like the Korean War, which was technically a United Nations police action.) External Affairs Minister, Lester B. Pearson explained that bringing Dr. Endicott to court might well make him a martyr, which would only rally more people to the side of the peace movement.

The media campaign against Jim continued. One newspaper ran a front page editorial proclaiming in bold print: "Dr. Endicott: Judas got 30 pieces of silver. How much did you get?"

This was undoubtedly the most stressful period of Mary's life but she was not lonely as she had been in China and her partnership with Jim was

文
月
華
的
中
國
日
記

on firm ground. They weathered the persecution together, supported by their immediate family and many new-found friends.

Mary continued to help write The *Canadian Far Eastern Newsletter*, develop ways of distributing the English language magazine *China Reconstructs* to hundreds of subscribers in the United States and accompany Jim on a number of international visits, including two more to China in 1956 and 1959. She was a member of the national executive of the Canadian Peace Congress and attended meetings right up to the year before her death. In all this she felt she was a co-worker with Jim even though he was the one in the limelight. She would go over a speech he was to give, pruning out unnecessary inflammatory statements, curbing the "firebrand" element in him. Then she would go to the meeting , like that night in Maple Leaf Gardens, and pray that in his enthusiasm he would not depart from his printed text with an impulsive ad lib. This was a reprise of the role bestowed on her in Chungking by Harold Swann back in 1926.

文月華

Mary's passion for peace was particularly kindled when she and Jim attended the annual peace festival in Japan in August 1958. Writing in the Endicotts' *Far Eastern Newsletter* she concentrated on how inspiring it had been for her to be welcomed by a crowd of 30,000 people in the seaside town of Kamakura not far from Tokyo:

> The loudest applause was given to the peace marchers from Nagasaki and Hiroshima, deeply tanned by their six weeks of travel, on foot and on bicycles. Their faces were grave from the solemnity of their mission but, as their leader said, they were not exhausted because of the wonderful support and gratitude they had found in every town and hamlet they had passed through. Everywhere thousands had marched with them for some hours or days and their meetings were always jammed, especially in the home village of the fisherman from the Lucky Dragon, who paid with his life for the first H-bomb experiment which showered him with ashes over the Pacific....
>
> The next day we went to a sports field on the outskirts of Tokyo....First in the procession came the gallant twenty whose sign proclaimed they had marched the 1000 kilometres from Hiroshima. Two of them were women and two were blind young men. Those from Nagasaki (twice as far away) were on bicycles and brought up the rear.

Mary responds to the welcome of foreign friends at a seaside peace festival in Kamakura, Japan, 1958.

文月華的中國日記

Right behind the Hiroshima marchers came the handful of foreign delegates who had arrived in Tokyo before the conference opened, ourselves among them. How proud we were to fall into line behind these determined and longsuffering people and in the van of tens of thousands from Tokyo. No, we international delegates did not go all the way with them but we would not have missed this experience for anything. It was not only the resolute throng with whom we marched, their banners and broad hats visible as far back as the eye could see, who thrilled us. Even more moving were the thousands who lined the streets for all those miles, becoming denser the nearer we got to the heart of the city....

The housewives from the tiny wooden houses which fill every space between drab workplaces, the mothers and grandmothers with the little children clustered around them, their eyes popping with wonder—they were the most moving evidence in the whole scene. They waved and smiled and bowed to us—these anxious little mothers looking for support in a problem too great for them to handle. The older women were often stirred to tears, perhaps because their memories of war go deeper and they cannot outgrow them. Gravely they bowed in Japanese custom, clutching the small girls and boys by the hand. Few of them could smile, for tears streamed from their eyes. I found it very rewarding to look directly into individual faces which lighted up as their eyes caught mine and they realized I, too, was

文
月
華
的
中
國
日
記

probably a mother and grandmother, feeling as they do, and pledging, by my presence, that we would all join hands around the world to stop the atomic terror. (*Canadian Far Eastern Newsletter*, 11, 184 [September 1958])

Mary had not forgotten the horrific Japanese bombings of Chungking. "Among the people we talked to," she wrote, "there is, of course, acknowledgement that it was their own country that started the war and they expressed special remorse for the crimes their military men committed in China."

文月華

As the decade of the 1960s began, her enthusiasm for this public work began to diminish with political shifts and the emergence of health problems. A conflict between the Soviet Union and China "muddied the waters." Various physical disabilities surfaced after the 1958 peace conference in Japan—angina, osteoporosis, unexplained chronic cystitis and fatigue. The stairs became too difficult for Mary. The birth of Norman's son Eric made a larger place imperative. The three-storey home on Glenholme Avenue was sold and the Endicotts moved to the ground floor of a triplex on Wychwood Avenue. Norman's family took the top floor.

Mary would now attend to "keeping friendly with herself," a hope she had confided to the Chungking Oxford Group in 1935.

26

The Winter Years

As premature aging and infirmity began overtaking Mary, her life, nevertheless, exemplified the words of Sean O'Casey: "Even the winter has her many beauties, even for the old who shiver."... One of these came unexpectedly from Jim in early 1960. He had gone to Rome to attend a meeting of the World Peace Council. For some reason he arrived a day early and took advantage of the extra time to write Mary a love letter. The sudden death of their friend and colleague Roscoe Rodd had prompted him to make this deeply felt review of their life together.

Mary My Love,

    I feel a long way from home and somewhat lonely tonight. The affairs of state will have to be considered tomorrow. I seem to have arrived one day too early and so this evening I shall enjoy the pleasure of devoting my thoughts and memories to you. I have just been reading a short American novel, one of those that rather overdoes the description of love-making but at least wants to make me leave it and write a love letter to you. About the most sensible thing in the book is the reflection of one character—"There is nothing in life that is better than this, lying beside the woman you love, in your own bed, in your own house."

    I have been feeling very deeply about you, with a certain tender respect which goes from the roots of my hair down to my toes, ever since the sad separation of Roscoe from Nora. I had a lot of time to think about it on the train but I did not have time to talk about it to you. Some of what I thought made me feel rather sad, because I have not given you the companionship of reading and conversation which you would have valued and found satisfying. And at a certain time of real crisis in my life I allowed a separation to take place which every now and then I find devastating to my self-respect. There are many things in my life which I just want to forget, completely and utterly black-out, when I get introspective I feel that I have made you miss a lot which would have made your life more vitally delightful.

文
月
華
的
中
國
日
記

You are really too good and wonderful a person for me and I feel that I have not measured up to the love and devotion which you so richly deserved and have given to me. It seems as if there has often been an inner core of pride which I never surrendered to you. My first awareness of it was during our engagement when I became angry when you challenged certain theological beliefs which I was determined to defend, for reasons not clear to me, but I suppose because I wanted to go to China and didn't want to disappoint my father.

Looking back on those years in China I can recall many periods of inner gloom, when I left you a stranger to my thoughts, because I was trying to prevent myself from thinking. When it finally cracked up you were not there. But when you came to Shanghai you were really wonderful, a gloriously lovely, tender and shining honest soul and I feel I let you down rather badly.

This is not at all the kind of love letter I intended to write when I first got the urge. I just wanted you to know that I love you with the same delight in my soul as it was in the beginning, and how deeply I respect and admire you as well and I hope to be home in 8 days and I wish it were eight minutes because it is time to go to bed.

Love to you, Jim (22 January 1960)

Two days later Jim wrote again:

Mary My Love,

We have just been debating a document. Shall we have a long one, or is it more effective as Ehrenburg says, to compel yourself to say the essence of the thing in a few slogans? While the political experts elaborated at length, I diverted myself in some private and enjoyable reflections, namely, how my soul taketh delight in Mary Austin. I love you. You are the real meaning of life, the most enduring delight and the most profound content, in short, the best thing that ever happened to me is you.

It also seems to be true that one is required to operate from such a treasure trove, outwards, towards the creative purposes of life and so—on with the peace movement. This meeting is the most inspiring for a long time....

Love, Jim

This letter was carefully placed in the red tooled-leather writing case that Mary kept in the drawer of her night table.

While she missed Jim when his work took him away in trips, Mary was not lonely as had been the case in the early China years. Her four children—

Norman, Stephen, Shirley and Philip (now "Mike")—all lived close by, with families of their own. The trend began early. As 1945 was drawing to a close, Norman wrote from England to say that he and his new bride, Kathleen Fouracre, were expecting a baby the following summer. Mary would be a grandmother at age forty-nine! After receiving the news, she declared: "I am too young to be called 'Grandma'—I will be 'Grandmary'."

And "Grandmary" she remained for the rest of her life—first to Suzanne Michelle, born August 9, 1946, and then to twelve other grandchildren over the next seventeen years. When Jim returned from China in 1947, Suzanne was a toddler and from her baby talk came his grandfather nickname, "Popeye." While to the world they were Jim and Mary Endicott, within the family they were "Grandmary" and "Popeye."

As her physical strength ebbed and she sensed her time would be short, her growing brood of grandchildren was a particularly important source of comfort. In 1964, she had a special Christmas card printed: a green Christmas tree with the faces of all thirteen grandchildren as lights. Suzanne Michelle was at the top while the others came down the tree according to their age.

Mary continued to work with Jim on the *Canadian Far Eastern Newsletter* and attend meetings of the national executive of the dwindling Canadian Peace Congress, sitting in a reclining chair when her body grew tired. However, by the time Jim's treasured 1960 love letter arrived, Mary's creative energy was focussed on other activities, to pick up other threads in her life.

She began taking non-credit courses at the University of Toronto. Her daughter-in-law, Lena Wilson (Stephen's wife), went with her to a poetry class in 1961-62, helping her sustain her enthusiasm as well as writing poems herself. One evening a fellow-student asked Lena: "How did you get such an interesting mother-in-law?"

Her magnum opus was a long narrative poem describing her harrowing trip down the Yangtze River in 1933. Given her many health problems, which, unknown to her included Parkinson's disease, the ability to concentrate on such a lengthy piece is remarkable. She also wrote a graphic poem about the day in the early 1930s when she witnessed young men chained together, members of a press gang being forced to join the army. The image of an elderly woman—"stumbling along on little bound feet/ wailing to heaven…"—had stayed with her for over thirty years. That particular horrific scene had not been reported in her letters; it must have been

文
月
華
的
中
國
日
記

cathartic finally to set it down in words. Now, too, she could compare that scary time with the new China, where soldiers were friends of the people, helping the old and weak, carrying their "water from the well as if it were an honour." Another poem described how she coped with the insomnia that increasingly plagued her. She would imagine herself floating like a water lily in an Algonquin Park lake, mentally singing Psalm 23:

> In waters green He leadeth me;
> My soul He doth restore.

文月華

The "winter years" also ushered in a remarkable ministry. A young man Mary knew was convicted of murder and sentenced to hang. Heartsick, she wished she had taken a greater interest in Ken (not his real name). Although the killing had occurred in another city, he was now incarcerated in Toronto's Don Jail, a cavernous old building that served as a "holding tank" for those refused bail—or waiting the gallows. She wrote the warden asking for permission to visit Ken—"if he wishes to see me." He did. Instead of the bright, optimistic youth she had met years before, Mary now sat opposite an ashen-faced prisoner, scared and deeply remorseful. She obtained his permission to call the new lawyer who was appealing his case.

Murder requires an "intent to kill," and the lawyer successfully argued that, since his client had been inebriated at the time of the crime, he could not have formed this intent. Ken was given a second trial. This new lawyer was delighted when Mary phoned and offered to testify.

In spite of her years of speaking out at Board of Education meetings, she was concerned lest her stammer reappear and hamper her presentation. Ken's life was at stake, so she prepared for this court appearance carefully, typing out a draft speech well in advance:

> I met [Ken] about ten years ago, in a group of young men with whom he was working—in another Ontario town. Ken was the youngest and his boyish, smiling face drew my attention and his eager happy way of talking. The others had been making their way in the world somewhat longer and were already a bit heavy in their manner.
>
> An older man, a writer, who was taking an interest in this group, talked with me about them and agreed that young Ken was the brightest and most promising among them. He told me about his background; it did not sound

like a good start—a broken home, from which he had been wandering so long he was not sure where his father was. The father's heavy drinking was part of the picture of a working man down on his luck.

Ken was studying at night school at that time and I heard from his instructor he was doing well in acquiring a trained skill.

It must have been two years when I saw Ken again. The writer friend telephoned to ask if he might bring him around for a chat. Ken had come to Toronto, fallen into heavy drinking and the writer was worried about him.

When they came I saw Ken had lost his boyish look but he was still very young, about twenty. He and the writer stayed for dinner with the family and everybody had a good time. I noticed Ken was eating very little. When I asked about this he was embarrassed and made excuses about having been up very late. I realized he was suffering from a hangover....

Before Ken left that evening I talked to him frankly about his drinking. I told him I believed he was a bright capable boy who could make his way in the world if he made up his mind and not to let drink drag him down....He seemed to be moved by my motherly talk and promised he would try to do as I suggested. Impulsively, as I shook hands with him, I put an arm around his shoulder and kissed him, and sent him off with a prayer that God would guide and strengthen him.

I never heard from him directly. Once or twice I met people who only knew that the drink had fastened itself upon him more and more. I suppose he was ashamed to come and see me or let me know where he was. When the dreadful news came last winter I felt I should have made more effort to find him and give him a hand now and then. That is why I have come here.

From my understanding of God as the Father of the sinful as well as of the good, I should like to see Ken Smith have a chance to redeem himself, even in prison. (autumn 1958)

The conviction for murder was laid aside; Ken was given a seventeen-year prison term for manslaughter. Mary felt her testimony about his drinking had helped convince the court that he was indeed inebriated at the time of the crime, giving credence to the lesser charge of manslaughter instead of murder.

Having helped to save him from the gallows, Mary felt a desire to keep in touch with Ken while he served his sentence in Kingston Penitentiary. She obtained permission to write weekly and to visit every three months (all the rules allowed), staying at the home of a friend.

文
月
華
的
中
國
日
記

She asked him to call her "Aunt Mary" and for the next six years Ken received letters urging him not to lose faith and to use his time in prison constructively, congratulating him when he took correspondence courses. She sent him books and newsletters. He heard about all the comings and goings of the Endicott tribe, from the latest analysis of the Cold War to the cute sayings of the grandchildren. At one family Christmas party, when each child was encouraged to sing or recite, a small grandson who did not want to be left out, counted from one to a hundred!

After several years, Ken asked "Aunt Mary" if she would consider visiting another prisoner, John (not his real name), who had been in and out of jail for many years and never had any visitors. She took John under her wing, writing and visiting both men. When John was released from prison—in the late spring of 1962—he came to stay with the Endicotts and Jim asked him to join the family at Beaver Lake to help build a new cottage. It would be a starting job, and Mary hoped that her caring and the outdoor setting would get him off to a good start. Within days, John left a goodbye note under the windshield wiper and vanished. Ken had predicted this outcome, but nevertheless Mary was devastated. To make matters worse, Ken himself soon succumbed to severe depression.

Mary with "John" after he was released from prison in late spring 1962. She is showing, with the mask-like look of her face, the early signs of Parkinson's disease.

文
月
華
的
中
國
日
記

Dear Ken,

Your letter…reached me yesterday and was read with deep interest, and some sadness. Yet I do not regard it as disillusionment, dear Ken, because you are the same person I have come to know in these difficult years; it is only another side of your personality that has come to the fore. We are all like that, really, only some of us are not tested in such ordeals as others and so our "dark" side never becomes prominent for long. And, don't forget, great souls have been unable to surmount the darkness and the cycle back to the light was prolonged or became permanent….

It is this turning of the wheel of life—from dawn through daylight to twilight, midnight and back to dawn—which is the background for the great drama and poetry. I don't think your present depressed state of mind indicates weakness of character, but only weariness of spirit under a long pull….

You are right to feel "free" of any burden of guilt towards me; you didn't say it that way but that is what you meant. Maybe we have talked at times in too high terms of what your future could be like, but there is health in hitching your wagon to a star, so long as you are not disappointed if you find it is a meteor with a limited path to follow. What I mean is, I shall not feel let down if you always live a very quiet, limited life, making a livelihood and finding satisfaction in friends and family, without striving for big income or a highly useful career.

Of course, I shall never give up the dream that you may turn your misfortunes into something good for you and helpful to others. I am sure you are capable of such a way of life, and would find your deepest satisfaction that way. What you are going through now is a phase, which may be of value to you when the time comes to give a hand to others or to illuminate a path, which our society needs to follow.

I know—you've been through it before, this period of boredom and cynicism, and it may come again. You can only meet it a day at a time, so look at it that way….

As ever,

Mary Endicott (summer 1962)

During the next seven months Ken only wrote once. The silence was hard on Mary but she continued her weekly letters. Finally Ken's morale improved and Mary's letters began to reveal more feelings about her own life:

文
月
華
的
中
國
日
記

Dear Ken,

Your letter received this week has given me a lift. You see, you give me optimism and confidence too insofar as you get it for yourself—and that is like some lines from Longfellow's "Evangeline," which I put into my chap-book when I was in my teens....

Talk not of wasted affection –

Affection never was wasted...

That which the fountain sends forth

Returns again to the fountain.

And it gives me refreshment to know that my friendship means something to you. Naturally the more your personality flowers in your adverse circumstances, the more refreshed I shall be as I find myself more and more withdrawn from activities that used to stimulate me, and more and more inclined to look back and ask myself what I have done with my life. Doesn't sound like much, compared to the great of this world, but fame exacts a heavy price, too, and I find myself content with my modest niche, mainly as wife and mother—and in the latter category I include you and John too, for you are more than ordinary friends to me....

As ever,

Mary Endicott (spring 1963)

Dear Ken,

Your appreciation of whatever my friendship has meant for you in these hard years reminds me of the beautiful poem by George Eliot....It is called "The Choir Invisible" and I copied it out for my chap-book when I was young. There were some lines that stuck in my memory and they come to me now and then:

To live in scorn for miserable aims that end with self,

...may I reach

That purest heaven, to be to other souls

The cup of strength in some great agony...

It was that line I used to wonder about when I was growing up: would I ever be in circumstances where I could be a cup of strength to such a person? I longed to be so, but in my sheltered life I could not imagine how it would happen and would certainly have been astonished could I have looked ahead 40-50 years and seen your agonized face in the dock, or the various moods in which you have talked to me through "the cage." It will not be long now before I come down—depending on the weather. I still have

234

quite a bit of pain in my back and I would like to get it reduced before I take the journey....

Affectionately,

Mary Endicott (winter 1964)

父月華的中國日記

By now Ken had been moved to a medium-security prison, raising hopes that he would be granted parole before too long. Her Kingston friend drove Mary to this new institution where, for the first time, Ken and Mary were able to visit without a glass barrier between them. She found him more relaxed and confident in the semi-privacy. Returning home, Mary wrote: "I am still half-living in your world, as I always do after a visit. I think of the things I wish we had talked about in that shortest of all hours."

Four months passed before Mary was able to make another visit.

Dear Ken,

You seem very close to me since our visit. There was so much to be talked over and thought about, it went all too quickly, as usual. I felt again the competition between my desire to hear more of your life and thinking and the time to talk to you about other things to refresh your soul, which did seem a little down this time....

I feel the need for more experience and study of your whole situation in order not to make any mistakes in advising you or encouraging you in what might seem to you as pressure of some sort. So, let it rest that you know I care for you deeply and that means for two reasons—for your personality which I have come to know since I have been visiting you, in an experience new to me—and for the tradition of the high value of the individual which I absorbed from my Christian training, as exemplified in the story of the lost sheep for which the shepherd searched all night in the storm.

As I travelled home I kept thinking that prison life is like a freezing and thawing process. The thawing is painful, as well as the original freezing process, but it is a necessary part of the experience and the new maturity acquired under duress must surely be a help in the process. It seems to me that the longer the freeze, the deeper it is and the more trying is the thawing. And yet, all the more necessary, especially as it is the prologue to the new life ahead.

I thought also that these months of waiting and uncertainty would go faster if you were working towards a limited objective—something or other that you want to accomplish—or, at the least, progress towards—during that time. Not knowing the limitations of your library, I cannot suggest anything definite but I think there must be enough scope to inspire you.

文
月
華
的
中
國
日
記

For instance, through the Extension Classes at the University of Toronto I have been reading more books and poetry than I have done in the last ten years—or longer. I've been concentrating on the ever-piling literature about our work to the extent that I felt as if I were being snowballed by it and needed to plunge into something else, with a limited goal each week, but hard to meet—and it was a great relief to me. If this was therapy for my problem something similar might be for you....

With love,

Aunt Mary (spring 1964)

Mary lobbied the Parole Board to have his application accepted. She was assured by the executive director that her letter was being included in Ken's record to ensure that her continuing interest in him would be taken into account. She told Ken she was trying "to get across 'telepathic' waves of thought" to encourage him to hold on.

In the interim, in two separate letters, Mary opened up heart to him about her own situation:

Dear Ken,

Shall I tell you a little of my own problems? Will my difficulties depress you or give you a sense of comradeship? The latter, I hope.

It is just this: I seem to be getting old much sooner and faster than I expected. It is not that I mind the idea of getting old and passing along. I don't. I feel reconciled to it. But I hate feeling so tired all the time, as if I were just recovering from an illness. I can't accomplish hardly anything because of that feeling, plus the pain, which comes in my back when I make much of an exertion. I just want to go and lie down, and there I am happy. But I don't want to do that all the time either.

I don't know whether I can learn to adjust myself better or not. How much to push myself so as not to grow—i [sic] forget the word but it means unable to do things—you know. Or how much to rest quickly when the body calls—and hope it will refresh me? Sometimes it does and sometimes not. Even to go for a short walk is more of an effort than it was and I get discouraged about it.

Then I think of all the people worse off than me—and begin to count all the blessings I have had, and still have—and my burden begins to lighten.

I know the whole thing is partly because of the atmosphere of tension in which I live—the state of the world, etc.—and now members of my family are on opposite sides of certain world questions and that solid family unity is gone—not that there is quarrelling or mistrust—but arguing ad infinitum. Sometimes I feel I must flee from it for a while—but, of course, I am too deeply concerned to be able to really forget what's going on in the world. Then there's my dear old Dad. My heart aches for him and there is so little I can do to relieve his desperate feeling of loneliness as extreme age saps his vitality....Well these are my prison walls—and I must live among them and learn how to take it with a smile—I'm trying that now.

Love to you,

Mary Endicott (summer 1964)

Dear Ken,

I am writing from my sister's cottage on Lake Erie near Chatham. It is the old house where we went every summer from the time I was thirteen. My father lives here with my sister in the summer. He is 95 now and not much like his old self, so that it makes me sad to see him, but he likes company while he waits "for the call."

I have brought with me the...last of Sean O'Casey's autobiographies which brings him to his old age. Here is a taste....

"Even the winter has her many beauties, even for the old who shiver; the crisper air; the cold mists of morning, the fretted framework of the trees against the sky....Even here, even now, when the sun had set and the evening star was chastely touching the bosom of the night, there were things to say, things to do. A drink first!...Here, with whitened hair, desires failing, strength gone out of him, with the sun gone down, and with only the serenity and the calm warning of the evening star left to him, he drank to Life, to all it had been, to what it was, to what it would be. Hurrah!"

Isn't that inspiring and comforting—to know that age and death can be faced with such joy and acceptance?...

In the title page of the book is this: "You cannot prevent the birds of sadness from flying over your head, but you can prevent them from building nests in your hair." (Chinese proverb)

As ever,

Mary Endicott (summer 1964)

The National Parole Board informed Mary that Ken had been denied parole. Almost immediately, he was sent back to the dismal maximum-security Kingston Penitentiary. Within days Mary went to visit him but left emotionally bereft. Returning home she poured out her feelings to her friend in Kingston:

文
月
華
的
中
國
日
記

It was a great shock to find Ken in a very depressed and discouraged mood. I have never seen him in anything approaching it, even in the early days. He thinks the only way is to forget about the future, drop all outside contacts and live only to get through the routine of each day. I don't know what he had thought about me but looking at his letter in the light of the conversation I should not have been surprised when *he asked me not to come again* (emphasis added).

You can imagine how I felt, and I knew it was hurting him a lot and making him feel guilty and a failure so I tried to accept the situation as well as I could. He says my visits disturb him because they make him think and then he cannot sleep. I could not tell him, in that mood, that unless he continues to wrestle with his thoughts and is able to mix with the thoughts of others, he will never be able to fit into the great world again....At present he is struggling not to have a breakdown and I spoke to his counsellor afterwards to give him all the help he could....

It was agreed that I would write a little, but that he would not answer so often. I guess I shall have to keep to incidental bits of news, and I won't know if they are reopening wounds or helping the intolerable loneliness....I feel washed out today but I'll recover. (fall 1964)

She thought about nothing else for several days, as demonstrated by her next letter to Ken:

I've been thinking of our conversation a lot and understanding it better all the time. When I re-read your letter I saw it was all there, indirectly, and I should not have been surprised at your change in outlook. You wrote that you had failed me and had not the courage to try again.

I can see now that I also failed you, in spite of the sincerity of my intentions. I was just not equipped by training or experience to give you the kind of help you need. *In my intensity I may even have added to your difficulties* (emphasis added). Well, failure is just one kind of experience and we can benefit by it, so I shall try to do that. For one thing I must be more casual in my approach and more conventional, perhaps. That is, wait for you to reply to my letter before writing again...

As ever and always,

Mary Endicott (fall 1964)

Mary never saw Ken again. After two years he resumed writing to her. She dictated short notes to him, for writing or typing were now beyond her abilities. Two days before she entered the hospital, he was granted parole, but not allowed to leave the Kingston area.

文月華

Before her "Penitentiary Ministry" began to peter out, Mary had begun another project which greatly helped her to "keep friendly with herself" during her declining years. In a letter to Ken she explained how, during the summer of 1963, she began writing her "Life with Jim" memoirs:

> Steve is at me every now and then to put down on paper the story of our life together, and when I give any of them a bunch of our letters from China to read they get clamorous. I'd like to do it, too, though I can't see clearly just what form it would take. What I would like to do is a personal account, much as I wrote it in those long letters from China when I was so lonely, and the letters, giving the details of our life, were my chief outlet. Steve suggested I do it quite informally, with the idea in mind that maybe only the family and a few friends would read it, and then, if it shapes up into anything that could be polished for publication some day, the groundwork would be done.

Reviewing her China letters sustained Mary through three years of declining health. That summer of 1963 she mysteriously fell over a board: her doctor mentioned arteriosclerosis (hardening of the arteries). However, at this time she was not told she had Parkinson's disease—perhaps her doctor did not know. She never had the tremor that is so often a symptom. However, the typical mask-like look is recorded on her face in a snapshot taken with John as early as the summer of 1962. Parkinson's disease explains many of the symptoms Mary had confided to Ken, but she did not learn she had it until the fall of 1966.

Her chief helper with her memoirs was her daughter-in-law Isabel MacIntyre, Philip Michael's wife. The letters were read out loud and Mary indicated the important paragraphs. Isabel then transcribed them on the typewriter. By 1965 Mary had begun having daily hallucinations, which she came to accept and befriend—so her "Life with Jim" project became an island of stability. In a memo dictated in anticipation of having a new physician, she recorded:

> I find [working on my letters] actually very satisfying. It is of necessity very slow and this is frustrating. When circumstances make it difficult to carry

文月華的中國日記

文
月
華
的
中
國
日
記

on work for a couple of days, I find it disturbing to my nerves. My general condition is such that I almost dread going out any place and sometimes have to leave early.... (October 1966)

The project was never completed, but material from these memoirs has been woven in with the earlier chapters of this book.

Epilogue

By February 1967, my mother suffered severe short-term memory loss, cognitive impairment and a constant sensation of being choked. She asked to be admitted to hospital so she could have round-the-clock care. I arranged for her to go to the psychiatric ward of the Women's College Hospital for observation. The nurses believed she had suffered a mild stroke just before she came in. Within three days she was disoriented and hallucinating all the time. She often complained there were RCMP secret agents on the ward plotting against her.

Still, there were moments of beauty even in those bitter days. Two memories stand out for me:

My mother had fallen asleep so I went out to the patient's lounge to eat my brown bag lunch. Suddenly a young woman sat down beside me. I recognized her as a patient on the ward who had been out of touch with reality several weeks before, but was now calmed down. She asked: "Are you Mrs. Endicott's daughter?" I nodded. Her face brightened as she said: "Your mother is the most intelligent woman I have ever met!"

I almost choked and asked: "How do you know that?"

"Because," replied the formerly psychotic angel-of-mercy, "I read poetry to her and we talk about it. She says the most interesting things."

Her admitting psychiatrist relayed the second episode to me. We had found a nursing home for my mother but, to my knowledge, had not yet told her of this. I was meeting to explain the arrangements.

"Shirley," the doctor exclaimed, "your mother was magnificent yesterday. It was the weekly Wednesday ward meeting. She was wearing her brocade dressing gown."

"That's the one her sister Jane gave her last week on her seventieth birthday," I said. "What happened?"

文
月
華
的
中
國
日
記

"She pulled herself up straight in her chair and made a speech: 'We must all face our future with courage. I myself am going to a nursing home and will never be with my family again. But we all must accept what is to come. Learn to be brave.' She talked about everyone—the patients, the nurses. They were all quiet and paid attention. It went on for almost ten minutes, then suddenly her energy was spent. She sank back into her chair and became confused again."

Mary Austin Endicott died early in the morning of August 9, 1967.

文月華

At her memorial service—which she had discussed with Stephen far in advance—Jim's two nieces, Joyce and Carolyn Gundy, played Purcell's *Golden Sonata*, the piece that had brought her so much pleasure in Duckling Pond as she accompanied my father and Captain Brotchie on the violins.

Lukin Robinson, a fellow-member of the National Executive of the Canadian Peace Congress, spoke of her personal contribution to the 1950s peace movement: "I wish I could describe to you her smile and her sense of humour. She enjoyed the work and made it fun. She loved people, her friends and co-workers, and we certainly loved her." Several of her poems were read, including her 1939 "Vignettes of Chungking." The service concluded with a recording of Paul Robeson singing Beethoven's "Hymn to Joy," and then we all sang the theme song of the peace movement, the hymn "These Things Shall Be." Finally, the large candle that had been burning was used to light two smaller candles and then extinguished. The ceremony symbolized my mother's concept of immortality: her spiritual energy passing on to others, especially her grandchildren.

Appendix A

Three Poems by Mary Austin Endicott

The First-Born

Spring comes to the Golden Valley
Rice fields gleam in the sun;
New green waves in the bamboo;
The time of waiting is done.

Frogs are piping this evening;
The moon climbs over the hill;
A sweet cry comes from the cradle,
Our hearts are glad and still.

Can it be that this is our baby?
This bit of peach-bloom and gold?
We are filled with the ancient wonder
Of a drama that never grows old. (1 April 1935)

Vignettes of Chungking

Encircled by blue misty hills,
Where rivers meet, and swirling over hidden reefs—
Race eastward to the sea.
A city built upon a rock
Defies the march of Time.
On its steep cliffs brown dwellings cling
Like barnacles; above the ancient city-wall,
Whose arch'd gateways have all but vanished now,
Tower modern skyscrapers.

文
月
華
的
中
國
日
記

Around its rocky base,
Vying for anchorage,
Crowd weather-beaten junks, among which sampans
Pole their way against the current's force
To find brief mooring.
Pitched sails move langorously upstream
A steamer whistles, and a plane wheels overhead.

"Life is more vibrant here than anywhere else,"
A traveller said, watching the teeming crowds
Surge through the streets,
Pressed by the panting coolies
Bearing great loads upon their shoulder-poles.
Up and down precipitous flights
That scale the river bank.

Around the southern sweep of shore
The lofty hills above green ridges rise,
Where one may walk amidst the old, unhurried China.
There, in fertile valleys golden in the Spring
Gleam tiers of watery crescents where brown shadows
Hold the fringe of field, the curve of darkened hill,
The tiny water-plant and grey clouds floating by.
(*The West China Missionary News*, May 1939)

When You Return

When you return, my love, I shall not ask
How you have spent your days, nor what joy
Gave you blue skies when clouds hung low;
I shall not want to know what each hour held for you
Of duty done, of terror overcome or friendly interludes.

What's been, has been, and what you wish to share
I'll gladly hear. The rest is locked with you.
All that I need to know is that you're by my side,
Your laughter in my ears, your eyes upon my face.
With this I'll be content.

From that glad day we'll build a life together,
Secure each in the other's love,
Yet granting, each to other, the right to be,
A person venturing through life by his own chart,
Guided by everlasting stars. (winter 1945)

文
月
華
的
中
國
日
記

Appendix B

Historical Background

Warlord China

1840-42: The Opium Wars were initiated by the British Empire to force China to import opium from India and ended with China's humiliating defeat—the Manchu Emperor was forced to sign UNEQUAL TREATIES. Foreign powers were allowed to impose their laws in "Concessions"—in Shanghai and elsewhere. Unequal Treaties also guaranteed freedom of missionary activities in China.

Era of Sun Yat Sen

1911: Manchu Emperor overthrown but revolutionary movement led by Sun Yat-sen fails to set up strong central government.

1920s: Numerous feudal leaders with private armies—WARLORDS—control most of China. Warlords oppress people with exorbitant taxes. Foreign powers (Britain, France, United States and Japan) support warlords.

1923: Sun Yat-sen forms Kuomintang Party (KMT), sets up revolutionary government in south China which includes Communist Party.

January 1924: KMT First National Congress starts new wave in Chinese Revolution. Slogans: "DOWN WITH IMPERIALISM!" "DOWN WITH FEUDAL WARLORDS!"

March 1925: Sun Yat-sen dies.

15 May 1925: Japanese factory guard fires on Shanghai strikers, killing one, wounding others. Students, arrested for demonstrating, to be tried in Foreign Settlement courts.

On trial date, 30 May 1925, 10,000 Chinese parade down Nanking Road in Foreign Settlement of Shanghai—to protest imperialism; British police open fire on unarmed demonstrators, killing twelve and arresting over 50. Shanghai is in turmoil, many strikes. Anti-imperialist demands include withdrawal of all foreign land and naval forces from China. Whole nation aflame with indignation against foreigners.

246

1 July 1925: National Government formally founded in south China city of Canton; Kuomintang still allied with Communists, but within KMT many say: "Raise your left fist to knock down imperialism and your right fist to knock down the Communist Party".

The Endicotts arrive in China 17 November 1925

文
月
華
的
中
國
日
記

The Wanshien Incident, 5 September 1926

The Wanshien incident arose out of a dispute between British shipping companies and General Yang Sen, the warlord in that city. The latter, claiming that one or two of his junks containing soldiers and silver had been sunk by the wash of a speeding steamer, the *Wanliu*, seized two steamers with their officers and demanded reparations. When negotiations failed, the British authorities in Hankow sent a comouflaged merchant vessel with orders to secure the release of the six officers by negotiation or force. Before the *Jia Ho* arrived, the gunboats *H.M.S. Cockchafer* and *H.M.S. Widgeon* were already on the scene. When the *Jia Ho* put her bridge alongside one of the captured ships, her three officers walked off unharmed.

After that no one was quite sure what happened, and, since all the responsible British naval officers were killed, no investigation was possible. Apparently when the commander of the expedition saw how easily the three imprisoned officers walked off, he decided on the spur of the moment to board and seize the ship. There seemed to be no Chinese troops ready for action. But there were troops hidden in the cabins and when the boarding party struck they opened fire. Meanwhile, the *Cockchafer* with a six-inch gun and the *Widgeon* with a three-inch gun bombarded the city, starting a number of fires; a large number of Chinese troops along the shore were killed by the use of machine-guns....A foreign observer estimated that three thousand civilians and troops had been killed before darkness fell and the gunboats departed for Ichang. (From Stephen Endicott, *James G. Endicott: Rebel Out of China*, University of Toronto Press, 1980, pp.93-95.)

The Hankow Incident, January 3-5, 1927

The Chinese first arranged a huge mob of labourers and ne'er-do-wells who invaded the concession and threatened foreigners. The British had armed guards there and the mob proceeded to throw stones and spit on them—small boys and girls, especially, were trying to provoke the soldiers to fire. The British refrained, being unwilling to fire once more on a Chinese crowd—as they had done earlier in Shanghai and Wanshien. Finally the Nationalist government stepped in and said we will control the mob for you if you withdraw your troops and your armed volunteers. This the British agreed to do and so the Chinese soldiers took over and the mob departed. (James G. Endicott, circular letter, 14 January 1927)

"Direct Method" English Course

The "Direct Method" English course, invented by Harold E. Palmer, "was based upon the theory that a second language should be learned by speech first, giving students an opportunity to hear, observe, and imitate the same way as a small child learns a language. The further object of the method was to teach students to read rapidly and to compose accurately without the medium of translating mentally from their own language." (Stephen Endicott: *James G. Endicott: Rebel Out of China,* University of Toronto Press, 1980, p. 117)

Japan Invades China

July 7, 1937: Japanese troops cross the Marco Polo Bridge, ten kilometres southwest of Peking. The local Chinese garrison opposes them. China's War of Resistance to Japanese Aggression has begun.

August 13, 1937: Japanese troops attack Shanghai on their way to the invasion of Central China. Chinese troops again fight back. It is a war of the utmost brutality: The enemy slaughtered the people indiscriminately. In the massacre after the fall of Nanking which went on for more than a month, no less than 300,000 defenceless civilians were killed. A great number of Chinese soldiers who had laid down their arms were machine-gunned in groups or burned alive. Rape cases were even more appalling. Neither girls of tender age nor old women escaped. In many instances, rape was followed by mutilation, murder and indescribable brutishness.

Britain and other Western countries were forced to withdraw from the treaty ports of Shanghai and Canton where the Nationalist Government had allowed them to stay. The Western powers adopted a policy of

"watching the tigers fight from a safe distance" [while] continuing to supply Japan with petrol, iron, steel, planes and other war materials. For four
years—until the Japanese planes destroyed United States naval ships in
Pearl Harbour, Hawaii on December 7, 1941—China was left on her own.

The Central Government led by Chiang Kai-shek moved its headquarters to Chungking. (Ho Kan Chih: *A History of the Modern Chinese Revolution*, Peking: Foreign Language Press, 1959, p. 313. Also 1998 TVOntario
documentary: *Soong Sisters: Destiny's Children*.)

The Berlin Blockade

This event marked the beginning of the Cold War.

At several conferences held during World War II, the anti-Hitler forces
had agreed that after victory Germany would be divided into four zones,
to be administered by the United States, Great Britain, France and the
Soviet Union. This was to be a temporary arrangement pending the uni-
fication of the country. The city of Berlin (100 miles within the Soviet
zone) was to be treated as a separate entity and it, too, was divided into
four zones.

Major ideological differences emerged between the three Western powers and the Soviet Union—the "Cold War." Some of the events leading up
to the "Berlin Blockade" are described in an official West German document: "The Soviet Union considered the western protests against her
advances in Eastern Europe and the refusal by the U.S.A. to grant her the
10 million dollars demanded as reparation payments to represent a policy
of encirclement by the capitalist nations and she openly pursued a policy
of securing her sphere of influence....On 12th March 1947, the American
President announced the Truman Doctrine, which marked the beginning
of a policy aimed at stemming the communist tide."

Now the United States took the initiative to merge the three Western
German zones, including those in Berlin, into one, which became "inte-
grated into the Western power system." By 1948 the East-West confronta-
tion centred over Berlin.

18th June 1948: Western occupation authorities printed a new west
mark for West Germany. The next day Soviet authorities declared that the
western mark would not be allowed to circulate in their zone, including
all of Berlin. The Western powers interpreted this as the Soviet Union
claiming the entire city of Berlin to be part of its zone.

文
月
華
的
中
國
日
記

June 22nd: The Soviets issued a new east mark and declared it to be the only legal tender in all of Berlin.

June 23rd: Western authorities secretly flew in 250,000,000 new west marks in cases labelled "whisky," "gin" and "brandy" and distributed them in West Berlin. A black market developed as people had more confidence in the western mark even though it was officially illegal.

June 24th: The Soviets imposed " a blockade on all land and water routes to West Berlin. The Western powers' response to this...was the Air Lift: for eleven months—until the blockade was lifted on 12th May 1949—the city with a population of two million was supplied exclusively from the air."

From *Questions on German History* (Bonn: German Bundestag Press and Information Centre, Publications Section, 1984) pp. 376-80. Details of the currency struggle from Frank Donovan, *Bridge In The Sky* (London: Robert Hale and Company, 1968) pp. 74-75.

Bibliography

Canadian Far Eastern Newsletter 11, 114 (September 1958) (peace rally in Kamakura, Japan) and 19, 198 (August 1967) (memorial service of Mary Austin Endicott). Bound copy of *C.F.E.N.* in National Archives.

Correspondence of Endicott family members in National Archives of Canada: 8320-James G. Endicott Fonds, includes Mary Austin Endicott letters, reports on children and personal jottings.

Endicott, Mary Austin, *Five Stars over China*, 1953 (self-published).

————, "My Journey for Peace," 1951 pamphlet.

————, uncompleted draft of "Life with Jim."

Endicott, Shirley Jane, *Facing the Tiger* (Winfield, BC: Woodlake Books, 1987).

Endicott, Stephen, *James G. Endicott: Rebel Out of China* (Toronto: University of Toronto Press, 1980), especially chapter 6.

Soong Sisters: China's Destiny, TVOntario 1998 documentary, for chapter 7.

Books in the Life Writing Series Published
by Wilfrid Laurier University Press

Haven't Any News: Ruby's Letters from the Fifties edited by Edna Staebler with
an Afterword by Marlene Kadar
1995 / x + 165 pp. / ISBN 0-88920-248-6

"I Want to Join Your Club": Letters from Rural Children, 1900-1920 edited by
Norah L. Lewis with a Preface by Neil Sutherland
1996 / xii + 250 pp. (30 b&w photos) / ISBN 0-88920-260-5

And Peace Never Came by Elisabeth M. Raab with Historical Notes
by Marlene Kadar
1996 / x + 196 pp. (12 b&w photos, map) / ISBN 0-88920-281-8

Dear Editor and Friends: Letters from Rural Women of the North-West, 1900-
1920 edited by Norah L. Lewis
1998 / xvi + 166 pp. (20 b&w photos) / ISBN 0-88920-287-7

The Surprise of My Life: An Autobiography by Claire Drainie Taylor with a Fore-
word by Marlene Kadar
1998 / xii + 268 pp. (+ 8 colour photos and 92 b&w photos) / ISBN 0-88920-302-4

Memoirs from Away: A New Found Land Girlhood by Helen M. Buss /
Margaret Clarke
1998 / xvi + 153 pp. / ISBN 0-88920-350-4

The Life and Letters of Annie Leake Tuttle: Working for the Best
by Marilyn Färdig Whiteley
1999 / xviii + 150 pp. / ISBN 0-88920-330-X

Marian Engel's Notebooks: "Ah, mon cahier, écoute" edited by Christl Verduyn
1999 / viii + 576 pp. / ISBN 0-88920-333-4 cloth / ISBN 0-88920-349-0 paper

Be Good Sweet Maid: The Trials of Dorothy Joudrie by Audrey Andrews
1999 / vi + 276 pp. / ISBN 0-88920-334-2

Working in Women's Archives: Researching Women's Private Literature and
Archival Documents edited by Helen M. Buss and Marlene Kadar
2001 / vi + 120 pp. / ISBN 0-88920-341-5

Repossessing the World: Reading Memoirs by Contemporary Women
by Helen M. Buss
2002 / xxvi + 206 pp. / ISBN 0-88920-408-X cloth / ISBN 0-88920-410-1 paper

Chasing the Comet: A Scottish-Canadian Life by Patricia Koretchuk
2002 / xx + 244 pp. / ISBN 0-88920-407-1

The Queen of Peace Room by Magie Dominic
2002 / xii + 115 pp. / ISBN 0-88920-417-9

China Diary: The Life of Mary Austin Endicott by Shirley Jane Endicott
2002 / xvi + 251 pp. / ISBN 0-88920-412-8